NEW POETS FROM OLD

NEW POETS FROM OLD

A Study in Literary Genetics

By HENRY W. WELLS, Columbia University

NEW YORK • COLUMBIA UNIVERSITY PRESS • 1940

Copyright 1940

COLUMBIA UNIVERSITY PRESS, NEW YORK

Foreign Agents: OXFORD UNIVERSITY PRESS, Humphrey Milford, Amen House, London, E.C. 4, England, AND B. I. Building, Nicol Road, Bombay, India; MARUZEN COMPANY, LTD., 6 Nihonbashi, Tori-Nichome, Tokyo, Japan

Manufactured in the United States of America

40-32476

TO
BORIS TODRIN

PREFACE

MY POINT OF VIEW IN THIS BOOK CAN BE VERY SIMPLY and pragmatically expressed. If anyone selects at random a dozen books from the copious literature on contemporary poetry, he will probably find that most if not all of them deal with this poetry virtually as a new thing quite unrooted in the past. If, on the contrary, a reader at all familiar with the history of English poetry reads carefully a dozen leading modern poets, he will presumably find that most if not all of them stand greatly indebted in their own art and thought to poetry of earlier periods. My object is to examine this largely neglected theme, to appraise the character, quantity, and worth of our poetical heritage in terms of its active use by our contemporaries.

My underlying assumption has seldom been expressed more wittily than by that sagacious master of metaphor, Robert Frost. He likens a poem to the pillar of a waterspout. Its top, which rests in the clouds, signifies the tradition of verse; its bottom, rising from the ocean, symbolizes the poet's direct contact with life.

This viewpoint will, I hope, prove refreshing to those who find that where critics are aware exclusively of either the moderns or the ancients the atmosphere not infrequently tends to become stuffy. There are numerous analogies. The typical picture gallery is academically arranged in chronological and geographical schools. Such is the great Metropolitan Museum of Art in New York City. How refreshing, by contrast, we find a visit to the neighboring Frick Collection, where in one of the rooms hang masterpieces from modern painting and from at least four preceding centuries. Good art always clashes with bad art, while inspired works of all periods are harmonious regardless of the greatest differences in manner. The more recent work is not a totally new structure but merely an addition in a somewhat different style to one edifice built through many generations. In a future volume, as a logical companion to this, I hope to discuss the never-exhausted theme of the innovations in modern poetry; the present volume, as I remark in my first chapter, deals with the conservative element in the radical writers.

The vast materials at hand for such a study present sufficiently formidable problems in organization; but I trust that my simplification will prove clear and satisfactory. Although I can obviously make no pretense to inclusiveness, most major authors both present and past are considered in some fashion. The first chapter reviews general problems of literary indebtedness and outstanding movements in our own poetry, new and old. The second deals with stylistic technique, the third with versification and genres of poetry, the fourth with the heritage of the spirit from the chief preceding periods, while a final chapter at least sketches some answer to the question of the true use and unfortunate abuse of our heritage as a whole. Since the first chapter is itself introductory and brief forewords are provided for later sections, I shall spare myself and my reader the superfluity of a long preface.

In the preparation of this book I have been aided by the kind and critical advice of many persons. Among them I wish to thank Charles Harold Gray, of all my friends the most devoted reader of modern verse, Edward Hodnett, Roger Sherman Loomis, Harry Morgan Ayres, Hoxie N. Fairchild, Lionel Trilling, Edward Ames Richards, Frederick Dupee, and Theodore Weiss.

I am obliged to numerous publishers and authors for permission to quote. Thus I wish to express my hearty thanks to

Jonathan Cape for permission to quote from *The Poems of W.
H. Davies*; to Duckworth for *Sonnets and Verse* and *Cautionary
Verses* by Hilaire Belloc and for *Collected Poems* and *All in a
Summer's Day* by Sacheverell Sitwell; to Faber and Faber for
Collected Poems 1909–1935 by T. S. Eliot, for *Selected Poems*
and *Look Stranger* by W. H. Auden, and for *Letters from Ice-
land* by W. H. Auden and Louis MacNeice; to Farrar and
Rinehart, Inc., for *The Fall of the City* and *Public Speech*
by Archibald MacLeish and for *A Draft of XXX Cantos* by
Ezra Pound; to Harcourt, Brace and Company, Inc., for *Col-
lected Poems* by E. E. Cummings and for *Collected Poems
1909–1935* by T. S. Eliot; to Harper & Brothers for *Collected
Poems 1918–1938* by Genevieve Taggard; to the Hogarth Press
for *Collected Poems 1929–1933* by C. Day Lewis; to Henry
Holt and Company for *Collected Poems* by Robert Frost; to
Houghton Mifflin Company for *Poems 1924–1933* by Archibald
MacLeish; to Alfred A. Knopf, Inc., for *Chills and Fever* by
John Crowe Ransom, for *Harmonium* by Wallace Stevens, and
for *Collected Poems of Elinor Wylie*; to Horace Liveright,
Inc., for *The Collected Poems of Hart Crane*; to The Mac-
millan Company of New York for *Collected Poems of Edwin
Arlington Robinson* and to both The Macmillan Company of
New York and Macmillan and Company, Ltd., of London for
The Poems of T. Sturge Moore and for *The Collected Poems
of William Butler Yeats*; to the Oxford University Press for
Poems of Gerard Manley Hopkins; to Random House, Inc.,
for *The Selected Poetry of Robinson Jeffers*, for *Poems* and *On
This Island* by W. H. Auden, and for *Letters from Iceland* by
W. H. Auden and Louis MacNeice; to Charles Scribner's Sons
for *Selected Poems* and *John Deth and Other Poems* by
Conrad Aiken, for *Vachel Lindsay, a Poet in America*, by
Edgar Lee Masters, for *The Poetical Works of George Mer-
edith*, and for *The Town down the River* by Edwin Arlington

PREFACE

Robinson; and to The Viking Press for *The Poems of Wilfred Owen*. E. E. Cummings, the family of Gerard Manley Hopkins, and Sacheverell Sitwell have also generously granted permission to quote.

HENRY W. WELLS

Columbia University
April 23, 1940

CONTENTS

NEW POETS FROM OLD

I: OUR POETIC TRADITION

IN ANY BOOK DEALING WITH THE POETIC HERITAGE of our contemporary poets, it is necessary to keep in mind that these writers are confronted by a new world demanding fresh forms of expression. Where the inner and outer life of society alter rapidly, as in modern farm and city, science and industry, philosophy and religion, the survival of any art depends on its power to meet a shifting world. Nothing quite like the masterpieces of the past can be reproduced, and even were such production possible, it could not answer our present needs. Perhaps more imperatively than any period of history, the modern age cries for new insight and new beauty. The striking developments in our music and painting are accompanied by as radical movements in contemporary literature.

While the most rational view of all the arts denies any steady progress, it assumes a constant evolution. It is clear that mankind is continually faced by new problems in language and literature no less than in metaphysics and transportation. The state of literature and poetry today is an uncommonly novel one primarily because society has lost its center of gravity. Shakespeare addressed all orders of society and even Longfellow and Tennyson exercised a wide social appeal. But our popular education has created an enormous reading public detached from old traditions by industrial and mechanical progress and well satisfied with inferior workmanship. At the same time that the popular taste has become increasingly vulgarized, the literature of the intellectual classes has become correspondingly rarefied and removed from the vulgar point of view. The poets most warmly hailed by the intellectuals address the smallest fraction of our enlarged population. And so various are the current ways

of life and thought that no single poet commands the wide ac-
claim achieved by many writers of earlier periods. The public
at large probably values poetry less than hitherto. Not only has
the reading of prose largely taken the place of the recitation
or singing of verse. No poet of commanding stature actually
reaches a popular audience. As a result the general public
casually reads or occasionally hears over the radio a fair amount
of inferior rhymes from which the names of no major authors
emerge. And with its horror of banality and insatiable urges of
the intellect, the more refined poetry grows more esoteric and
obscure. So far as the general public is concerned both Archibald MacLeish and T. S. Eliot might as well write in Latin as
in English. Such are the outstanding developments in modern
verse, occasionally paralleled in earlier periods but never closely
approximated in recent centuries.

Where modern poetry has risen with some distinction to
meet the needs of our complex times, it has generally done so
by an ever-growing complexity. It is, indeed, possible that this
movement toward subtler forms may be approaching its end.
In both the fascist and the socialistic states a more popular
audience for literature at present exists than that now belonging
to the great democracies. But this book is not primarily concerned with prophecy, ominous or otherwise. Modern poetry
means here the chief English and American poetry of today and
not poetry in the world of tomorrow.

Although no one really believes a mere puzzle or riddle to
be a poem, most intelligent persons today very naturally prefer
their poems to be in a variety of ways a little puzzling. In the
first place we have a fondness for psychological subtleties. In the
second place our learned allusions can be more learned than
ever, since the world has never before possessed an accumula-
tion of knowledge comparable with that today. Thirdly, much
of our poetry at its best presents a new subject matter, with
reference to new scientific, mechanical, political, and philosoph-

ical developments. In the fourth place the imagery of modern poetry is oblique rather than direct: a well-known volume of modern criticism (with ironical reference, perhaps, to Ruskin's *Seven Lamps of Architecture*) is entitled *Seven Types of Ambiguity*. Finally, the most familiar meters from preceding centuries are superseded by patterns not only less obvious but often positively obscure. Free verse is frequently used, and where the term is not generally applied, the verse pattern often remains so irregular as to be quite unintelligible to all but the highly trained ear. There is even a well-warranted opinion that writing printed as verse is at times prose.

In many of its basic qualities this undeniably elusive modern verse has, then, no real ground in any literary tradition whatsoever. In his recent book, *Modern Poetry and the Tradition*, Cleanth Brooks argues that this poetry conflicts with a rationalistic tradition dominant for nearly three hundred years, from Hobbes to approximately 1918. But the author says little to indicate that Elizabethan or medieval verse stands closer to our own times than does Augustan or Victorian. However much our poets may lean upon the past, they undoubtedly have, for better or for worse, certain marked achievements of their own— a conclusion with which Brooks himself is certainly in agreement.

Many of the ablest modern poets seem content with their restricted audience. While they may believe that they possess an imaginative understanding of the community as a whole, they can hardly expect their verse to be read by more than a small minority of the public. Books of verse in almost unbelievable number are published annually, many of them distinctly creditable; but no one volume is likely to reach a great number of readers. The few true poets who have attempted to popularize their art in a generous way with the masses, as did Vachel Lindsay, have thus far invariably bruised their own heads against a wall.

Perhaps the poet of the future may reach a larger and more appreciative audience by his living voice over the radio than by a printed page. Perhaps new art forms will arise in this new poetry of the air. Emerging from the ocean of the commonplace, a few distinguished works, notably the verse dramas of Archibald MacLeish, have been broadcast. But no poems thus far written for this purpose have differed in any notable way from the work of the same authors composed for the usual type of publication. Only current forms and current ideas have thus far flowed in these wholly new and almost miraculous channels of communication.

When the modern poet faces the world, he generally depends in part upon recent achievements and in some degree at least upon a traditional literary past. He consciously discards one or the other at his own risk. A few poets, to be sure, succeed with a minimum of indebtedness either to their contemporaries or to their predecessors in verse. Thus Merrill Moore borrows little but the sonnet form in his volumes inspired at times by the theory and application of modern science and above all by his fresh and lively contact with life throbbing about him. Nevertheless it is inevitable that even in rapidly moving and emotionally stirring times like our own we should, in Auden's words, call upon the noble dead.

> Yet though the choice of what is to be done
>   Remains with the alive, the rigid nation
> Is supple still within the breathing one;
>   Its sentinels yet keep their sleepless station,
>   And every man in every generation,
> Tossing in his dilemma on his bed
> Cries to the shadows of the noble dead.

It is the nature of many who write our most modernistic verse to crawl backward with a rapid and crablike motion towards an idealized past, as do T. S. Eliot and Ezra Pound. And there are poets with a historical perspective to be taken much more seriously than Pound or Eliot. Whenever a breakdown occurs in the present—a state of affairs hardly to be denied today—thinkers naturally turn backward for aid to build a better future. The imagination of a dynamic present becomes haunted by the images of a significant past. The foundations of society are today explored by anthropologists, and their conclusions found stimulating to the poets. Old myths are retold with new meanings. The ideals and especially the achievements of earlier cultures are studied with hope for our own. It is thought that a new reading of history may in some unforeseen way aid us in our predicament. Acutely aware of recent and disastrous errors, we turn from the nearer to the farther past, from the great Victorian era, in which the germs of our present ills first became apparent, to the remote eras where at least those ills nearest ourselves seem farthest removed. Moreover, the historical sense has never been so critically minded as today. Other cultures than our own may have lived more in a legendary past; none has ever known anything like so much about a historical past. Research has drawn more vivid pictures of every century in English history, from the time of the Venerable Bede to the French Revolution, than have ever been enjoyed before. The republication and reëxamination of our literary classics proceed at no leisurely pace. All these developments have powerful impacts upon living poets. Whether as a whole recent poets have depended too much or too little upon their forerunners is probably a larger question than can be answered satisfactorily. But in any case it is incontestable that the great majority of them have read widely in the verse of several centuries and assimilated much of this reading. Their frequent desire to break with the nineteenth-century conventions has itself led them so much the more eagerly to earlier periods.

In seeking freer metrical forms more expressive of our dynamic life than the regularized verses of our nearer predecessors, these poets have consulted a Middle English or even an Anglo-Saxon versification. In their love for a difficult imagery and a scientific subject-matter they have found valuable suggestion and inspiration in Donne. From Shakespeare they have sought the ancient freedom of imagination untrammeled by bourgeois didacticism. From Webster they have learned the difficult lesson of speaking tersely. From Chaucer they have discovered that true poetry is not without humor; from Marvell they have found it not without wit. Dryden and Pope have taught refinements in technique and a more realistic vision of society. Blake, offering an escape into infinity, has only recently been discovered to disclose metaphysical and mystic heights and depths unknown to more prosaic minds. Keats affords a sensuous power which for reasons difficult to analyze was often lost to the understanding of his immediate successors. Even the Victorians have on reëxamination been found to possess enviable virtues quite as great as their obvious faults, and Arnold, for example, is, if possible, more suggestive today than thirty years ago. It is not difficult to discover that with good reason the modern poets have reëstimated and newly utilized the treasures of English poetry. Some names have been drawn from obscurity and anonymous poems recovered to fame. Less fortunate productions have been allowed to sink further toward threatened oblivion.

The scholar-poet is a common figure today. In some cases the poet's dependence upon books is so great as to arouse charges of pedantry and willful obscurity and sorely to tempt ridicule. Ezra Pound may stand as a convenient symbol of the extreme literary-mindedness. And the procession follows with T. S. Eliot, who inhabits a world of old books, the three Sitwells, who live in old houses, Archibald MacLeish, eagerly devoted to anthropology and to *Beowulf*, and such men as Robinson Jeffers who, bringing up the rear, show small outward evidence in their work of the fact that they, too, are studious men. In our eminently self-conscious and nervously critical age most of our chief poets have engaged in literary criticism, as, for example, Allen Tate, T. S. Eliot, John Crowe Ransom, Conrad Aiken, Edith Sitwell, C. Day Lewis, and William Butler Yeats. The larger number of leading poets in both America and England have specific ties with the literary life of the universities. Most of them have studied within college walls, and a large number have lived, lectured, and taught in the shadow of these institutions. This is true not only of older men, such as Bridges, Hopkins, and Frost, but of a younger generation of poets, not only at Oxford and Cambridge but in Louisiana and Tennessee. More than one British poet has been inspired by the sound scholarship of Nevill Coghill at Oxford. And it is hardly irrelevant to recall the large number of notable books of recent verse published by university presses, as by the Oxford Press in England and the Yale Press in America. A traditional intercourse between scholar ship and poetry flourished in the ages of Chaucer, Spenser, Ben Jonson, Milton, Dryden, and Pope. For a brief time romanticism obscured what seems to be a natural state of affairs. But for better or for worse the scholar-poet has of late returned all too clearly into his own.

Specific evidence of the lively interest taken by well-read poets in their forerunners is discernible in the large number of anthologies gleaned from considerable periods of literature by prominent modern poets. Comprehensive collections of verse have been made, for example, by Conrad Aiken, W. H. Auden, William Rose Benét, Laurence Binyon, Robert Bridges, Robert Graves, John Masefield, Walter de la Mare, Herbert Read, Carl Sandburg, Edith Sitwell, Genevieve Taggard, Mark Van Doren, Robert Penn Warren, and William Butler Yeats. The list might easily be enlarged. This activity implies a lively interest on the part of the editor in the work of his antecedents; indeed, it presumes a certain connoisseurship. Such labor and enthusiasm can hardly be without significance for the poetry of the compiler himself.

Before investigating the relation of modern poets to their predecessors, it is useful to consider briefly who are the predecessors and who are the modern poets. The historical subject is logically the first to examine in order to bring some arrangement into so vast and cumbersome a field. For the purpose of reference in this book, English poetry will be considered under five major chronological divisions, each subdivided and each in turn especially attractive to a group of modern poets. Since the present historical treatment and terminology differ slightly from the conventional one, a brief description of each period may be helpful in itself and save repetition in later chapters.

English medieval literature is conveniently divided into two periods, the Old English or Anglo-Saxon and the Middle English, determined equally by the character of the language and of the literature. The Anglo-Saxon period dates from the sixth century to the Norman Conquest in 1066. The Middle English period is roughly comprised between the Conquest and the commencement of Elizabeth's reign in 1558, although in some respects the later Middle Ages had retreated before the Renaissance much earlier. The neoclassical age or the Renaissance proper is likewise divisible into at least two periods, an earlier and a later, the first or most dynamic age colorfully called Elizabethan or Shakespearean and extending from about 1559 to, say, the death of Shakespeare in 1616, the second, here called the Augustan, extending from the latter date till the triumph of romanticism at about 1798, the year of the *Lyrical Ballads* by Wordsworth and Coleridge. Although it is not customary to speak of the Augustan or second phase of the neoclassical period as commencing quite as early as 1616, and thus including Milton and the Cavaliers, this broader description best serves the purposes of the present study. The spacious period itself accordingly contains several stages, as the Cavalier age, from the death of Shakespeare to the Civil Wars, and the Restoration, from 1660 to the death of Dryden in 1700. The early eighteenth century, often called the Age of Reason but perhaps in poetry better described as the Age of Sentiment, is represented by Pope and Thomson, while the later eighteenth century, or age of dawning romanticism, is characterized by Cowper and Burns. The romantic movement itself, broadly envisaged, extends from the rise of Wordsworth and Coleridge approximately to the First World War and in some quarters has, of course, not yet spent its force. It, too, consists of marked stages, as the period of the early romantic poets from Wordsworth to Shelley, that of the early Victorians, and, finally, the more cosmopolitan movement which reached its height at the end of the nineteenth century and the beginning of the twentieth.

Life can never be stretched evenly on the rack of time. At any period there flourish authors behind or ahead of their times, a few men of genius hard to associate with any literary movements whatever and men whose early and later work belong in essence to two different generations. Thus Chaucer and William Langland are contemporaries, but Chaucer in some respects looks forward to the Renaissance while Langland looks more frequently backward to the patristic period, or the early Middle Ages. Of the two contemporaries Edmund Spenser and Shakespeare, the allegorical poet is the more inclined to be medieval, the playwright the more disposed to be modern. The incisiveness of Swift seems modern beside the elegance of his friend Pope. Thomas Lovell Beddoes imitated the Elizabethans at approximately the same time that the radical Shelley rejoiced in his romanticism. And Gerard Manley Hopkins was writing in a distinctly modern idiom while Swinburne was employing a comparatively obsolete one. Today some poets, as John Masefield, seem to us reactionary, while others, as William Carlos Williams, exasperate certain of their readers by extreme modernity. Only in a general way, therefore, is it possible for convenience' sake to speak of the periods of poetry. Our own eclectic age more than any other baffles definition. One explanation of this condition today is the conspicuous indebtedness of some poets to one preceding age and others to another. The occasional assumption of some critics that only one or two periods of the past remain today a vital influence is untrue: all are still actively felt, although certain poets from each age are rapidly gaining in importance and others as speedily declining.

What are the qualities in each period which attract or repel the modern poets? A few of these poets, to be sure, are catholic-minded enough to find all periods stimulating and suggestive, but as a rule a writer discovers that one or two ages are most appealing to him and relatively neglects the rest.

There are many qualities which Anglo-Saxon verse quite obviously has not to give. It lacks lightness, flexibility, social alertness, intellectuality, narrative power, and much else which come only with the maturing of English civilization. But an intensity of feeling, an apocalyptic vision, a tragic nobility, and a rhetorical power to carry all these to effective conclusions the poetry of the Anglo-Saxons does possess. It has appealed to modern poets of a religious inspiration, such as Hopkins, to writers, like MacLeish, interested in primitivism and anthropology, and to poets like C. Day Lewis and W. H. Auden, who bring new energy to an effete culture. Its chief use has been to enrich the language of modern poetry with a rhetorical power long forgotten. From the Old English our contemporary poets have learned much of the metrical freedom which they seek as a vehicle for new delicacy, strength, and expressiveness; and in its strong alliteration they have discovered a new energizing factor for modern verse.

Although much Middle English verse is on a lower plane aesthetically than the Anglo-Saxon, the legitimate value of the period of Chaucer has also risen greatly in the eyes of modern poets and their readers. The left-wing poets who have struggled to deliver modern verse from its wasteland of esoteric piddling and to address the modern public in what MacLeish terms "public speech" have turned to the simple and forthright style of Chaucer, Langland, and many other of their contemporaries. Skelton, who flourished a long, dull century after Chaucer, has enjoyed a resurrection quite as marked as that of Langland and from the same cause. These men are at once humorous, satirical, witty, and worldly. They write with a keen eye and no little zeal for social reform. Modern poets attempt to recapture the tricks of their style—their racy colloquialism, their flexible rhythms, and their vigorous verse music. The old ballad also is still occasionally echoed in modern verse. In short, the medieval poets have qualities which the moderns wish and need and can study nowhere to better advantage than in medieval verse. Auden has in particular profited from this intercourse.

Medieval allegorical symbolism has also attracted some attention, especially in poets of a metaphysical cast of mind. The introspective and religious poetry of the Middle Ages chiefly excels in such a style, and while the provincial Langland is even here a remarkable figure, the cosmopolitan figure of Dante (who in a sense may be considered no more Italian than Beethoven is German) rises above all others. A later part of the following chapter shows how surpisingly close to the symbolism of the *Divine Comedy* is that of Hart Crane's *Bridge*.

Although some students of more sanguine faith than historical judgment speak glibly of the spirit of the Middle Ages, and these centuries indeed seem to us by no means dark, the character of their light is strangely removed from our own. Their religious ideas, popular superstitions, feudal and civic organizations, and primitive modes of living differ so widely from ours that with the best available information and the most active imagination we find it almost impossible to grasp the age in its entirety or to become really intimate with its culture. The Middle Ages at best are vast, baffling, miraculous. Details stand out most vividly, as the spires of Chartres prick a glowing sky or a lonely figure in stone miraculously escapes the ruin that has overtaken its neighbors. Hence while the Elizabethan, the Augustan, or the romantic spirit comes down to us in a fair degree of clarity, it is not so much the spirit as the remarkable style of the medieval poetry from *Beowulf* to Skelton that impresses us today, especially since the modern poet and the majority of his readers have really no leisure to acquire a vivid and rounded understanding of the medieval world. While an Anglo-Saxon rhetoric and a Middle English lack of rhetoric have both deeply influenced modern verse, there are subtleties of both the Anglo-Saxon and the late medieval spirit which have as certainly escaped us all. Therefore in this book the medieval heritage is considered in chapters on technique and form, and a chapter treating more general and spiritual inheritance deals with much of the heritage from Elizabethan, Augustan, and romantic times. Thus forms, rhythms, symbols, rhetoric, and the lack of rhetoric come down to us from the Middle Ages while much of the old spirit remains unknown. This does not mean that a great medieval poet, as Dante or Chaucer, is essentially obscure to us. Precisely because he is a great poet Chaucer is much nearer to us and more human than the sententious Addison. But Addison's world is much nearer and clearer to us than Chaucer's. The spirit of a dim cathedral is of necessity further removed from us than that of a Queen Anne coffeehouse.

The Elizabethan age is best considered as a remarkably brief and fertile period of literary accomplishment dominated by the spirit of the early Renaissance, where the medieval and the modern meet through the relatively inobtrusive mediation of ancient Rome. It is the age of Sidney, Spenser, Shakespeare, and Marlowe, of the great Elizabethan and Jacobean dramatists, and of the first great wave of lyricism, here naïve, there sophisticated, which swept across the English mind shortly after the fall of the Middle Ages. The dramatic movement had spent its main vigor by the time of Shakespeare's death. Some critics prefer to regard Donne as representative of the Cavalier school and of the poetry which flourished a generation or two after his death, from Randolph to Marvell. But the powerful Donne belongs properly to the age of Chapman, Webster, and Tourneur, to the period of Shakespeare, in which he actually flourished, rather than to the paler and less nervous years which followed. Again, most critics regard Herrick as a Cavalier, recalling his activity during the period of the Civil Wars, but when viewed more critically he is seen to carry on the lyric of sentiment as practiced by Campion in the first years of the seventeenth century. Both the sentimental lyric of Shakespeare and the intellectual lyric of Donne are thus Elizabethan in a familiar and legitimate sense of the word. The influence of all these writers may therefore properly be called an Elizabethan influence. The chief difficulty is raised by Ben Jonson, the most ambiguous figure in English literature. In rude and gigantic strength, in exuberance and enthusiasm, he, too, is an Elizabethan. But as an arch-champion of rationalism, realism, form, and control he is at least the prophet of the Augustans. It would be pedantic to quarrel over his position, and unfortunately he has not exercised the influence upon modern poetry which might be hoped. The Elizabethans have, however, profoundly influenced our own age, Shakespeare giving modern poetry much of its tragic and imaginative vigor, Donne much of its metaphorical and intellectual subtlety, and the slighter poets, as Dekker, Campion, and Herrick, some lyric charm. Jonson, Middleton, and Marston have aided in developing in a few modern writers of high rank an animated and imaginative colloquial style. The Elizabethan age in poetry is essentially creative, encouraging by its example the most aesthetically creative of modern minds.

A new sense for form and restraint, a new social consciousness and literal-mindedness, enter into the characteristic poetry of the Augustan age. The writing is typified by a sobriety of feeling and smoothness of tone, the first quality equally agreeable to the Puritan and the Cavalier, the second to the general advance of a polite and largely Gallic culture in England. In his lonely splendor recalling something of the first freshness of the Renaissance as typified by Spenser, and yet anticipating the sober taste of such men as Young and Cowper, Milton stands between two ages, in stature as great as an Elizabethan, in temper perhaps nearer to the aesthetic philosophy of Dryden and of Addison. In this rough and broad classification it seems better to think of him as an early Augustan than as a belated Elizabethan, that is, so far as such lofty genius can be classified at all. And the considerable company of minor poets who regard form at least as highly as content, reaching back even to Shakespeare's times, are fundamentally best regarded as belonging to the Augustan phase of the neoclassical movement. This general group includes Carew and Marvell, Herbert and Vaughan.

The entire Augustan movement from the mid-seventeenth century to the late eighteenth century has received of late careful attention and reëstimation. Such poets as Sacheverell Sitwell have learned much of their art from Milton and Marvell, while such versemen as Hilaire Belloc imitate the school of Pope, Gay, Prior, and Swift. The early eighteenth-century taste and philosophy of character have influenced Aldous Huxley, Osbert Sitwell, and others. The close of the period presents odd and restless contradictions. On one side are pale and fastidious preromantics, as Collins and Cowper, on the other side Hogarthian realists, as Churchill and Burns. In eighteenth-century England are met decorum and indecorum, Gallic suavity and native vigor, a maximum of affectation and rhetoric, and a maximum of directness and ease. Although echoes of the Augustan rhetoric are still more or less faintly heard in modern verse, it is the great vigor of the later eighteenth century that lasts best. Today a Rowlandson commands a better price than a Flaxman.

The poetry of the nineteenth century is more often used than praised by the poets of today. It is customary to attack Shelley but impossible to forget him. Especially our minor poets imitate

Keats. Wordsworth and Coleridge are now read more for their emotions and ideas than for their technique. Poe is still a vital force among the introspective and the morbidly fastidious. And it would be almost banal to observe how strong a force in American verse are Walt Whitman, the patriarch of free verse and of a new impressionism, and Emily Dickinson, the prophetess of a new delicacy, sensitivity, and subjectivity. The gravity of Arnold as a social philosopher in verse and the approximations to prose in the more analytical and discursive poems of Browning's later years entered directly into the manner of such poets as E. A. Robinson. Romantic idealism motivated almost all the poems of Vachel Lindsay; romantic introspection has directed almost all those of Conrad Aiken. Thus, as even its bitterest enemies admit, the romantic spirit dies hard. The nineteenth century has in fact produced English and American poems far too powerful to die for many generations to come. For example, the poetic idiom and intricate symbolism of Meredith's *Woods of Westermain* are still of assistance to modern writers striving for substantially the same goal. Whether we like it or not, we are still the children of the last century, and more radical changes are sometimes attributed to the War of 1914–18 than the facts warrant. Although much of the nineteenth century has already fallen leaflike from the branches and more is daily being swept away, still more gives promise of remaining for a long time. While the chief tendencies of the present times, in poetry as well as in life, point undeniably away from the Victorian temper, this temper is not neglected wholly and cannot be so neglected. The Victorian period, like all others, remains still a strong, positive force on our creative writers.

This summary reveals that each age has not only enriched our libraries with literature as durable as the language itself (in the case of the Anglo-Saxon, really more durable), but is still a living influence. And here is reached the first and most obvious conclusion of the present book. A doctrinaire criticism extols one school of verse more highly and degrades other schools more severely than is historically justified. Any individual has the right, of course, to prefer one age or one type of poetry or of poetic influence to another. But undeniably active and powerful minds continue to operate on a broad front, using a great range of materials. A brief list of the most diverse modern poets who have received an undoubtedly discriminating recognition shows how wide is their sensitivity. These circumstances should surely discourage dogmatic partiality. One severe critic derives "all the charm of all the muses" from Virgil, another from Shakespeare, Milton, Keats, or Donne. The last mentioned has in recent years received a warmth of admiration not so much in excess of his deserts as contaminated by a variety of aesthetic bigotry. Just as there were great poets before Homer, so there were witty ones before Donne. Our critics are just beginning to discover that Skelton, for example, was one of them. And there have been witty poets in many ages after. No poet or poetic movement has sustained an entirely unique poetic quality. The objective evidence that good verse is produced in virtually all periods of English history is seen not only in the circumstance that some verse from each movement is remembered but in the fact that it is repeatedly incorporated as a literary influence into new poetry of the same language or even of foreign tongues. Modern poetry is thus much more catholic and less doctrinaire than a great deal of modern criticism.

This book aims to show the conservative element in radical writers. It aims to make modern poetry more significant to those who have already enjoyed much of the older verse but have overlooked the common ground between the old and the new. It attempts incidentally to make the older poetry more significant to those lovers of modern verse who have wrongly supposed the latter to be in essence unique and thus have missed the modern as well as the universal elements in the older poets. It is, to conclude, a study in literary genetics.

It is of interest to note, as one line of thought consequent on such an investigation, the divergence between the rank assigned to poets by the literary historians, almost always conservative, and the station which the older poets actually hold in the minds of contemporary poets themselves. Thus, while medieval historians recall Gower and Lydgate, modern poets remain almost wholly insensitive to these men as literary influences. Conversely, historians give relatively less importance to Langland and Skelton than these authors hold in the eyes of the modern poets.

Modern scholarship has produced thousands of pages of commentary on Spenser. A century ago he still exercised a lively influence upon English verse; today he seems left almost wholly in the tireless hands of the scholars. T. S. Eliot may at times quote from him, but such casual allusions only emphasize the superficiality of his present influence. The Spenserian stanza barely exists today as a living verse form, while on the other hand the older alliterative measures are undergoing a distinct revival. The vogue of Donne rose with amazing rapidity twenty years ago. So far as the poets are concerned it seems hardly to have declined. But other Elizabethans resembling Donne have gained greatly in favor among the poets. Chapman, Middleton, Marston, and Jonson are also beginning again to come into their own. Our investigation will frequently lead us to these men, much less widely used by poets even ten years ago than now. Emphasis also changes, of course, on the individual works of the same author. Shakespeare's sentimental comedies, such as *The Merchant of Venice, As You Like It,* and *Much Ado about Nothing,* seem to mean relatively less to the poets now active; his satirical plays, as *Measure for Measure, Troilus and Cressida,* and *Timon of Athens,* mean more. Although Marvell and Vaughan generally occupy similar space in histories and anthologies, the former is certainly the more often remembered by the poets. Both Dryden and Pope have gained in popularity, while Thomson and Young have unjustly, I believe, fallen into scorn or, what is worse, neglect. The sententious authors of the eighteenth century are generally in decreasing favor, the witty or realistic poets, as Prior, Gay, Swift, and Churchill, are happily recalled with increasing frequency. Byron's graver poems are neglected, his light verse is beginning to be an influence again. Wordsworth's thought and feeling are coming to be esteemed above his art. Coleridge the metaphysician and critic is outdistancing Coleridge the poet. Keats's letters are now almost as well remembered by the poets as are his poems. Whitman is more praised than imitated, Emily Dickinson even more imitated than praised. Of the Victorians, Arnold and Browning seem far more influential than Tennyson and Swinburne. It is difficult to escape the view that the poets feel the shifts of taste more quickly and strongly than the professional critics or scholars, who plod their repetitious way head downward, none too keenly aware of the atmosphere around them. The musing historian discovers that he has been uncomfortably hot for the last hour without thinking to notice it or that he has got uncomfortably wet without observing the rain. The best way to anticipate the critical opinion of tomorrow is to observe what the poets are thinking today.

The modern poets are legion. In an attempt to give a fair general view of their literary heritage, some selective process becomes inevitable. The question therefore arises, who is a modern poet? And the answer must be, not one who writes today, but one who writes in a spirit to a certain extent representative of today or peculiar to it. In one sense every great poet of the past is a modern, and every poor poet, no matter if he is writing at the present moment, a dead one. While we cannot well push a working definition to this extreme, for the purposes of this book there is reason to disregard many persons now writing fairly good verse simply because their work belongs in spirit to an earlier age. Thus there will be little to say of the conservative Masefield, who is still active, but much of the radical Hopkins, who died fifty years ago. The extreme radicals of today, on the other hand, will be somewhat slighted, partly because their meaning still remains obscure to most readers of verse and because what little indebtedness they may have to the past is also uncertain. But since recent years have witnessed more radical experiments in prose than in verse, relatively few writers will be overlooked on this score. That an author died yesterday through some unfortunate accident seems no reason to exclude him from the role of the moderns if his verse is of the necessary quality. Moreover some older men, as E. A. Robinson, attained a modern idiom at a remarkably early period. The object here is to include the modern rather than the most recent writers. This is partly due to the circumstance that, where reference must often be made brief, it is more useful to cite a well-known poet whose works are accessible and published in a collected edition than a young poet perhaps equally talented but as yet unhappily not widely read. For this reason I have written little of some poets whom I greatly admire, such as Boris Todrin.

Too brief a statement regarding any poet or poem invites superficiality. I have accordingly focused the greater part of the discussion upon something over a score of conspicuous names. At the present time twenty of the poets here considered at some length are living and six have died, most of these quite recently. Fifteen are of American birth, nine of English, and two of Irish. But since 1914 nationality means increasingly little in art. T. S. Eliot, for example, has long been living in England, while several British poets have lately taken up residence in the United States and the literary Irish are exiles almost by tradition. The language means vastly more than merely geographical distinctions. Since it has seemed most useful to organize the study along critical rather than biographical lines, the poets chosen for special study have been not only those with a highly literary style but those with some definite leanings. A few able poets of unusually catholic tastes, as Mark Van Doren, are treated only casually because an ampler discussion of their position would almost inevitably lead to diffusion.

Of special note is the number of well-known poets, several of them much to be admired, who are rarely if ever mentioned because their verse bears such faint signs of literary indebtedness. Among these writers are some of the freshest, liveliest, and most creative minds in verse today. With this praise I should hail the aforementioned Merrill Moore. James Stephens and Stephen Spender stand for present purposes in this category. The significance of such work in the general theory of literary indebtedness will be briefly but more critically considered in the last chapter of this volume, when it will be possible to make new and fresh comparisons between the more and the less literary of the poets.

Frequently one or two poets are closely examined in respect to a single literary influence. Thus Hopkins and MacLeish are studied in relation to Anglo-Saxon rhetoric, Auden and Lewis in relation to Middle English colloquialism, and Eliot to Elizabethan blank verse. Frost is examined in respect to dialect verse, Belloc as an example of Augustan borrowings, and Crane for his mystic symbolism. The influence on Jeffers of Elizabethan and medieval tragedy is studied, and likewise the relation of the three Sitwells and Wallace Stevens to the Augustans and the use made by Aiken, Lindsay, and Robinson of the romantics. In studies on the general heritage derived from the prosody and poetic genres of the older verse are considered a much larger number of poets, both old and new—Ransom, Cummings, De la Mare, Yeats, and Elinor Wylie the most emphasized among the moderns.

A primary object in assembling these authors for considera-

tion has been a maximum of diversity, in short a picture of
modern verse showing the greatest range of legitimate accomplishment which poetry has achieved in recent years. To present
a balanced and comprehensive view it is necessary to include
notable poets of all schools. A spokesman for conservative art
and society, as Hilaire Belloc, appears beside a radical such as
C. Day Lewis. There are distinctly lyric poets, as W. H. Davies
and Walter de la Mare, and others who excel in narrative, as
Jeffers and Robinson; there are mystics such as Hopkins, popu-
larizers such as Vachel Lindsay, and esoteric metaphysicians
such as Conrad Aiken. No age of English poetry, not even the
most prolific age of Shakespeare, achieves as great variety as our
own. A thesis of this study is that good verse is being written in
almost every possible style, with indebtedness to every major
epoch of English literary history. So far as the study is directed
against any previously asserted views, it combats the doctrinaire
opinion that poetry of our own day is without wide and
far-reaching roots in the past and fails to serve highly various
functions in modern life. There is no poetic capital of the
English-speaking world, in London, Oxford, New York, Boston,
Chicago, Ohio, Tennessee, or Louisiana. Naturally and rightly
poets form circles of congenial minds bent upon similar tasks.
Occasionally a man or a woman even possesses the magnetism to
stand in the center of such a circle. But there is no grosser error
than to mistake a brilliant constellation for the entire sky.

To estimate the fruitfulness of a poet's reading is not easy.
Doubtless the systematic and prosaic scholarship led by German
academicians of the last century, which examined the "influences" of a poet or painter, often exaggerated and perverted the
truth. A poet's major "sources" are, for his subject, his knowledge of life itself and, for his technique, the spoken language.
Purely personal factors of no literary nature whatsoever determine the greater part of his work. Poetic technique is in no
sense so technical as the craft of sculptor, painter, architect, or

musician. The natural and unimaginative tendency to limit one's view to the particular form in which the writer himself excels grows misleading. He is often more influenced by prose writers than by other poets; novelists sometimes prefer news-papers; and occasionally a playwright has a passion for reading lyrics. Literary as well as personal inspiration proves thoroughly capricious. Among the amusing paradoxes is the frequency with which poets borrow important ideas from authors whom as a whole they dislike, as though it were more praiseworthy to filch from an enemy than from a friend. Fond of fostering an illusion of pure inspiration and secretly hostile to the prying critic, the poet not uncommonly throws his readers off the scent. He agrees with Chaucer, who pretended to translate "Lollius," when, it seems, his true master was Boccaccio, or with that American Chaucerian, E. A. Robinson, who in a poem will suggest Brown-ing and in a letter will affect a distaste for him. A poet quite as often becomes a follower of one whom he dislikes as of one whom he admires, hastening to correct an error, but despairing to imitate perfection. Only the poorer of the eighteenth-century poets or the better writers in their youth attempted close imita-tion of the matchless manner of Pope. The sagacious artist in-stinctively realizes that what has been poorly done needs redoing and what has been supremely done needs not, and can-not, be achieved again.

In the interests of objectivity and clarity, the literary relation-ships viewed in this book are almost wholly conscious. A mere similarity between the work of a modern poet and that of a poet belonging to some earlier age warrants no mention here. It is not enough that the poet if confronted with a comparison should recognize it as sound. He must have recognized it already. But to follow this course rigidly would be pedantic and even impos-sible. We shall be less concerned with the identity of particular passages of modern poems and particular passages in old ones than with the impression which an earlier school of writing has made upon our contemporaries. While it seems picayune to gloat over parallel passages, it is surely intelligent to observe literary movements not so much mechanically parallel as organically related. In a few rare instances, to be sure, a poet follows a tradition which he has found hovering in the air rather than lying on specific shelves of a library. Perhaps the tradition is so essential a part of the national character or of Western civilization as to persist without tangible ties. Although in such instances we stand almost as far removed as possible from the enumeration of parallel passages, we may still speak of a definite cultural inheritance.

Unlike the present survey, a comprehensive study of literary inheritance would introduce the more spacious field of comparative literature. Especially in the case of a few living English authors, it has been argued that French poetry exercises a deeper influence than all other literary traditions. But a poet will presumably be deeply in debt to his own language. The more distant focus would be to the detriment of a detailed view of the English and American foreground, and the relative neglect of foreign literatures should sharpen the focus of our study. Home fields offer enough and to spare.

The most open and overt imitation is actually of small interest. Although many major poets have at early stages of their careers aped the style of others, as when the young Pope wrote rhymes avowedly in imitation of Chaucer, Spenser, Cowley, and Waller, such obvious imitation plays no important role in the annals of verse. Every sound artist not only recapitulates more of the past but also anticipates more of the future and expresses more of himself and of his times than the bookworm who lives solely upon the past. The servile imitator is no legitimate heir of the past but merely a parasite upon it. More interesting than direct imitation, because more original, but still of secondary value, is the art of parody. The subordinate place accorded parody in this book, however, is due not so much to any triviality in that sprightly art as to the circumstance that most poets parody their contemporaries, not their more distant predecessors. And the present study deals not with the tendency of contemporaries to imitate one another and thus to form schools of art, but with their debt to their more widely removed antecedents.

There is a type of literary influence of greater interest than meticulous imitation, humorous parody, or the natural intercourse of contemporaries. This occurs when a poet becomes at once historical in his subject matter and archaistic in his technique. Such a course has been more fruitfully followed in the historical novel than in verse. Nevertheless some notable exceptions occur. Both in his lyrics and in his "epic drama," *The Dynasts*, Hardy shows an extraordinary preoccupation with the past. In some dramatic fragments and minor poems he not only selects classical topics but is at pains to follow far more scrupulously than most of his contemporaries both the classical spirit and the details of the classical technique. Similarly, when writing poems ultimately of a medieval inspiration, he typically chooses meters reminiscent of medieval Latin—once, for example, he definitely states his model to be the Sarum liturgy. He lays scenes for his poems in the seventeenth century and carefully reproduces the spoken or written idiom of the times. The scene of his *Dynasts* is in the period of the Napoleonic Wars. Both in the prose and the verse passages he frequently gives the flavor of a speech a hundred years before the writing of his own work. He translates into blank verse much of the parliamentary eloquence of Canning, Sheridan, and Pitt, freely using phrases culled from actual speeches and debates. The language of the mercantile classes and of the Dorset farmers he is even more skillful in recapturing. The style of his masterpiece resembles the woodwork of a well-preserved house a century or more old, with quarters for both gentry and servants. Such faithful or archaistic reproductions are, however, outside the scope of our study because they show that an entire literary movement has actually survived, because they are, in such forms as Hardy employs them, rare, and because to anyone reasonably well read they become self-evident, calling for no comment. Little sport can be found stalking such obvious prey. It is with the subtler recapturings of the old verse theories and technique that this exposition deals: not with the complete survival of the old, but with the chemical compound of old and new.

In his admirable biography of E. A. Robinson, Hermann Hagedorn observes that at the height of his career the poet's favorite and almost sole serious reading consisted of the Bible, Shakespeare, and his own works. A certain body of reading in prose and verse may, indeed, be assumed for almost any poet; and the interest here lies not in what the poet reads but in how he reads it and in what way he utilizes his knowledge. Besides language itself there is the communal poetry of the people, consisting of familiar phrases, quotations, and proverbs. And there are even the dictionaries and books of reference, whose importance is not to be slighted. In all English-speaking countries, at least until quite recently, a good knowledge of the Bible could be assumed; and something of the dignity of this supreme textbook of poetic language long molded the English tongue. At least a few reminiscences of Shakespeare have for three centuries been discernible in the writing of almost every man of any pretense to literacy. In a preliminary sketch of a poet's literary background, these and similar sources of enlightenment may be assumed. A poet's literary background becomes of special remark to us only as he shows fondness for a book not universally read and as he puts to uncommon use the books which everybody reads. Throughout the following pages some attention will be given to what the modern poet is reading and more to why he selects this reading; but we are primarily concerned only with what active use he makes of the English and American poetry known to him.

In the literary education of a poet, which begins when he learns the meaning of words and ends only with his death, his studies in the poets of his own tongue constitute much of his most valuable activity. From this poetry he almost certainly learns more than from formal criticism or literary biography. Handbooks on versification are for the schoolroom rather than for the mature poet; entertaining as some prose criticisms of style may be, a creative artist is primarily his own critic of both his own compositions and those of others; and it cannot be too much stressed that while formal critics from Aristotle to the present day have doubtless made important philosophical comments on poetry, the poets themselves, especially in the more self-conscious, recent centuries, have written on the subject, often in verse, in an ample, impassioned and sympathetic manner far more likely to attract one another. The poets may not be the best witnesses to their actual activity, but they at least say better than the professional philosophers what they really believe their ideals and standards to be. Since it is precisely this long-established belief which we seek, we do best to go directly to the poets themselves.

The notorious unreliability already mentioned of the poets in discussing their own literary background has led in this book to a minimum of reference to their own statements on this subject. Perhaps not a single poet has systematically examined his own sources. Moreover, the artist has traditionally been led to minimize the importance of his indebtedness and to exaggerate his spontaneous inspiration. He apparently works at his best when most confident of his own creative powers and least conscious of his very real dependence upon his forerunners. The romantic tradition still dominant in many ways further instructs the poet to make a mystery of his trade. The artist grows shy and uncomfortable when he feels the critic probing the roots and secrets of his art. So conversations, notebooks, and prose works of the poets, though occasionally useful, reveal more of their views of other poets than of their own actual methods of composition. The author is not as a rule the best witness to this phase of his activity. He may not even know as much about it as his observant friends. And what he does know remains, like a trade secret, concealed. Consequently we are thrown back upon the first and most obvious recourse: the search for what, on the evidence of poetry new and old, the modern author has learned from his predecessors.

II: THE HERITAGE OF TECHNIQUE

IN THE CRITICISM OF POETRY IT HAS LONG BEEN THE practice to recognize as constituent parts of any poem its style, its larger contours of form, as versification and general structure, and finally its spirit or, in other words, its personal and social significance. Indeed, few of the common terms of literary criticism are sharp or ideal tools for the tasks assigned to them; but perhaps it is best to speak of the style of a poem as technique, of larger structural outlines as form, and of a general human significance and relation to human society as spirit. The poetry new and old examined in this book is viewed under these three heads.

There are two rocks to be avoided in steering a judicious course—well known but not easily escaped. On the one hand is the danger of viewing these three facets of the subject as mutually exclusive. To observe them overrigidly, although the simplest and most orderly method, only speciously appears the best course and proves in fact the most sterile and misleading. Since style and form are begotten by spirit, neither technique nor form can be seriously examined without constant reference to spirit. On the other hand so dependent upon style and form is any work of art that a close realization of them both becomes essential in the understanding and definition of the soul. So all three aspects are merely parts of the same organism. Stylistic and formal elements are leaves and branches of a tree, while the spirit is the root and trunk from which the foliage proceeds. To understand even one of the phases of a poem it becomes necessary to grasp all three. But in any prolonged analysis it is also expedient to place the emphasis now in one and now in another direction. To neglect the categories altogether, running one indiscriminately into another, is as disastrous as to abide by them pedantically.

The material falls, accordingly, into three chapters, each emphasizing one of the three major aspects of poetry although never entirely neglecting the others. This chapter deals with six phases of poetic technique or style, stressing in turn our heritage from Old and Middle English rhetoric, our tradition of colloquial ease as derived from the late medieval and early Renaissance poets, our dialect poetry inspired by more recent developments, our tradition of rationalism as drawn from the late Victorians, our heritage from Augustan or eighteenth-century eloquence and wit, and, finally, our ageless debt to religious and mystical symbolism. In each case the heritage, deeply as it springs from personal and social experience and admirably as it conveys the poet's meanings, is principally envisaged as a traditional use of style or technique.

POETIC RHETORIC

The words poetic rhetoric may at first seem a contradiction in terms. They are used here to mean any of the more clearly artificial aspects of poetic language with the exception of versification itself. Any heightening of diction falls under this head, while it excludes simpler and often subtler shadings of style basically the same as prose. The concept is a large one. Obviously no detailed view of the poetic rhetoric of twentieth-century writers and their forebears is possible within reasonable space; this phase of our discussion must remain highly selective. Since, on such evidence as we possess, the earliest English poets are among the most rhetorical, the relation of these writers—especially the Anglo-Saxon—to our contemporaries will be examined. It seems only natural to start with a review of the very earliest poets; and a distinctly interesting use of their work by the most radical of modern poets becomes apparent, a development not as yet much discussed by critics of modern verse.

The spirit of Anglo-Saxon, or Early English, poetry, ranging approximately from the sixth century to the eleventh, is not easily grasped today. The literary records are richest for about the ninth century. From this period we have a fair quantity of notable verse, while the prose is less remarkable for quality and by no means voluminous. We have no really adequate record of common speech. And since we suffer an imperfect view of how men spoke, it is difficult to judge just how artificial the poetic language really was. Nevertheless what evidence there is points to a strongly rhetorical flavor. The characters in the verse stories and didactic narratives joyously engage in poetic rants. The entire verse tradition seems highly conventionalized and artificial. "Nature, be thou my goddess!" was no prayer of these early men. The religious poems are based on the more miraculous parts of the Scriptures, the liturgy, and the thoroughly standardized saints' legends. The secular pieces belong largely to the epic saga, already with foreshadowings of the artificial medieval romances. The two finest long poems are Cynewulf's *Christ*, a religious effusion on the Advent, the harrowing of hell, and the Last Judgment, and the tale of Beowulf, an epic story of marvel and magic carried to England in the migration of the Germanic tribes. Both are highly heroic in theme and correspondingly exalted in diction.

The first few lines of *Beowulf*, even in translation, give some notion of this highly rhetorical poetry. Gummere's version of the poem begins as follows:

> Lo, praise of the prowess of the people-kings
> of spear-armed Danes, in days long sped,
> we have heard, and what honor the aethelings won!
> Oft Scyld the Scefing from squadroned foes,
> from many a tribe, the mead-bench tore,
> awing the earls. Since erst he lay

friendless, a foundling, fate repaid him:
for he waxed under welkin, in wealth he throve,
till before him the folk, both far and near,
who house by the whale-path, heard his mandate,
gave him gifts; a good king he!

A comparison with the original may be helpful to some readers
of this book:

Hwæt! we Gar-Dena   in gear-dagum
theod-cyninga   thrym gefrunon,
hu tha æthelingas   ellen fremedon.
Oft Scyld Seefing   sceathena threatum,
monegum mægthum   meodo-setla ofteah.
Egsode eorl,   syththan ærest wearth
fea-sceaft funden: he thas frofre gebad,
weox under wolcnum,   weorth-myndum thah,
oth that him æghwylc   ymb-sittendra
ofer hron-rade   hyran scolde,
gomban gyldan: that wæs god cyning!

Cynewulf's passage on the Last Judgment gives some idea of
his style. Gollancz's translation preserves very little of the alliteration but does suggest the spirit and general structure of the
original:

He shall sweep the victor-sword with His right hand,
that the devils shall fall down the deep abyss
into swart flame; the bands of sinful ones
into earth's realm beneath; the fated spirits
into the camp of foes; the guilty shoal,
damned to perdition, into the prison-house,
the devil's death-hall. Ne'er shall they seek again
remembrance of the Lord, nor 'scape their sins,
but, crime-stained, they shall there, bewrapt with flame
endure destruction; vengeance for their sins
shall they see revealed; that is eternal death.

Cynewulf's own words in this passage follow:

> Swaped sige-mece   mid thære swithran hond
> thæt on thæt deope dæl   deofol gefeallath
> in sweartne leg   synfulra here
> under foldan sceat   fæge gæstas
> on wrathra wic   womfulra scolu
> werge to forwyrde   on wite-hus
> death-sele deofles.   Nales dryhtnes gemynd
> siththan gesecath   synne ne aspringath
> thær hi leahtrum fa   lege gebundne
> swylt throwiath   bith him syn-wracu
> andweard undyrne   thæt is ece cwealm.

This explosive alliterative verse has itself the rhetoric of an inspired oratory. Alliteration, a formal part of Anglo-Saxon versification and decidedly more important than rhyme in Middle English, was by the latter period generally used as ornament and rhetoric. In the beginning an alliterative sequence helped to define the line, seldom sweeping beyond to include two or more lines. Alliteration remains regularized and organic in the great fourteenth-century poem, Piers Plowman, and in a score of important productions. But it became increasingly a device of poetic rhetoric, not of versification, occupying in Spenser a position similar to that in Tennyson. For this reason all survivals of alliteration in modern poetry will be regarded as occasional and rhetorical devices and not as a part of the pattern of the versification.

As the foregoing citations have shown, the older poetry shows a fondness for many tricks of eloquence—full-flowing compound words, circumlocutions, participial phrases, dangling, redundant, or appositional phrases which prolong as well as obscure the sentiment, and an uncommon number of expletives and exclamations. The best of the Anglo-Saxon poets are chary indeed in the use of articles, prepositions, and the small change of vocabulary generally. As a result the translations from Anglo-Saxon are almost always much wordier than the originals. Even when the translator does his best to retain the stylistic flavor of the original, he commonly increases the number of words by well over twenty percent. The compounding of words in the original by no means accounts for all the original terseness. Thus if all compound words, whether in the old or the modern English, are counted as single words, *Beowulf* uses fifty-four words where Gummere uses eighty-three and Cynewulf uses sixty where Gollancz uses eighty-five. Of course a terse style today need not be derived from Anglo-Saxon. It may be quite native with its author or derived from any number of sources; Housman, for example, unquestionably learned much from the lyric poets of antiquity. But many expressions simultaneously used and characteristic of the practices already mentioned as distinctively Anglo-Saxon betray relationship between the oldest and the newest English writers. And here a more general principle in the study of so-called literary sources may be intruded. It may not be clear whether the recent author knows his Anglo-Saxon in the original, in a literal translation, or not at all. He may have been attracted to another poet who himself is one or two stages removed from the Old English. Frequently all that can or need be said is that in one way or another a genuine tradition is ascertainable. The newer poet could scarcely have written as he has if the older poets had not written as they did.

Of Gerard Manley Hopkins's claim to be regarded as a modern despite his lifetime within the nineteenth century, little need be said. His brief works were first published in 1918, thirty years after his death. He is still probably many years in advance of our own times. While he inevitably picked up something from his contemporaries, he lived on the whole a remarkably detached life, partly in the arms of an enthralling and ancient tradition, partly on the strength of his own creative genius. He had much less in common with Victorian England than had

Emily Dickinson with nineteenth-century America largely because he was a deep scholar, which the recluse of Amherst certainly was not. He led, first, the life of the devout and scholarly
Roman Catholic in religion and in art, the life of the Church
Militant of the Middle Ages, medieval in every phase of
thought, and, second, the life of a saint whose miracles are per-
formed posthumously at his shrine, a life that really commenced
a generation after his death. He has been acknowledged as a
master by C. Day Lewis; more has probably been said of him
by Robert Bridges than should ever be said of a mortal man.
Auden, Spender, and other younger and more enterprising
British poets have acclaimed him. Such a poet is clearly an exception to rule, and whether we like him or not, we must acknowledge his work as fundamentally one of the most important phenomena in the world of postwar verse. Whether his
influence will wax or wane cannot, of course, be said; but he
seems assured of a high place in our literature, to use Yeats's
words in another connection, along with Landor and with
Donne.

As a matter of fact, critics have been all too eager to assert
his undoubted modernity. A close examination can only ac-
centuate the venerability of his inspiration. Never a pedant,
since his poetic and personal inspiration clearly came from
within, he indisputably pastured his mind upon the poetry and
philosophy of a distant past. His notes on his literary activity
show him to have been an enthusiastic student of classical and
medieval metrics. What only an inspection of his brief poems
themselves can prove, however, is his indebtedness to both the
spirit and the rhetorical form of Anglo-Saxon verse. He has in
every way more in common with the patristic age of Cynewulf
than with the more genial age of Chaucer.

Even when the aim is a study of his rhetorical inheritances,
we do well to consider first his cultural heritage. To some extent, of course, a Victorian and a man among men, Hopkins
was at heart an ascetic, a saint, a dreamer, and a rhapsodist.

Like Cædmon, he was born essentially not to be a priest, but to seize an angelic harp and sing his Creator's praise. Of all the figures in history, he declares in one of his sonnets, he loves Duns Scotus best. But it is with the religious poets of the earlier medieval period that he has most in common. He is himself no scholastic, as Bede was, any more than Bede, despite his brief *Hymn*, was presumably a major poet. He is not a poetic scholastic, but a scholastic poet; not a brother of Albertus or Aquinas, but of Dante and Cynewulf. As Cynewulf in his *Christ* sings the patristic vision in a poetic rhetoric combining the ideas of the saints with the language of the sagas, so Hopkins combines the feelings and ideas of the holy men of Lindisfarne with the language and rhetoric of both the secular and divine poetry of their age. Hopkins was, interestingly enough, not only a churchman and a visionary but a provincial and a patriot. This accounts for his passionate singing of the universal doctrines of the Church in so eminently English an idiom. Like Cynewulf and Cædmon, he is fired in the most ecstatic form with Christian devotion, combining his praise of Christ and his enmity to the world, the flesh, and the devil with an acute awareness of the splendor of nature and, in particular, with the terror of the sea. Hopkins shares with Cynewulf the same spiritual and sensuous vision.

No true poet—and Hopkins deserves this honor—follows ultimately any star besides his own. That Hopkins merely derived occasional inspiration and suggestion from the Anglo-Saxon poets shows at once his sagacity and his own stature. His poetry, like that of every major author, contains evidence of widely spaced origins. His play on words is often palpably Elizabethan, his stanzaic forms generally derive from the Cavalier age, his clinging to the basic outline of the sonnet form despite all his metrical virtuosity shows his eclecticism. His fondness for anapaestic feet, his love of elaborate rhyme, his profuse nature imagery and preoccupation with nature, even indicate a certain indebtedness to the romantic tradition as exemplified in the most fecund poet of his own day, Swinburne. Thus his Anglo-Saxon investment is merely a part of his poetic capital. But it cannot well be ignored and has too often been slighted.

The important use of literary heritage in such a poet lies not so much in direct borrowing of ideas, plots, or phrases as in the totally new working of old themes. The wise author translates the past into the language of the present for the needs of the present. Thus the statement of a specific relationship between a passage by one poet and a passage by another poet, although comforting to the academic mind, has relatively small interest to the poetic mind. The later passage is usually indebted not to one but to a thousand antecedents. Of greater consequence is a similarity of mood and technical achievement. Lest, however, the comparison between the first English poet and one of the most recent seems fantastic, a rare example of a passage in which Hopkins did stoop to paraphrase an Anglo-Saxon poem may be given. In the midst of a very pagan poem Hrothgar preaches an eloquent sermon (Gummere's translation of Beowulf, lines 1761–68):

> The flower of thy might
> lasts now a while: but erelong it shall be
> that sickness or sword thy strength shall minish,
> or fang of fire, or flooding billow,
> or bite of blade, or brandished spear,
> or odious age; or the eyes' clear beam
> wax dull and darken: Death even thee
> in haste shall o'erwhelm, thou hero of war!

The Second Part of Hopkins's longest poem, The Wreck of the Deutschland, begins vigorously as follows:

> "Some find me a sword; some
> The flange and the rail; flame,
> 'Fang, or flood" goes Death on drum,
> And storms bugle his fame.

But we dream we are rooted in earth—Dust!
Flesh falls within sight of us, we, though our flower the same,
Wave with the meadow, forget that there must
The sour scythe cringe, and the blear share come.

Parallels might be adduced to other passages in Anglo-Saxon poetry besides the lines quoted from *Beowulf*, but these obviously comprise the nucleus of Hopkins's stanza. The metaphor of the flower which comes first and most briefly in the epic is used by Hopkins last and most elaborately. But in writing of death both poets use the word fang—"fyres feng" in Anglo-Saxon—both use the word flood, and both write of the sword. The sequence of the same or similar words cannot be accidental. This most Christian passage in the English epic was obviously one which would be likely to attract Hopkins and linger in his memory. The closeness to the Anglo-Saxon suggests that this rather than a translation was uppermost in Hopkins's mind. His published notebooks show him to have been thoroughly familiar with the original. Gummere's version, which at the date of its appearance was by far the most faithful to the letter and spirit of the original, appeared over twenty years after Hopkins's death.

Since, as we have seen from quotations, the prevalence of imaginative compounds becomes one of the most conspicuous features of Anglo-Saxon poetry, a few instances in Hopkins will assist our view of his heritage from this quarter. In a single stanza of *The Wreck of the Deutschland* nine compounds occur:

Now burn, new born to the world,
Double-naturèd namè,
The heaven-flung, heart-flushed, maiden-furled
Miracle-in-Mary-of-flame,
Mid-numbered He in three of the thunder-throne!

Not a dooms-day dazzle in his coming nor dark as he came;
    Kind, but royally reclaiming his own;
A released shower, let flash to the shire, not a lightning of fire
    hard-hurled.

Especially the sensuous vigor of the last phrase combined with
the ascetic fervor of the first suggests the degree to which Hopkins had drunk at the earliest springs of English verse.

Typical of Hopkins's word-building in the old manner are the
opening lines of his sonnet *Duns Scotus's Oxford:*

Towery city and branchy between towers;
Cuckoo-echoing, bell-swarmèd, lark-charmèd, rook-racked,
    river-rounded;
The dapple-eared lily below thee . . .

Representative also of his Anglo-Saxon heritage are the first
lines of *The Caged Skylark:*

As a dare-gale skylark scanted in a dull cage
    Man's mounting spirit in his bone-house, mean house,
        dwells—

The compound "bone-house" comes directly from the Anglo-
Saxon "banhus," used in *Beowulf;* and to call it a "mean house"
is likewise in the Old English manner.

A stanza especially close to the Anglo-Saxon style appears in
The Loss of the Eurydice:

A beetling baldbright cloud thorough England
Riding: there did storms not mingle? and
        Hailropes hustle and grind their
Heavengravel? wolfsnow, worlds of it, wind there?

The apocalyptic language of Cynewulf breathes again in such
words as these:

. . . so some great stormfowl, whenever he has walked his while
The thunder-purple seabeach plumèd purple-of-thunder . . .

Or again, as he writes of the constellations: "The bright bor-
oughs, the circle-citadels there!" He has phrases such as "sea-
swill" that, if not actually taken from Anglo-Saxon, have the
flavor of it fully. A memorable passage on a storm has the same
feeling:

> And the sea flint-flake, black-backed in the regular blow,
> Sitting Eastnortheast, in cursed quarter, the wind;
> Wiry and white-fiery and whirlwind-swivellèd snow
> Spins to the widow-making unchilding unfathering deeps.

His use of alliteration might, to be sure, be derived from
Middle English as well as from Anglo-Saxon, although he makes
free with it in the more generous manner of the older writers.
Two or three additional quotations show how well he reproduces the representative four-beat line with alliteration on the
first three stressed syllables:

O Deutschland, double a desperate name! . . .

With the gnarls of the nails in thee, niche of the lance, his . . .

Burden, in the wind's burly and beat of endragonèd seas.

The older poetry comes to us bodily and in a rush through the
one word "endragonèd."

A close-packed style, typical of Anglo-Saxon diction at its
best and bare of all linguistic small change, also marks Hopkins's
poetry. Here again only examples can prove how strongly reminiscent of Old English his manner is. In his *Pied Beauty* we
find the line: "With swift, slow; sweet, sour; adazzle, dim."
Again, in his well-known *Windhover*, we read: "Brute beauty
and valour and act, oh, air, pride, plume, here . . ." *The Lantern
Out of Doors* ends:

Christ minds; Christ's interest, what to avow or amend
* There, eyes them, heart wants, care haunts, foot follows kind,*
Their ransom, their rescue, and first, fast, last friend.

The concluding line of *The Wreck of the Deutschland* proves an excellent instance of the same technique: "Our heart's charity's hearth's fire, our thoughts' chivalry's throng's Lord." In the same poem occur the equally extraordinary and reminiscent lines:

> Oh,
> We lash with the best or worst
> Word last! How a lush-kept, flush-capped sloe
> Will, mouthed to flesh-burst,
> Gush!—flush the man . . .

Each of the preceding passages bears at the same time strong marks of Hopkins's own somewhat precious personality and of his desire to escape the prolixity of Victorian verse style in favor of the firmer muscle and bone of the early Saxon.

Hopkins's reliance on the early school of poetry so dear to him included a love both for specific words and for the indefinable spirit. It is an affection for an old word (as well as the thing) which led him to end his sonnet *The Starlight Night* with the word "hallows," meaning saints: "Christ home, Christ and his mother and all his hallows." Rather in the spirit of the strongly onomatopoeic style of Anglo-Saxon is the line, "the rash smart sloggering brine." Especially the last line of one of the stanzas in *The Loss of the Eurydice* breathes the old fragrance. Of the ship he writes:

> She had come from a cruise, training seamen—
> Men, boldboys soon to be men:
> Must it, worst weather,
> Blast bole and bloom together?

The laconic phrasing of Early English poetry is used to describe the disaster in the same poem: "Too late; lost; gone with the gale." Both the startling abruptness and the alliterative phrase, so highly effective, have many analogues in Anglo-Saxon. Finally,

the love of Old English poets for a terse ironical phrase to conclude a bout of eloquence, as shown in the last words of each
of the recently cited passages, is well duplicated in a passage in
The Wreck of the Deutschland:

> *The breakers rolled on her beam with ruinous shock;*
> *And canvas and compass, the whorl and the wheel*
> *Idle for ever to waft her or wind her with, these she endured.*

Nor do we need to look far for exclamations so typical of Anglo-
Saxon verse. The first phrase of *The Wreck of the Deutschland,*
like the first word of *Beowulf,* contains an instance. The device
is too common in Hopkins to require exemplification.

One notable ingredient in Hopkins's magical brew, then, is
the tradition of Old English poetic rhetoric, surprisingly emer-
gent during the latter years of the nineteenth century. The
authors whom Hopkins admired for style he also admired for
spirit. Every feature of technique enumerated as representative
of the Anglo-Saxon poets appears conspicuously in Hopkins,
and every one contributes to the heightened, ecstatic, and
strained feeling. Something of the similarity in style between
old and new is owing, no doubt, merely to this similarity of
purpose—though Hopkins emphatically stated his own indebtedness. One of the most progressive, experimental, and original
of modern poets sought and found refreshment in wells of
English much earlier and less defiled than Chaucer. Just as anthropology has advanced modern political theory, a revival of
Anglo-Saxon studies has inspired some of the liveliest English
verse of the twentieth century.

Not all Hopkins's followers have been as good scholars as he,
with the result that they have relied less upon the more remote
Anglo-Saxon and more upon the more accessible but hardly
richer vein of alliterative poetry in the Middle English period,
approximately from 1100 to 1500. The chief school of alliterative verse during these years flourished in the latter half of

the fourteenth century, reaching its fullest flower a little earlier than Chaucer. Its masterpiece is Langland's *Piers Plowman;* there are many other notable poems, heroic romances, saints' legends, and didactic verses. C. Day Lewis, an avowed admirer of Hopkins, has expressed his warm interest in Langland and his desire to emulate his poetic style. The author of *Piers Plowman* was a less affected and a less rhetorical poet than Cynewulf. He combined alliterative verse with the simplicity, though hardly with the translucence, of Chaucer. A good example of the naïve but telling eloquence found from time to time in Langland's poem may be taken from a description of the throngs of people—largely laborers—on the "fair feeld ful of folk."

Barons and burgeises, and bonde-men als,
I seigh in this assemblee, as ye shul here after;
Baksteres and brewesteres, and bochiers manye;
Wollen webbesteres, and weveres of lynnen,
Taillours and tynkers, and tollers in markettes,
Masons and mynours, and many othere craftes.
Of alle kynne lybbynge laborers lopen forth somme,
As dikeres and delveres, that doon hire dedes ille,
And dryveth forth the longe day with Dieu save dame Emme.
Cokes and hire knaves cryden, "Hote pies, hote!
Goode gees and grys! Gowe, dyne, gowe!"
Taverners until hem trewely tolden the same,
Whit wyn of Oseye, and reed wyn of Gascoigne,
Of the Ryn and of the Rochel, the roost to defie.
Al this I saugh slepynge, and seve sithes more.

Such is the background for the style of the younger Englishmen. Lewis indicates his receptive attitude toward the past in two suggestive lines:

> *But we seek a new world through old workings,*
> *Whose hope lies like seed in the loins of earth . . .*

Here one of the most lyrical of English social radicals uses an image from his favorite field—the modern mine—with implications which the student of his poetry does well to keep in view. Like Hopkins, he experiences with the Anglo-Saxon poets the fascination of the sea and ships, nor is the style materially altered by the circumstance that the radical poet prefers steamships to sailboats. In a spirited passage rich in reworkings of the old alliteration and the old rhetoric, this exuberant poet likens the radical political minority in England to a ship—not the ship of state, but (shall we say?) the ship of the opposition:

> Many months have gone to her making,
> Wood well-seasoned for watertight doors,
> The old world's best in her ribs and ballast,
> White-heat, high pressure, the heart of a new
> In boiler, in gadget, in gauge, in screw.
> Peerless on water, Oh proud our palace,
> A home for heroes, the latest of her line;
> A beater to windward, obedient to rudder,
> A steamer into storm, a hurricane-rider,
> Foam stepper, star-steerer, freighter and fighter—
> Name her, release her, anoint her with wine!

The four-stress line running upon uneven feet, the frequent alliteration, the appositional phrases, exclamations, and metaphorical compounds all derive from the older poetic realm.

In contrast with the slightly specious eloquence of the foregoing is a more poetical passage, no less medieval in style, but inspired with a vein of fervent and imaginative satire exploited more richly by Auden. Lewis inveighs against the conservative classes:

> Getters not begetters; gainers not beginners;
> Whiners, no winners; no triers, betrayers;
> Who steer by no star, whose moon means nothing.
> Daily denying, unable to dig:

At bay in villas from blood relations,
Counters of spoons and content with cushions
They pray for peace, they hand down disaster.

The syntax of this passage even more than the alliteration betrays its obligations to the past. The ideas touch Langland; rhetoric touches still earlier poets.

In some further details Lewis finds support in the old authors. In one passage, for example, he amusingly adapts from Langland the trick of coining allegorical compound names. Thus, if I may borrow from my own modernization of *Piers Plowman,* Langland had written:

Piers' wife was called dame Work-while-I-am-Able;
His daughter was Do-this-or-thy-Dame-shall-beat-thee;
His son was Suffer-thy-Sovereigns-to-have-their-Wishes,
Dare-not-Judge-them-for-if-thou-Dost-thou-shall-Dearly-Abide-it.

Lewis more succinctly lists the misguided persons opposed to radical reform:

Lipcurl, Swiveleye, Bluster, Crock and Queer,
Mister I'll-think-it over, Miss Not-to-day,
Young Who-the-hell-cares and old Let-us-pray,
Sir Après-moi-le-déluge. It is here
They get their orders. These will have to pay.

This trick of begetting allegorical and hyphenated names was also cultivated, of course, by Bunyan; but the versification and alliteration here point unquestionably to the Middle English

Lewis's poetry reveals a particularly charming Irishman with an imagination more remarkable for its freshness than for its profundity. W. H. Auden is obviously the more deeply inspired, as he is clearly the less ingratiating author. His interest in the form and spirit of medieval literature began early in his career. His friend Christopher Isherwood observes that Auden's first play, *Paid on Both Sides,* was written under the influence of the Norse sagas. Echoes of the Old English style are especially notable in the choral passages, archaistic even in their absence of punctuation. Unusual capitalization marks the caesura:

> Shot answered shot Bullets screamed
> Guns shook Hot in the hand
> Fighters lay Groaning on ground
> Gave up life Edward fell
> Shot through the chest First of our lot
> By no means refused fight Stephen was good
> His first encounter Showed no fear
> Wounded many.
>
> Then Shaw knew We were too strong
> Would get away Over the moor
> Return alive But found at the ford
> Sturton waiting Greatest gun anger
> There he died Nor any came
> Fighters home Nor wives shall go
> Smiling to bed They boast no more.

Auden has even acquired the reputation of being something of an authority on medieval poetry. In the Criterion for 1932-33 he reviewed editions of the Middle English poets Skelton and Dunbar and a volume by Bertha Phillpotts entitled Edda and Saga. Two years later he wrote an essay on Skelton in a collaborative volume, The Great Tudors, edited by Katharine Garvin.

Auden's admirable anthology of light verse (not all of it as light as might be supposed) significantly begins with a generous selection from Middle English poetry, some of the pieces being by no means among the more widely known. This selection indicates the most important medieval influence upon Auden's own verse, an influence not from the rhetorical but from the colloquial poems. Auden's poetry shows no evidence of the poet's indebtedness to Beowulf: it strongly suggests his familiarity with Langland and especially Chaucer. Hence in the section immediately following which deals with the colloquial style in modern poetry we shall observe Auden's most significant departure from the romantic tradition in the direction of the late Middle Ages. Auden's contact with the alliterative poets and their more rhetorical idiom calls, however, for some present attention. Even in his choice of themes he shows his medieval background—so much more genuine and less sentimental than that of Tennyson, Swinburne, or Morris. Langland and many other poets of his age, for example, used the formula of an imaginary last will and testament to lend mock heroic energy to their verses. Auden and MacNeice return to this device in one of the cleverest and most ambitious of their poems in their joint volume, *Letters from Iceland*. Again in his poem *To My Pupils* Auden proves himself a follower of Langland and his school by writing satirically and realistically of the Seven Deadly Sins.

Auden has many lines conforming strictly to the pattern of the old four-stress line alliterating on all but the final stress. Two instances may be cited: "Luxury liners laden with souls"— a sardonic metaphor for the British cathedrals—and "Learning the laws of love and sailing." The medieval idiom itself is better represented in the following stanza:

> *Picnics are promised and planned for July*
> *To the wood with the waterfall, walks to find,*
> *Traces of birds,*
> *A mole, a rivet,*
> *In factory yards*
> *Marked strictly private.*

The phrase "walks to find" is good Middle English, hardly good modern English, but it commends itself to the poet apparently because it seems fresher, terser, and more emphatic than a more current expression.

No small part of the pleasure of reading Auden's verse is to encounter a vigorous phrasing strictly medieval used to express an action or an idea thoroughly modern. The Victorian medievalists, following quite the contrary method, not uncommonly used new and flaccid rhetoric to express thoroughly obsolete ideas and emotions. The instances of the better way in Auden are numerous. Thus a highly alliterative long-line stanza amusingly ends with the terse phrase "Gone with a suitcase" quite in the old manner. It is a delight to see Langland's art alive again in such lines as these:

> Tourists to whom the Tudor cafés
> Offer Bovril and buns upon Briton ware
> With leather work as a side line: Filling stations
> Supplying petrol from rustic pumps.

The building-up process of Langland's rhetoric reappears in the following:

> I see barns falling, fences broken,
> Pasture not ploughland, weeds not wheat.

The participial construction characteristic of the older English poetry becomes equally vigorous in such lines as these:

Past boys ball-using: shrill in alleys.
Passing the cinemas blazing with bulbs: bowers of bliss. . . .
Look left: The moon shows locked sheds, wharves by water . . .

Auden is one of the most typical, as he is one of the most brilliant and widely acclaimed, of British poets today. He proves in no way more representative of his fellow poets than in his eminently fruitful acquaintance with the fresh and liberating idiom of fourteenth-century verse. Breaking in important respects with the romantic tradition, these younger men are all the more firmly grounded in England's literary past. It would hardly be expected that as a group the American writers should show an enthusiasm which in the Englishman often seems a thoroughly natural manifestation of an intelligent patriotism. Nevertheless a few of the more intellectual and scholarly Americans have rivaled and possibly surpassed the Englishmen in profitable excursions into the older medieval fields. William Ellery Leonard has translated *Beowulf* in what he deems the original meter, and Robinson Jeffers has echoed the alliterative meter in *At the Birth of an Age*, a play inspired by the Volsung Saga. No American, however, has in this respect been more enterprising than Archibald MacLeish, a writer happily something of a scholar and even more a true poet.

MacLeish combines a sensitivity to books and to men; he is equally concerned with literature and reality, with past and present. This breadth of mind has manifested itself in all his writing since he reached maturity with his metaphysical poem, *The Hamlet of A. MacLeish*. Rather more than a liberal in politics, he has never been disposed to discard bodily and impulsively the past of poetry. His first important poem consists in variations upon themes by Shakespeare. As a lyric poet he shares much in common with the metaphysical school: indeed, one of his best known lyrics, *You, Andrew Marvell*, acknowledges this relationship. His realistic satires on the social and economic order have slashing strokes which remind us of the great age of satire from Swift and Pope to Churchill and Byron. He evokes a perfect mirror of baroque imagery in his poem *Men of My Century Loved Mozart*. That he cherishes the art of the best romantic verse appears in *Dover Beach: a Note to That Poem* where he writes a not unworthy sequel to one of Arnold's most moving compositions. MacLeish has been quite unjustly accused of lackeying to contemporary fashions—a perversion of the case, since like greater minds than his he has sincerely shared in the common movement of the human spirit from year to year. Of greatest interest, however, is the fact that distance in time seems rather to increase than to diminish the vitality of his assimilative powers. He has felt the influence of

Middle English; directly or indirectly he has come still more under the spell of the Anglo-Saxon tradition; and above all general anthropology has exercised a continued fascination for him. He is a gardener who has enriched his beds with the most exotic as well as with local plantings. His work in many subtle ways represents as fully as that of any living writer the continuity of the poetic tradition. And this becomes all the more refreshing since he has to date resisted all temptations to fall into the easy ways of the academically uninspired.

To appreciate the spirit of his important assimilations from the earliest English poets it is useful to glance at his strong leanings toward that singularly poetic member of the family of the social sciences, anthropology. In *The Hamlet of A. Mac-Leish* are allusions to the dim history of the Near East, to migrations of tribes in Central Asia, and to the sex customs of savages. He shows the anthropologist's vision in a number of poems which meditate upon the time when the present century of the Christian era will be a dark and disputed age among future anthropologists. One of his longer poems, *The Pot of Earth,* deals with adolescence in the light of discussions in Sir James Frazer's *The Golden Bough* and similar works. His admirable and characteristic poem, *Land's End,* bears subtitles *Geography of This Time* and *Response of the Ancestors.* It supplies an allegory of modern life in terms of a primitive past. MacLeish describes a seafaring race not fully adapted to its environment because of stubborn ancestral memories of a period when the tribe lived among inland hills. Just so are we unable to adjust our own past to our present. Where other poetry has brooded over the fate of the individual, poem after poem by MacLeish is haunted with the sense of the transience of race itself. He appears to have drawn this speculation into his lungs with the odors of camp and field in the War of 1914-18. America herself he views as a dangerous experiment in civilization whose present destiny is either to perish or to move forward. His longest poem, *Conquistador*, commemorates the Indians of Mexico and the early conjunction of Indian and Spanish cultures in Central America. In *The Fall of the City*, an excellent radio drama produced in 1937, dealing primarily with the menace of fascism to democracy, he still turns to a setting learned from his study of primitive cultures. Hitler appears as a new conquistador, weaker than the old, but conquering an even more decadent Inca civilization. MacLeish's anthropological interests are themselves framed by his still wider broodings upon the temporal destiny of the human race, the earth, and the heavens. Geography, geology, and astronomy have in their turn exercised their spell over him. With such an appetite it becomes only natural that MacLeish should turn from time to time to the poetic riches available to him in the first English poets. Nor is he above the fascination of their rhetorical exuberance. Hopkins appreciated best the dazzling apocalyptic element in the old poetry with its electrical fervor. The genial Lewis and Auden see more superficially into the primitive rhetoric. MacLeish shows an instinctive sympathy for the old eloquence begotten of the old melancholy.

The themes in MacLeish's verse help to show at once his genuine interest in the Middle Ages and his stronger leanings toward the earlier half of the period. The literature and art of the later Middle Ages, to be sure, have clearly attracted him. In *The Hamlet of A. MacLeish* is a long passage elaborated from Malory's *Morte d'Arthur*, but with a keener appetite for mythology than the moralizing Malory possessed. MacLeish has composed an allegorical poem with modern reference based on the *Song of Roland*. He has written one of the briefest and best lyrics on that apotheosis of medieval art, Chartres Cathedral. While his sharp satire mocks the poet who squanders his talents in a false and sentimental medievalism, no part of the medieval tradition seems alien to him. MacLeish is no worshipper of the noble savage or the law of nature—no quester after the primitive with the fopperies of Gauguin. But because he has trained himself to think in the broadest sociological perspective he naturally steps backward before leaping forward. Old English rhetoric appeals to him and resumes vigorous life in his own verses, vastly enriched by this subtle contact.

In *Conquistador* the case becomes transparent. MacLeish is writing an epic episode, or saga, of much the same length and spirit as *Beowulf*. The Mexicans deified their conqueror as the Anglo-Saxons glorified their dead hero. The exploits of Cortes seem, indeed, almost as fabulous as those of the conqueror of Grendel. Each hero meets death tragically. By ways best known to himself MacLeish came under the spell of the early poetry considerably before he produced his narrative masterpiece. It is necessary to take the entire body of his poetry into account in connection with the dominant characteristics of the Anglo-Saxon rhetoric described earlier in this chapter. He artfully draws most upon the Old English rhetoric when his theme takes its coloring from anthropology.

Borrowings in vocabulary, as the most obvious type of indebtedness, at once strike the reader's attention, especially where an old word is accompanied by archaism of syntax. MacLeish, together with Auden and Lewis, has a liking for the colon to indicate a rhythmical pause, reminiscent of the Anglo-Saxon rather than a conventional mark of punctuation. All these features appear in three lines from *Conquistador*:

We that to west now: weirdless: by fates faring
Follow on star-track: trust have we neither now:
Traceless this ground: by the grazing deer by the hare crossed:

The archaism of "weird" is repeated a few lines further on: "Nevertheless it was ill weird for a man." The word "star-track" is a compound thoroughly Anglo-Saxon in spirit, while used as it is without the article it all the more strongly suggests the old poetic rhetoric.

Other words commencing with "w," such as "wold" and "wealed" carry a strong Anglo-Saxon savor. They are to be found in *Conquistador* as follows:

Wold was that country under heaven: woodless:
A crow's pasture and a bitter ground:
Tehua they called it: stones of that city stood. . . .
And we sent them word they were well wealed: and to think of
   it:

The animal imagery, realistic or fantastic, has a medieval aspect, as in the simile, "Fry on his bib like a glibbed boar in a bucket." It is hard to believe that in the episode of Bleheris in MacLeish's *Hamlet* the poet failed to recall the Grendel of *Beowulf*:

Loose fingers groping, cropped, no arm there, grey,
The nails gone, shriveled, a dead hand, and droop
And close about the vessel.

The spirit, imagery, and word formation of the age of *Beowulf* are reflected in lines such as these, eloquent of seafaring:

She moved, wind in the sail top, rolling to the long
Swell, the land against the wind, the skystain
Spilling from trough to trough of the dead waves.

That was the third night and the morning stormy,
Rain and the wind gone east, the gear wet . . .

The word formation attracts similar interest here:

In praise of autumn of the far-horn-winding fall
I praise the flower-barren fields . . .

The omission of the article proves a small but really important stylistic feature in Old English as well as in MacLeish. He uses, for example, excellent alliterative phrases such as "quail out of corn," "stars over stubble," and "rest by roadside." The phrases resemble such Old English expressions as "secgas on searwum," meaning "heroes in harness."

The participial phrases characteristic of the Anglo-Saxon are much cultivated by MacLeish. He writes, for example:

> And I struck the sea with the oars but the ship lifted,
> Grinding on gravel, and the bow fell off . . .

> Eighteen mile on the granite anticlinal
> Forty-three foot to the mile and the grade holding:

> Sea ruffled with squalls: ships scattering:
> And we held her northward as the weather wore:
> Heeling the gusts: her head down: the hoits slatting:
> Standing with morning to an island shore . . .

> . . . used
> Long to the wave-lift: wind-led: sea-suffered:
> Beached now on this last land . . .

> Strange as it is that men: wanderers: wretched:
> Deceived often; misled: their way lost: thirsting . . .

> . . . and Montezúma
> Clad in the gold cloth: gilded: and he smiled . . .

A close-packed construction with frequent appositional phrases derives from Anglo-Saxon:

> This priest is a learned man: is not ignorant:
> And I am poor: without gold: gainless. . . .
> I: poor: blind in the sun: I have seen. . . .
> I: poor as I am: I was young in that country:
> These words were my life: the letters written
> Cold on the page with the spilt ink and the shunt of the
> Stubborn thumb: these marks at my fingers:
> These are the shape of my own life . . .

The Thirteenth Book of *Conquistador* ends with six lines redolent of the earliest heroic English poetry:

And we saw well what weapon was our guard:
And now there was none: only the night: and the ways were
Barred before us and the ditches barred
And the dykes down by the banks and the water-breaks
Open and armored and they held the roads:
And nevertheless we had the choice to take them! . . .

The first poem of *Public Speech* contains syntax as distinctly reminiscent: "Fix our eyes also: waylost: we the wanderers . . ." And in *The Fall of the City* the terseness of the alliterative poetry appears agreeably in the last words of the following brief verse paragraph:

> Let this conqueror come!
> Show him no hindrance!
> Suffer his flag and his drum!
> Words . . . . win!

The Anglo-Saxon practice in expletives accentuates Mac-Leish's poetry on many occasions. The first pages of his *Poems, 1924–1933*, contains the line: "Ha, but the sun among us . . ." In his highly anthropological poem, *Land's End*, occur the words, "Ho! they are free, they can sleep where they will." The *Sunset Piece*, a poem rich in Anglo-Saxon elements and based on an image of seafaring, commences:

> Christ but this earth goes over to the squall of time!
> Hi but she heels to it—rail down: ribs under: rolling
> Dakotas under her hull! . . .

To use this device it is necessary to remember no more than the first words of *Beowulf*—"Hwæt! we Gar-Dena."

Occasionally, too, he ends a passage with an abrupt exclamation, as when in harmony with the old manner he writes, "that was a victory!" We recall *Beowulf*, "that was a good king!" or the phrase in Cynewulf, "that is eternal death!" MacLeish's verse at times even comes so close to the Old English as to suggest unintentional parody.

Enough quotations have been given to illustrate how alliteration, chiefly a phase of versification in Anglo-Saxon, becomes a largely rhetorical feature in MacLeish. Nevertheless some further citations suggest how effectively and frequently MacLeish uses the basic alliterative line with four measures, changeable in character and number of syllables, having alliteration on the three earlier stresses. A few representative lines may be suggestive:

It is strange to sleep in the bare stars and to die . . .

A little light left over the tree top . . .

Hooked horse when he heard of the heft of the platters . . .

And he had no hope of the harvest of that ground . . .

And no man's name was needful to those wars . . .

We heard the rain in the reeds and the rear-guard halted . . .

From furthest off frontiers of foreign hours. . . .

The warders of wealth will admit him by stealth. . . .

Freedom for fools: force is the certainty! . . .

So did we lie in that land in the long days . . .

Sun-bright birds up—and the beat of sound . . .

Sour and smelling of spent milk and their children:

(And the smell of the smoke is sour in such places)
And we ate nothing or ill: and we ate roots: and our
Bellies were bitter for bread among those mountains . . .

Like the Anglo-Saxon poets, he uses not only this basic pattern,
but a number of variations. Especially in *The Fall of the City*
he shows a fondness for the usual rhythmical line alliterating,
however, ABBA. This rhetorical device he employs so frequently
as to suggest affectation. It may be illustrated thus:

Murder your foe and your foe will be murder! . . .

Once depend on iron for your freedom and your
Freedom's iron!
Once overcome your resisters with force and your
Force will resist you! . . .

A current of people coiling and curling through people . . .

He knows what he wants for he wants what he knows. . . .

Hinting and shadowing: sly in his hiding.

Like many other poets MacLeish employs alliteration for emphasis. So the concluding line of his largely anthropological *Pot
of Earth* reads: "Settling and stirred and settling in an empty
room."

Finally, one observes with pleasure how flexibly and easily
he handles fresh patterns of alliteration using types of versification not inherited from the old English. A poem on the economic depression in America entitled *1933* derives its imagery
from the *Odyssey* and is spaced in couplets. For four stanzas the
poet alternates alliterative and nonalliterative lines:

Till you come to a clean place
With the smell of the pine in your faces and

Broom and a bitter turf
And the larks blown over the surf and the

> *Rocks red to the wave-height:*
> *No sound but the wave's:*
>
> *No call of a cock from the*
> *Windward shore nor of oxen—*

In *The Fall of the City* occurs an even more obvious pattern:

> *Lay up your will with the gods!*
> *Stones cannot still you!*
>
> *Lay up your mind with the gods!*
> *Blade cannot blind you!*
>
> *Lay up your heart with the gods!*
> *Danger departs from you!*

Such, then, is the curiously indirect and strangely pervasive influence of the Old English poetry upon one of the younger Americans. His radio drama, *The Fall of the City*, impelled by political propaganda, shows that the Anglo-Saxon rhetorical devices are still literally in the air about us. From the foregoing exposition of his adaptations of medieval usages it must not be assumed that this is necessarily his chief source of literary inspiration. He acknowledges his deep debt to modern French verse as well. And no inclusive criticism is here intended. The Middle Ages in all aspects probably mean less to him than they meant to Hopkins and relatively no more than to Lewis and Auden. It is a pleasure, however, to see MacLeish's art frequently enriched and never burdened by the revival of interest in the earliest English verse. He uses this heritage organically, never pendantically. Of his indebtedness to the versification and other aspects of Old English poetry we shall speak later. But to the rhetoric he certainly owes much. That such relationships have seldom been remarked in modern criticism is doubtless owing to the unhappy circumstance that the enthusiasts for the newest English poetry are all too seldom readers of the oldest.

COLLOQUIAL IDIOM

Just as literary style swings between two extremes—oratory, artifice, rhetoric, and naturalness, simplicity, colloquialism—so does poetry. While a single author and even the same work may exhibit both veins, the distinction is easily drawn. At one end stands the language of self-conscious learning, at the other the unliterary and familiar speech of the people. Perhaps the most palpably rhetorical style used in the course of English literature is the prose euphuism of the sixteenth century; passages of equally pure low or colloquial language occur in the lighter dialect poems by Burns. Of course a dialect literature may be equally conspicuous for heights of rhetoric and valleys of linguistic familiarity. As a rule, however, a dialect is the language of a minority removed in space or cultural privileges from the main linguistic stem. Hence dialect verse supplies outstanding examples of colloquial verse.

Writing simply and familiarly in rhyme might seem to be no great task and to demand small aid from tradition, but often it is more difficult than writing elaborately.   Colloquialism no less than eloquence is a matter of custom and tradition; and, as Pope observed, those walk easiest who have learned to dance. Although the more familiar types of expression derive largely from the poet's observation of life aided by his superior imagination, even in these cases tradition proves useful and the great masterpieces are inspiring. Tom, Dick, and Harry imitated Pope's overt rhetorical mannerisms, but only true artists profited in their own works from his verses delicately attuned to the conversational tone.

Upon the threshold of the twentieth century, rhetoric threw herself down, panting and exhausted. The high style had done its uttermost; the language was due for a period of deflation. The great orators who had stirred England and America from pulpit, rostrum, or stage were dead or retiring into the background. Gladstone and Booth were already gone, Bryan and

Irving on the wane. English verse was more than willing to bid farewell to the age that begot Tennyson, Swinburne, Rossetti, Morris, and Francis Thompson. America, to be sure, had produced more luscious prose than verse; but after the turn of the century men wearied of the inflated style in all fields. Both countries witnessed an interlude in which the need vaguely felt for a naturalizing of the language of verse appeared in the vogue of second-rate poets with their sentimental and speciously simple idiom. Kipling began his dialect poetry a little too early to be acclaimed by the more Brahmin critics. But when John Masefield followed his *Salt Water Ballads* with *The Everylasting Mercy*, the critics were prepared to hail a new period in English poetry. The modern poet was to speak the language of the people—even of the submerged classes. Echoes of the more polished world had ceased to satisfy. Realism plotted his assignation with democracy in Saul Kane's barroom.

As the present century advanced, a loosening of the ideals of literary decorum and a thinning out of Victorian ornament have been increasingly evident. Distinguished verse deeply in debt to the spoken idiom of all social classes has been produced, just as novelists and playwrights of all shades of ability have exploited the cockney eloquence of London, the rich brogue of the Dublin streets, the archaisms of New England farms, the slang of New York subways, and the lyrical prattle of the cotton fields of the South.

This development raises the question of how far the new movement toward the vernacular in verse has been inspired by books and how far by a direct contact with contemporary life. Certainly much of the nineteenth-century rhetorical tradition was derivative, although no poets, orators, preachers, and actors exactly like those of the romantic age had flourished earlier. It remains to be seen how far the poets of our own century using a colloquial diction go beyond contemporary speech to draw encouragement, suggestion, and inspiration from predecessors. Doubtless the rhetorical school was the more literary. Doubtless, too, life has inspired more good writing directly through human contacts than indirectly through literary ones. But the latter are always too important to be neglected; because in certain fields they are peculiarly elusive and subtle they have often been overlooked by critics and through their very shadowiness all the more fully repay pursuit.

From all periods literary sources for colloquial poetry lie open to the twentieth-century writers of English verse. All the best of Chaucer is in an easy and familiar style. And the same may be said of Langland and the greater part—though not the whole— of Middle English verse. The restless and eclectic Elizabethans composed not only vast amounts of rhetorical verse but great quantities of colloquial verse. Their dramatic blank verse moves between the wildest fustian and the most graceful conversation. Many of their lyrics possess a simple and limpid purity of expression. Although some Cavalier poets, such as Cowley, tend to extreme artificiality, many notable passages and poems of that period are in a delightfully direct and natural language, notably the work of Suckling and Wither. While Pope and his school can be superbly (or absurdly) rhetorical, they can also be remarkably chatty and unaffected. Burns wrote as familiarly of the life of Ayrshire as Pope of London society. Vers de société still held a high level in Praed. Byron reached his greatest maturity in the light verse of the latter cantos of Don Juan. In this domain Byron and Praed were heirs of Pope and Prior. The stream of easy and graceful social verse which flowed lustily in all periods of English poetry since Chaucer tended to dry up in the nineteenth century, killed by the exalted romantic philosophy of the poet, by the luscious rhetoric of the romanticists on the one hand and their insidiously artificial sentimentalism on the other. The romanticists, fascinated by dreams and obsessed by spiritual problems over which they held no mastery and in encountering which they often lost both dignity and integrity, kept too far from the objective realities of life to cultivate the informal style and the special discipline in diction which are demanded. Some memorable colloquialism is, of course, to be found in the verse of the age, both serious and light—in a few sonnets by Elizabeth Browning, for example, or in Lowell's *Biglow Papers*. But the poet at the dawn of the present century seeking a skillfully turned poetry in the language of current speech would be likely to look past the Victorian and mid-romantic poets to almost any period of English poetry from Chaucer to Burns. He might listen to the talk in Saul Kane's barroom with the pleasant and profitable awareness that Burns, Gay, Prior, Suckling, Shakespeare, Skelton, and Langland had, so to speak, been there before him.

Many English and American poets have studiously examined the potentialities of a fresh and colloquial verse style. A landmark in such study appeared in 1938 in the form of *The Oxford Book of Light Verse* edited by W. H. Auden, the most brilliant of the younger English poets, which contains over five hundred specimens of verse from all periods since the thirteenth century written almost entirely in the colloquial vein. Auden's own poetry from his student years to the present illustrates the steadily increasing fruitfulness of such reading. We may conveniently begin our review of this field with Auden and his group of young poets chiefly sensitive to medieval influences, and so proceed to poets who have felt the fructifying effect of the Elizabethans, the Cavaliers, the Augustans, and, in a less degree, the romantics. Many poets are, of course, sufficiently sensitive and well read to come under the spell of a few writers from each of these periods.

Auden and the school of young poets in England have sought more or less consciously to strip English poetry of servility to all traditions subsequent to the Middle Ages. Eliot they find too Elizabethan, Yeats too metaphysical, Belloc too Augustan, and Masefield (despite his conscious efforts to the contrary) too romantic. They revive something of the idiom of Kipling, changing the political point of view. But they are forced back further, to find any age generally acceptable to them in literary style. Middle English serves best. Religious and other differences for the time being weigh little. They discover affinities in social aim and aesthetic outlook. The later Middle Ages from Langland to Skelton abound in "Satires on the Times." They afford a congenial object for the younger poets, on which their eyes rest with manifest pleasure.

Two substantial quotations, one from Chaucer, the other from Auden, help to show the colloquial style as it appears in a fourteenth-century and a twentieth-century poet. The passages are the more comparable in having a similarity in subject matter. In one a young student from Cambridge persuades a miller to give him a night's lodging, in the other a young man arranges for his lodging in a modern hotel. Each passage is equally remarkable for its easy, graceful, and genuinely conversational tone. The first is from *The Reeve's Tale*, the second from a play partly in verse, *The Dog beneath the Skin*. It is not maintained that Auden based his passage on any single passage in Chaucer, but merely that his general knowledge of Middle English materially helped him in writing as he did.

Chaucer wrote:

> *Thus pleyneth John as he gooth by the way*
> *Toward the mille, and Bayard in his hond.*
> *The millere sittynge by the fyr he fond,*
> *For it was nyght, and forther myghte they noght;*
> *But for the love of God they hym bisoght*
> *Of herberwe and of ese, as for hir peny.*
> *The millere seyde agayn, "If ther be eny,*
> *Swich as it is, yet shal ye have youre part. . . ."*
> *"Now, Symond," seyde John, "by seint Cutberd,*
> *Ay is thou myrie, and this is faire answerd.*

I have herd seyd, 'man sal taa of twa thynges
Slyk as he fyndes, or taa slyk as he brynges.'
But specially I pray thee, hooste deere,
Get us som mete and drynke, and make us cheere,
And we wil payen trewely atte fulle.
With empty hand men may na haukes tulle;
Loo, heere oure silver, redy for to spende."
　This millere into toun his doghter sende
For ale and breed, and rosted hem a goos,
And boond hire hors, it sholde namoore go loos;
And in his owene chambre hem made a bed,
With sheetes and with chalons faire yspred . . .

The modern play contains the following dialogue between a
young man named Alan, a hotel porter, and a page:

<blockquote>

Porter: I'm glad you've come, sir.
　　　　You want a room, sir?

Alan:　Please.

Porter: I'm sorry to be a trouble, sir:
　　　　A single or a double, sir?

Alan:　A single, please.

Porter: I'm still in doubt, sir.
　　　　With bathroom or without, sir?

Alan:　With bathroom, please.

Porter: Just sign your name, sir.
　　　　And date the same, sir.
　　　　Here, quickly, page boy,
　　　　Or you'll put me in a rage, boy.
　　　　Show this gentleman up to
　　　　Room 132.

Page:　Let me take your bag, sir.
　　　　It'll save you fag, sir.
　　　　Please follow me, sir.
　　　　I've got the key, sir.

</blockquote>

That the influence of one colloquial poet upon another is often real yet hard to trace appears in the relation of Auden to Middle English writers. He does not in any literal sense borrow from them; and perhaps fearing the charge of pedantry he deliberately hides from his readers if not from himself how much he has felt their presence. A typical instance of his shrewd use of his sources may be traced in his poem printed in *On This Island* without title and beginning, "Here on the cropped grass of the narrow ridge I stand." This piece describes the poet as meditating from a hilltop upon the present corrupt state of English life. The hill is a sharp-edged crest of cropped grass molded by British earthworks, looking to the west into Wales, to the east over the Midland plain with its rivers and cathedral towns. Small birds are in the air, cinemas in the town at his feet. The Cotswolds lie in the distance. A priory clock breaks the stillness and terminates his musing. This can be no other priory than Malvern; (on its first publicaction the poem was called *The Malverns*); and here the poet is musing on the state of England with a memory of the great medieval poet Langland, who in like fashion and with similar alliterative lines mused "meatless and moneyless on the Malvern hillside." The whole ode is Langland brought up to date. It is a poor example of Auden's colloquial manner, but a good instance of the really subtle ways in which the chief verse satirist of our times follows in the footsteps of his first distinguished predecessor.

Auden has of late written some charming light verse, but he has not always done so. His earliest poems, of which he speaks slightingly in his latest, are, for the most part, in a highly cryptic and artificial idiom, painfully congested in both thought and expression and intelligible only to a small audience not always including the present writer. In any case their involutions considerably exceed my own patience. Auden was at this time philandering with autocratic and aristocratic theories of government. Shortly, however, he turned with youthful zeal to champion a radical view of society. And as a natural accompaniment to his change in political philosophy there went a violent shift in style. A poet who had excelled his rivals in writing esoterically now commenced to excel in writing democratically. Auden's more recent poetry is not all easy reading, but the more colloquial aspect of Middle English verse chiefly affects his own simpler pieces.

In these poems his passionate desire for a healthier society than that now existing in the civilized world impels the writing. He addresses the whole community on the subject of its wellbeing. If not properly speaking a Communist, he is at least a communalist. A concern for the common man and the gift to speak in his behalf characterize the great Middle English poets, Chaucer and Langland, and Auden and his associates such as Lewis and MacNeice in only less measure. It seems natural that the latter should turn to the former as forerunners who succeeded in molding superb art out of congenial theories.

The politically radical writers today are inspired by the medieval sense of social solidarity; the conservatives are chiefly attracted to medieval literature as belles-lettres, as religious expression, or as political doctrine. Thus, Ezra Pound, who admires medieval poetry chiefly as belles-lettres and as an apology for the autocratic state, reads and carries away from what he reads very much what Longfellow did before him. Pound's variations upon the troubadours closely resemble Longfellow's *Tales of a Wayside Inn.* Again, T. S. Eliot believes as fervently in the medieval church as Pound in the medieval state, and yet Eliot is far less indebted to medieval than to Renaissance literature. The poets who stand closest to Middle English poetry today in style as well as in social outlook are unquestionably the radicals and even the Communists. Langland discusses communism as he understands it (involving the abolition of private property) and condemns it. But this apparently makes small difference to C. Day Lewis, who gains much from Langland as a poet and has quite possibly overlooked their differences in economic theory. This position of Lewis and his associates is historically speaking a happy one. The Victorian poets steeped themselves in themes from the old romances, retelling medieval stories. They assiduously cultivated medieval verse forms. But they failed to follow the most vital qualities in Chaucer, Langland, and their school: their artful but colloquial style, their humor, and their satire. This is also why the first part of Masefield's *Reynard the Fox*, in meticulous imitation of Chaucer, becomes as unlike Chaucer as possible. In the sober Masefield, Chaucer's salt has not merely lost its savor; it has wholly vanished. The same salt which escaped Masefield has been skillfully preserved by Auden.

One of the most widely quoted and admired of Auden's poems is the unnamed piece beginning, "Get there if you can and see the land you once were proud to own." It is in the meter of *Locksley Hall* as the first line alone might suggest, but, it is wholly devoid of the rhetoric of Tennyson, or, indeed, of any poets whatsoever. The language has a starkness, an earnest address to the objective fact, hardly seen in English between the fourteenth century and the World War. Its serious, direct pleading closely resembles the impassioned harangues of William Langland. Style is neither softened and enriched by the Elizabethan tradition, polished and refined by the Augustans, nor dilated and adorned by the romantics. The poem stands in important respects close to Langland, and Auden himself can hardly have overlooked such indebtedness.

In collaboration with the like-minded Louis MacNeice he wrote one of his longest and brightest poems, *Auden and MacNeice: Their Last Will and Testament*. The two young authors cannot have failed to remember the Middle English authors in whose footsteps they trod here: the many poets who left imaginary wills in verse, as Langland, Lydgate, Lyndsay, and Skelton. The relation, to be sure, is a general one, lying in the nature of the theme and the general spirit of the colloquial style rather than in borrowing specific ideas or phraseology. It is not unfitting, however, that among their ironical bequests they "leave to Stanley Baldwin, our beloved P. M., the false front of Lincoln Cathedral."

Important as the Middle English influence is on modern writers of colloquial verse, one must give some recognition to other periods as well. Auden himself shows in his anthology a wide and impartial acquaintance with verse in the lighter diction. His poem beginning, "Brothers, who when the sirens roar," is palpably an imitation of Burns, not only in versification, but in racy, popular idiom. It continues, in part:

> Ah, what a little squirt is there
> When of your aren't-I-charming air
>   You stand denuded.
> Behind your subtle sense of humor
> You hide the boss's sense of stuma,
> Among the foes which we enumer
>   You are included.
>
>   .   .   .   .
>
> A host of columbines and pathics
> Who show the poor by mathematics
>   In their defense
> That wealth and poverty are merely
> Mental pictures, so that clearly
> Every tramp's a landlord really
>   In mind-events.
>
> Let fever sweat them till they tremble
> Cramp rack their limbs till they resemble
>   Cartoons by Goya:
> Their daughters sterile be in rut,
> May cancer rot their herring gut,
> The circular madness on them shut.
>   Or paranoia.

It is hardly too fanciful to remark that were Burns living today he would be pleased to have written these stanzas.

Of chief interest are the subtle assimilations; but direct imitation or parody need not pass unregarded. Some of Auden's lightest as well as raciest verse appears in the volume written with MacNeice, *Letters from Iceland*. The greater part of Auden's contribution consists of a Letter, in five installments, to Lord Byron. It is a direct imitation of the marvelous later cantos of *Don Juan*, which are less romantic verse than the perfection of the society verse of the Augustan school of Swift and Prior. The Letter opens in the usual colloquial vein:

> *Excuse, my lord, the liberty I take*
> *In thus addressing you, I know that you*
> *Will pay the price of authorship and make*
> *The allowances an author has to do.*
> *A poet's fan-mail will be nothing new.*
> *And then a lord—Good Lord, you must be peppered,*
> *Like Gary Cooper, Coughlin, or Dick Sheppard.*

Not every poet proves so catholic in his tastes as Auden. In tracing the influence upon twentieth-century verse of the colloquial style from Shakespeare to W. S. Gilbert, one will generally be content to follow the indebtedness of each modern poet to a single age of literature. The verse of T. S. Eliot, for example, shows clearly his special fondness for the Renaissance. As we observe his repeated paraphrases of the Scriptures and liturgy, chiefly from the King James version of the Bible and the Anglican Prayer Book, and note his more secular reminiscences, principally from Shakespeare and the minor Elizabethan dramatists, his outstanding obligations to the Renaissance period become apparent. In almost all his poetry Eliot is shamelessly bookish, so much so that his verse is often nearly as academic as Ezra Pound's. His more rhetorical flights derive chiefly from religious sources, his more colloquial passages from the Elizabethan stage.

The more recent of his plays, notably *The Family Reunion*, show his profound debt to the eclectic Elizabethan blank verse, in both its ornate and its familiar passages. Indeed, the happy and logical evolution of his art becomes singularly clear in his last drama. But his contact with the Elizabethans began early. In his first verses he was treading the same paths. And since this book deals chiefly with nondramatic poetry, or with drama only as this affects style in nondramatic writing, the story may be sufficiently traced by considering Eliot's *Collected Poems* as published in 1936. His chief literary obligations are unquestionably to modern French verse, as his own published experiments in French verse amusingly indicate. Nevertheless, he early realized that the freedom from Victorian rhetoric which he sought could be learned by familiarity with the Elizabethans. Swinburne, to be sure, had fancied himself heir to Shakespeare and Marlowe. Eliot, however, interpreted the old playwrights differently. While Swinburne and Tennyson had sought in the Elizabethan dramatists the necessary inspiration for their rhetorical flights, Eliot considered them chiefly as masters of a genuinely colloquial tone. Especially in the satirical passages of the old playwrights he found much that was congenial to him in thought and style. For in Shakespeare, Marlowe, Webster, Ford, Chapman, Middleton, Marston, and their associates occur many bitter scenes of disillusionment with high ideals, couched in a language at once colloquial and poetic, realistic and imaginative. The best of Eliot's literary criticism has been directed not toward the French, but toward Donne and the English dramatists of the seventeenth century. Eliot has contributed greatly to the revival of interest in these men, their thought and style. His enthusiasm for Webster, master of a realistic dialogue in tragedy, he has shared with many writers of recent years, including a poet as different from himself as the romantic Rupert Brooke. His special interest in the dry, bitter, ashen language of Middleton and Marston proves equally significant. He could have turned to no writers of verse who had succeeded more fully in doing what he had himself set out to do. By exposing himself to such influences he cultivated a new and imaginatively virile colloquialism, at the same time that he was weeding out all traces of Victorian rhetoric and sentimentality. From a popular taste that preferred Wordsworth and Shelley, he turned to Middleton and Marston.

To an impartial student of the Elizabethans, the contrast between the strong venom of the old playwrights and the singularly harmless, futile, and diluted disillusionment of the author of *Ash Wednesday* must indeed be striking. The one casts the sinister shade of a gigantic pine, the other the melancholy shadows of a sentimental willow. Were they brought to life again, the Elizabethans would probably construe Eliot as a ridiculous courtier in one of their minor dramatic satires. But at least in point of style the relationship remains close. Eliot's verse is on important occasions a neurotic child begotten by the ghost of Elizabethan satire on the body of postwar enervation, an illegitimate offspring more fascinating than many less exotic heirs.

We shall do well to recall in more detail the phase of Elizabethan poetry closest to Eliot's colloquial manner. Being unprecedentedly eclectic, the old dramatists wrote both highflying poetry, rich in all varieties of poetic rhetoric, and low-pitched scenes in easy verse and, at times, even in prose. Their verse and prose, in fact, interchange with gradations almost too subtle for notice. The scene between Hamlet, Rosencrantz, and Guildenstern is typical of the best of such writing. At once colloquial and poetic, it represents one of the ripest developments of the imaginative Elizabethan stage. Marlowe's Mephistopheles and Jew of Malta, Webster's satirical characters, Flamineo and Bosola, Tourneur's D'Amville and Vendice, Middleton's De Flores and Bianca, and Marston's Malevole and Lampatho combine in their racy talk a sharp observation of the physical world, a bitter disillusionment with the moral world, an active fancy, and a concrete imagery as do the characters in Eliot's poems. In addition to the major cynics of the Jacobean stage are a large number of equally odious and ineffectual characters resembling Lucio in *Measure for Measure*, Apemantus in *Timon*, Parolles in *All's Well*, as a rule empty-headed, immoral, and contemptible followers of the great, the antithesis of a tragic nobility. They reflect, like Eliot's most typical characters, the ultimate disintegration following a materialistic and cynical philosophy. Their speech gnaws with a rat's tooth at the tottering fabric of the humanistic ideal. Here were already prepared for Eliot much of the sense and virtually all of the style which he desired. He hastened to take advantage of the models his keen and classical criticism had placed at his disposal.

Eliot is a better son of the Elizabethans for being himself eclectic. He imitates them in their most paradoxical aspects, notably in their religious idealism and their withering self-criticism. In Donne he finds epitomized the qualities more generously exhibited in the dramatists. His own works, as we have observed, vacillate between echoes of the Tudor prayer book and the Tudor stage; when he imitates the Tudor translation of the Missal and adaptations of Seneca he becomes literally the echo of an echo. In his earliest poems he attains his purest achievements in the colloquial manner reminiscent of the dramatists. As his thought has grown more theological, his poetry and drama have naturally exhibited ample borrowings from the unctuous rhetoric of the first generations of Anglican divines. Consequently it is to his youthful poems that we turn here.

The title poem of his first volume, *The Love Song of J. Alfred Prufrock*, exhibits in mature form the type of colloquialism thus far described, betraying the Elizabethans as at least one of his several sources:

No! I am not Prince Hamlet, nor was meant to be;
Am an attendant lord, one that will do
To swell a progress, start a scene or two,
Advise the prince; no doubt, an easy tool,
Deferential, glad to be of use,
Politic, cautious, and meticulous;
Full of high sentence, but a bit obtuse;
At times, indeed, almost ridiculous—
Almost, at times, the Fool.

And with a return to modern imagery in the next lines:

I grow old . . . I grow old . . .
I shall wear the bottoms of my trousers rolled.

"I grow old," echoes Falstaff's words to Doll.

Portrait of a Lady, the next poem in this group, is Eliot's masterpiece in the truly colloquial vein. In his own words, "this music is successful with a dying fall." The "dying fall" is, of course, from no less obvious an eminence than Shakespeare. It is a part of Eliot's allegiance to the Renaissance humanism of Spenser and Ben Jonson to incorporate numerous passages from his predecessors, thus creating a learned and somewhat esoteric poetry. Portrait of a Lady is one of several of Eliot's poems prefaced by a quotation from the Elizabethan drama, here from Marlowe's Jew of Malta. Scarcely in their own dramatic dialogue do the Elizabethans themselves surpass the combination of poetic feeling and complete colloquialism attained in this poem. The author perfectly catches the idiom of sophisticated talk in the world of London aesthetes. Whatever flights of language occur are quite within the range of polite conversation. The boldest excursion repeats favorite images of the Elizabethans who delighted in dancing bears, parrots, chattering apes, and tobacco. A fool in Ben Jonson might have spoken thus:

> And I must borrow every changing shape
> To find expression . . . dance, dance
> Like a dancing bear,
> Cry like a parrot, chatter like an ape.
> Let us take the air, in a tobacco trance—

The poem has been well recognized as marking a notable discovery for modern verse. It shows that Eliot rediscovered for English literature an art of colloquial poetry perfected in England over three centuries ago.

The familiar idiom and sordid imagery of other pieces in the same volume, such as *Preludes, Rhapsody on a Windy Night,* and *Morning at the Window,* likewise evince the nourishing root which Eliot's tree has flung out into the rich Elizabethan soil. Of his later productions, one of the most interesting in the familiarity of its idiom is *Sweeney Agonistes.* Much of the language is in keeping with the spirit of Elizabethan low comedy; but the final chorus is still more indebted to a vastly superior patter song in *Iolanthe.* In most of Eliot's other poems, even the briefest, the desired excitement is produced by the startling juxtaposition of unctuous rhetoric and colloquial vulgarity. *Sweeney Erect,* prefaced with a baroque passage from *The Maid's Tragedy,* begins with two verses clearly in this idiom before passing to the low register. This is Eliot's mock rhetoric, used for purposes of contrast:

> Paint me a cavernous waste shore
>   Cast in the unstilled Cyclades,
> Paint me the bold unfractuous rocks
> Faced by the snarled and yelping seas.
>
> Display me Aeolus above
>   Reviewing the insurgent gales
> Which tangle Ariadne's hair
>   And swell with haste the perjured sails.

This ultrarhetorical poetry is set against colloquial lines such as the utterance ascribed to Mrs. Turner, "It does the house no sort of good." Eliot apparently considers the contrast both profound and amusing, discovering his own life to be a tension between contemporary vulgarity and classical art, a tension relieved only by the Anglican Church in the role of *deus ex machina*. The Waste Land is merely an extension of the dilemma more succinctly presented in *Sweeney among the Nightingales*, while *Ash Wednesday* is wholly sacred and entirely baroque. As the poet has grown increasingly serious in his faith, he has occasionally found simple and almost colloquial language fit to carry his conviction, which is scarcely the case in his earlier religious poems. The important discovery made in *Portrait of a Lady* he has at times elaborated, at times ignored, but never improved. From the standpoint of technique, and from such a standpoint only, that poem may be held one of the most refreshing works in the evolution of modern poetry. In the central period of his career Eliot was inclined too much toward pedantry to be felicitously colloquial. His gifts in colloquial style he is at present employing rather in drama than in other forms of poetry.

That a poet may follow a great tradition without pedantry appears in the powerful pages of Robinson Jeffers. This writer not only inherits a theory of tragedy which we shall examine later, but a practice of style calling in the same poem for an exalted and familiar language. His many long poems show three general levels of style: a heroic vein evoked by passages of choral meditation; a medium vein, wherein the general narrative is conducted in the poet's usual manner; and a truly colloquial vein serving chiefly for realistic dialogue. Jeffers has been attracted, though less ardently than Eliot, to Elizabethan tragedy. Here he has found something of his doctrine of tragedy, as well as suggestions for his free use of various levels of style. In two of his recent poems he has quoted from Marlowe. But quotation or citation is itself weak evidence of a profound tie between the earliest and the latest master of tragedy in the English tongue. With a boldness hard to match outside Elizabethan tragedy, Jeffers gives to the same character lines of heroic elevation and plain homeliness. He allows the forces of thought and passion to determine the quality of the speaker's words. On the whole Jeffers excels in description, whether of the physical or psychological universe, rather than in close reproduction of speech. The minutae of speech so fascinating to Robert Frost hold no particular charm for him. Notwithstanding all this, his colloquial dialogue used with other language levels has the honor to call for comparison with Shakespeare and the other Elizabethans.

It is not alone through its drama that the Renaissance has enlivened the natural and colloquial tone heard frequently in modern verse. The lyric has exercised a considerable influence. Two universal tendencies in poetry took in the Renaissance lyric uncommonly sharp, divergent courses. On the one hand is the emotional lyric represented by the Elizabethan madrigalists and by Robert Herrick, on the other hand the intellectual lyric represented by Donne and such metaphysical poets as Thomas Traherne. Although a spoken idiom occasionally animates the intellectual type of verse, this species is too ingenious and high-pitched to be properly colloquial. The easiest and most natural diction is accordingly found among the singers addressing the heart rather than the mind. It is this type of song which chiefly influences the most blithesome of modern poets, W. H. Davies. We shall examine his indebtedness more broadly when considering the Elizabethan lyric tradition as such; his allegiance to colloquial tradition calls for less extended reference. The singular purity of diction in the verses of this lyric wanderer indicates that he is much more at home in books than a casual inspection of his life and writing lead one to suppose. Davies's poems abound in verbal echoes of the simplest lines in the lyrics of Shakespeare, Herrick, Marvell, Suckling, and the other masters of the most colloquial and unaffected of lyric diction. No living poet has a purer tone, although with him colloquialism is occasionally drawn to thinness. But many others who also excel in the simple and conversational vein are in debt to the Elizabethans, as, for example, the charming scholar-poet, John Crowe Ransom. It has clearly been the aim of Walter de la Mare, both in his children's verses and in his more serious poetry, to recapture the more pellucid tones of the mid-seventeenth-century lyric poets, while Yeats has succeeded in emulating those lyrics of the same period that occasionally combine, as do many short poems by Ben Jonson, an intellectual and a colloquial temper.

A conversational level, often without the reproduction of actual conversation, is achieved with high success in Osbert Sitwell's book of eclogues, *England Reclaimed*. The poet has many pleasant influences often indirectly playing upon him. His combination of swift, lucid language and rustic theme suggests the minor Elizabethan William Browne. Belloc in his light verse finds inspiration in the colloquial ease of minor eighteenth-century poets such as John Gay.

Many poets have been remarkably successful without using a colloquial style, while others have employed it at their own peril. E. A. Robinson wrote hundreds of pages of verse, much of it in dialogue form, with scrupulous stylistic standards of his own and small interest either in reproducing the tones of actual speech or in his predecessors as they have achieved such reproductions. The usually rhetorical Edna St. Vincent Millay in one long poem at least, *Conversation at Midnight*, essayed colloquial ease; but the drab and incoherent talk leads one to conclude the title truer than the author intended. To win distinction in the colloquial style in verse is really as difficult as it appears to be easy. Like a sonata by Mozart its treacherous simplicity smiles upon the artist and more often than not beguiles him into failure.

The reëmergence of naturalness and simplicity, of the tones of common speech and familiar cadence in poetry today, indicates a growing weariness with barren elaboration. Although it would be rash to ask poets to curb their fancies at all times to this humbler level of style, the tendency as now often evinced is an encouraging one. And although many great poets in the long course of English verse have from time to time excelled in the familiar style, none has done so as consistently and brilliantly as Chaucer, and in this respect no school as a whole has equaled the Middle English poets. Even the Augustans, who enjoy the advantage of being nearer to ourselves, are less fruitful, for they fail to rest content for long with their *vers de société* or their downright satire and revert repeatedly to their formal eloquence. Hence no poet affords such strong inspiration as Chaucer for those who wish to write simply and well; and to those who make this their goal no period in English verse is so congenial as Chaucer's age.

DIALECT IN VERSE

The colloquial style in verse enters its most striking phase in dialect poetry, with a notable tradition behind it and many distinguished practitioners in the present century. At first glance the dialect poet may seem to go directly to human nature without literary intermediaries. But in fact most dialect poetry stands on a considerable foundation of impressive precedent. No dialect poet, in any case, need feel that he writes without the authority of tradition. Hardy and D. H. Lawrence in England, Yeats and Synge in Ireland, Hugh MacDarmuid in Scotland, and Lindsay, Sandburg, and Frost in America have given renewed dignity to a practice well known to Chaucer, Spenser, Shakespeare, Burns, Tennyson, and many others of hardly less fame. Indeed, scarcely any type of language has a stronger precedent in verse. The lover of poetry in the Hellenic world frequently found himself confronted with verse in a dialect not his own, written in a more primitive or rustic language than that commonly spoken by the poet himself. Such poetry flourished the most luxuriantly among writers of pastoral eclogues in what appeared to the majority of its readers a slightly quaint style. From the stylistic viewpoint the author of *North of Boston* merely carries on the tradition of the Greek pastoralists.

How far do most dialect poets envisage themselves as traditional? The answer obviously varies with the poets themselves. Thus in the Renaissance about half of the leading practitioners of pastoral poetry used dialect in direct imitation of classical models. This is conspicuously true, for example, of Spenser's *Shepherd's Calendar* and of some of the pastoral scenes in Ben Jonson. A century later John Gay in his spoofing pastorals carried on the tradition. The most interesting of later pastoral and rustic poets in England is the Dorset author, William Barnes. The chief of rustic poets is, of course, Burns. The question of their conscious imitation of earlier authors in the use of dialect cannot be answered with complete finality, but Burns felt himself fortified by this most venerable of traditions and Barnes, a scholar in many languages, certainly enjoyed such support. Among Barnes's works is a translation into the Dorset dialect of a rustic Italian pastoral by the Renaissance poet Sacchetti.

The use of dialect may, of course, be either naïve or sophisticated. The poet may live so completely in a provincial society and be so innocent of the main stem of national or continental literature as to use dialect from necessity rather than choice. Few distinguished poets, if there are any, have been so illiterate, unless we admit to the rank of distinction authors of anonymous ballads. The sophisticated writer of dialect is a cosmopolitan who either by birth, education, or travel has acquired familiarity with dialectal peculiarities which he imitates in writing. So a novelist or playwright may introduce a dialect character in a minor role. In poetry the most familiar condition is neither an extreme of innocence nor of sophistication. The most memorable dialect verse is written by men who have possessed from childhood a familiarity with a certain dialect, often their native tongue, and who after a liberal training persist in using this long-familiar language in their poetry. Dante's apology for Italian as the speech dearest to his heart, learned as a child and used by his neighbors, indicates the attitude of the best dialect poets. Such men inherit the dialect, acquire the standard speech, and profit by the long literary tradition which wisely sanctions in the poet the use of the native and maternal accent.

The observer of these matters must resist the beguiling temptation to view the poet as the simple swain which he may superficially appear to be. One artifice of the pastoral poet is to hide his literacy. He must seem simpler than he really is. We are to fancy that we hear not the poet but the shepherd speaking. While the classical tradition has certainly waned in the last century, English poetry has a new and sparkling fountainhead of dialect poetry which has itself the vigor if not the dignity of a classical source. It is a plausible hypothesis that the greater part of all good dialect verse in England for over a century has come at least under some influence from Burns. In considering this case we must recall that the dialect poet tries to preserve an air of innocence. When Burns wrote his rustic epistles he did not advertise his relations to Horace; he stole in silence. The cross-fertilization from one dialect to another is a disturbing thought as it intrudes upon the aesthetic experiences of the poem itself. The poet may even learn his art of beguiling the public by first beguiling himself. He may not himself know how far underground his roots actually go or by what subtle suggestions he comes to write as he does.

The instance of Robert Frost is interesting not only because he occasionally writes exceptionally good dialect poetry but because so much of his best art lies in his manipulation of language. His intellectual subtleties belong essentially to the last century; he is not above sentimentality; his doctrine is comforting only to those who are content to see the passing hour pass without change; in short, he rejoices in a horse-and-buggy mind, but he remains one of the liveliest and best of American poets because of his mastery of words.

Frost is certainly not one of the poets depending most upon dialect. He has never written a poem in which more than a small fraction of the words and phrases are definitely provincial. If we divide his work roughly into ten parts, approximately one part is clearly New England dialect, two parts are Americanisms, three parts general English colloquialisms, and the rest standard literary English. But statistics cannot give us the truth. Virtually all of his mature writing is remarkably successful in conveying an impression of the spoken voice. In the chemistry of his art, the element of dialect resembles a capsule transmitting its own powerful coloring and flavor to the whole. New England dialect is not the whole body of Frost's language, but it is the heart. Even where the words and phrasing stand on the printed page as perfectly normal English, the reader tends to hear these words as spoken with much of the delicate patina of dialect which the poet himself uses as he reads aloud. His own reading during his earlier and most creative period was especially rich in an indefinable colloquialism. He consistently expresses the New England temperament in printed words attuned to New England speech. His fondness for reading his own poems to public audiences cannot be set down to vanity or acquisitiveness: he takes obvious pleasure in bringing to those who have either a vague idea or no idea of the New England idiom the curiously knotty, apple-tree language it really is, at once gracious and grotesque.

But to return to the problem of Frost's actual debt to other dialect poets. He did not start his career as a dialect poet. A *Boy's Will*, his first book, is a collection of several commonplace and a few perfect lyrics, without marked provincialisms. In his next and most surprising volume, *North of Boston*, he made an about-face, writing over a dozen rustic eclogues, with many traces not only of racy colloquialism but of actual dialect. The volume is thoroughly consistent with itself. It represents a step deliberately taken by an artist who knew his aims thoroughly. As he reflected on the possibility of success, he must have realized that the public of 1915, unlike that of 1715, was willing to take provincialisms seriously, in fact almost eager to do so. A tradition had been sanctioned to this effect. Though this knowledge must have been encouraging, no such attitude of the public was, of course, definite enough to shape the actual contours of his art. From whom did Frost actually learn? Hardly from some of the local sources lying near at hand. Lowell had surpassed his own romantic odes and sentimental lyrics in the political satires of his highly dialectal *Biglow Papers*. But Frost, to whom as a poet the New England Town Meeting means nothing, shies from politics as all-too-human and would hardly be inspired by Lowell's more intimate picture of the New England farmer. Frost is in a sense the more classical poet. Although he makes no allusion to Burns in his poems, it is hard to believe that he had not read and learned from him. The author of *The Exposed Nest*, which depicts farmers deploring a nest exposed in mowing, surely must have remembered another nest uncovered in Ayrshire. Unlike Burns as Frost is in temperament, philosophy, background, and lyrical technique, in speech technique they stand as close as it is possible for a New Englander to stand to a Scotsman—which is fairly close. In each poet we find a pungent, earthy language, sharp in imagery, tender in feeling, and often grotesque in humor. Burns would probably find some of Frost's poetry painfully slow; but no doubt he would be immensely excited by such writing as Frost's fine melodramatic piece, *The Witch of Coös*. This is one of his most dialectal poems, almost as racy in the New England manner as *Death and Doctor Hornbook* is in the Scotch.

In temperament Frost shares more in common with Barnes, the Dorset pastoralist and spokesman for a part of England whence many early settlers of New England came. Barnes and his school had used themes and devices thoroughly familiar in the first decade or two of the twentieth century and ready for the use of a really inspired poet, such as Frost, when he appeared. Barnes, for example, has several eclogues in anapaestic verse remarkably similar in movement, charm, and naïveté to Frost's *Blueberries*. Frost's admirable *In the Home Stretch*, depicting a family on moving day, resembles in theme and feeling several of Barnes's better-known and more effective pieces. These men succeed as pastoral poets precisely where Wordsworth proves weakest. Wordsworth's *Excursion* is the most gigantic of all pastorals. The first episode (once an independent poem) bears considerable resemblance to Frost's *Black Cottage*. Happily for Frost, he uses a much racier and more colloquial language than Wordsworth, who always remained a poor spokesman for the farmers because in denial of his doctrines he never really reproduced their language. Burns, Barnes, and Frost, often speaking the tongue actually used in rural Ayrshire, Dorsetshire, or New Hampshire, enjoy an initial advantage in linguistic vitality.

While no poet in recent years has acquired wide reputation by poems largely or wholly in strict dialect, more than might be supposed have, with Frost, made significant departures from standard English. In America, for example, Vachel Lindsay was brought up in a town loud with the voices of racy Westerners and illiterate colored folk, to which he listened attentively and profitably. Many of his best-remembered poems reflect these dialects, especially that of the Negro. E. E. Cummings records in striking poems the harsh and unpleasing slang of New York's downtown streets; Carl Sandburg faithfully records Chicago slang. Dialect has seldom been used in verse more pungently than by these two authors. In England some of the most vigorous hands have composed dialect poems. It was inevitable that so keen an observer of the common man as Kipling should when writing verse have accurately recorded his speech. More illustrative of the favor in which such poetry has been received in recent years are the poems with an Irish brogue by James Stephens, occasional racy sketches by so fastidious a poet as Lascelles Abercrombie, and a few poems recording the language of the cockney in the trenches by such a profound artist as Wilfred Owen. All these, too, have their precedents. Swift in verse had recorded the brogue of Irish servants; Byron, in *Don Juan*, of the London cockney; and Shakespeare, the rough speech of soldiers from Wales, Scotland, and England on the fields of Flanders. Although never pedantic in imitations of their predecessors, these modern poets in the practice of dialect can hardly be thought of as writing without the support and inspiration of predecessors. English verse enjoys a catholic tradition. Since Chaucer's *Canterbury Tales* it has been the custom of poets to float not only upon the main stream of literary English, but down tributaries through pastoral hill and urban gutters. Poetry should employ the thought and speech of an entire people: not only the conversation of such urban aesthetes as Eliot sketches in his *Portrait of a Lady*, but the colloquial English of all members of the community. By encompassing the whole it has kept, and does keep, fully alive. Just as the diction of the more literary poetry is continually refreshed by the introduction of the colloquial, the colloquial itself is greatly enlivened and whetted by the use of dialect.

THE ANALYTICAL TRADITION

By the middle of the Victorian period a number of powerful poets were leading a trend away from Parnassian idealism and cloying sentiment to realistic analysis in verse. Such authors, whether or not they were true poets, were essentially psychologists reasoning about ideals, analyzing emotions, and dissecting personalities. While Keats and the romantic poets had sought truth through beauty, these radicals now sought beauty through truth. Life demanded of them a strenuous laboratory analysis. The poet no longer waved the magic wand of Prospero; more magical in its promise and effect was a style suggestive of the instruments of the surgeon. Sick society required not a romantic bouquet of roses but the scientific service of poet-physicians. Vulgar and difficult their work might appear to the reactionary, but in their own eyes and those of their public it offered a new hope.

The movement was led by Robert Browning, aided by George Eliot, and materially advanced by the verse of two men who during the nineteenth century were primarily novelists: George Meredith and Thomas Hardy. No figures of comparable stature engaged in quite the same task in American poetry; but along slightly different lines the difficult soul-analysis in the poetry of Emily Dickinson was soon to prove even farther in advance of the times. Living poets and critics today are certainly justified in acknowledging their debt to Emily Dickinson; but it remains regrettable that, because of changes in idiom not always fundamental, the part played by the great Englishmen just mentioned has often been overlooked. Browning's contribution is on the most cursory consideration too obvious and important to require lengthy exposition. That all traces of an elevated style (especially in his later poems, such as *Parleyings with Certain People of Importance*) have been discarded in favor of a fluid, mundane, and analytical one is at once apparent. Browning delights in the analysis of a personality or an idea with the fervor of an ardent psychologist or dialectician. Repeatedly his poems seem creative quite as much in the spirit of science as of poetry. The proximity of his verse to Victorian prose admits no question. Hardy subjects destiny herself to the hard and dry analysis which Browning applies to men and women. He performs an autopsy on a defunct universe. Critics such as Edmund Gosse found Hardy prosaic, questioning the merit of his poetry. Indeed Hardy himself came to view much of his early verse as experimental and perfected his philosophical and psychological poetry only during the latter years of his active life, over a third of which was passed in the present century. The historical importance of the role of the more cheerful Meredith is at once greater and less widely recognized. He dealt in verse with the same subject matter which attracted him in prose, writing, for example, both in verse and prose an essay on the comic spirit as well as numerous works on social problems of the age. He rashly composed odes that are treatises on political theory and narrative poems actually dissertations on psychological theory. Meredith became the laureate of Darwinism, science and rationalism directing the spirit of his style no less than his doctrine. His verse in all respects resembles his prose except that the former is more difficult because more abrupt and succinct. His *Sage Enamoured* was once declared to be the most obscure of all English poems, and even today few are harder to unriddle. Although no poet could be more sentimental than Meredith on occasion, in many cases he outstripped all his contemporaries in intellectuality. Even where his ideas are not profound, his style remains something of a puzzle. He enjoys teasing his reader with a meaning wrapped in tantalizingly oblique expression. Frequently making matters doubly arduous, to a cryptic style he adds a cryptic allegory. This holds true for two of his most genuinely inspired poems, *The Woods of Westermain* and *A Faith on Trial*. Although some of his moods and mannerisms are peculiarly Victorian, so much of his work proves highly modern that he deserves more than any other British poet of the nineteenth century to be regarded as the historical progenitor of the twentieth.

This intellectual type of verse, bordering upon prose, may, then, best be illustrated in Browning and Meredith. Quotations of some length from each of these poets give the best evidence of the Victorian origin of a style that with unimportant variations persists today. In his *Parleyings with Certain People of Importance*, Browning writes about the eighteenth-century poet Christopher Smart in the following highly elliptical style:

> *Was it because you judged (I know full well*
> *You never had the fancy)—judged—as some—*
> *That who makes poetry must reproduce*
> *Thus ever and thus only, as they come,*
> *Each strength, each beauty everywhere diffuse*
> *Throughout creation, so that eye and ear,*
> *Seeing and hearing, straight shall recognize,*
> *At touch of just a trait, the strength appear,—*
> *Suggested by a line's lapse see arise*
> *All evident the beauty,—fresh surprise*
> *Startling at fresh achievement? "So, indeed,*
> *Wallows the whale's bulk in the waste of brine,*
> *Nor otherwise its feather-tufts make fine*
> *Wild Virgin's Bower when stars faint off to seed!"*
> *(My prose—your poetry I dare not give,*
> *Purpling too much my mere gray arguments.)*

A gray argument indeed, shot through at times, however, with strange flashes of imagination. Similarly in Meredith's poem *Napoleon*, we read the following intellectually inspired verses:

> *His Policy the act which breeds the act*
> *Prevised, in issues accurately summed*
> *From reckonings of men's tempers, terrors, needs:—*
> *That universal army, which he leads*

Who builds Imperial on Imperious Fact. . . .
His dispense
Of Justice made his active conscience;
His passive was of ceaseless labour formed.
So found this Tyrant sanction and repose;
Humanly just, inhumanly unwarmed.
Preventive fencings with the foul intent
Occult, by him observed and foiled betimes,
Let fool historians chronicle as crimes.
His blows were dealt to clear the way he went:
Too busy sword and mind for needless blows.
The mighty bird of sky minutest grains
On ground perceived; in heaven but rays or rains;
In humankind diversities of masks,
For rule of men the choice of bait or goads.
The statesman steered the despot to large tasks;
The despot drove the statesman on short roads.
For Order's cause he laboured, as inclined
A soldier's training and his Euclid mind.

And Meredith was not the only nineteenth-century poet who looked on beauty bare.

Some passages in Shakespeare and George Chapman, to mention two representative Elizabethans, are stylistically far from transparent. The most obscure style in English prior to the modern symbolists is undoubtedly that of the school of Donne and the seventeenth-century metaphysicals. But Shakespeare, more studied than ever, has been less a direct influence on verse in the present than in the preceding century, while Donne and the metaphysical poets have influenced the basic theory of modern poetry even more than its verbal practice. The intellectual style cultivated by Cowley and his followers in their so-called Pindaric Odes and verse epistles was followed in ode and didactic poem by many a belated lover of the Cavalier school—Francis Thompson, for instance. Nevertheless, as the analysis in this chapter will help to show, modern tendencies to intellectualism, realism, and analysis are owing more to the persistent pressure of the radical Victorians than to the belated revival of radical sixteenth- or seventeenth-century writers.

These lustier influences might be traced through a number of poets but nowhere more readily than in E. A. Robinson, who began his career well before the revival of interest in the school of Donne and terminated it when that movement had already passed its peak. That Robinson is to some extent representative hardly needs urging; he has been as much imitated as admired. This particular phase of his style and imagination is but one of his many aspects commanding our attention. Few American poets have in recent years done so much distinguished work. So varied, indeed, are his mind and achievement that the precise place of his analytical style in his poetry as a whole merits attention, lest we appraise it for more or less than the truth.

Much of Robinson's poetry is free from this analytical tendency. Especially among his earliest volumes appear several examples of sentimental verse. Throughout one of his popular poems, *Isaac and Archibald*, he consents to imitate Wordsworth's most bucolic manner. On occasions he writes a singularly straightforward or even colloquial style. *Richard Cory*, one of his best-known pieces, is no more obscure than a ballad by Kipling. Once his use of the word "wonderful" in *King Jaspar*, his last poem, appears positively banal. On the other hand a few passages in *Captain Craig* reflect the extravagant and grotesque eloquence of Carlyle. Particularly sensitive as he was to the power of Shakespeare and the Bible, many passages betray earlier forces than those of the radical Victorians. Such ornamental phrases as "the wingless crawl of time" and "embellished rhetoric of regret" are heirs of Shakespeare's eloquence. The analytical element in Robinson is only a little stronger than the colloquial in Frost: in short, passages well marked by this style comprise a minority of his actual lines, but leave a strong coloring upon the whole. Robinson was at first widely admired for his more conservative qualities; but when the radicalism of yesterday becomes the orthodoxy of tomorrow, he will presumably be best remembered for his flights of analysis. *Tristram*, his only poem to have a wide popular appeal, marked a notable departure from the major part of his work. The longest and most romantic of his trilogy of Arthurian romances, it is written with a warmth and expansiveness unusual to the New England poet. It is much more heavily indebted to the Elizabethan and pseudo-Elizabethan tradition than any of his other verse novels, such, for example, as *Roman Bartholow* and *Matthias at the Door*. In this conspicuous work, then, Robinson achieved a popular success precisely by discarding his native dryness. The nine psychological tales in verse, six of which were written after *Tristram*, although never winning during his lifetime a comparable triumph, much better represent his favorite manner. Not all his poetry, therefore, can be described as difficult and dry in coloring, but much of it can be.

A bristling rationalism struck congenial soil in the fields of New England, Robinson's style resembling a thistle springing in her fields: a silken flower and a prickly leaf. It is a pity that Hagedorn's biography fails to appreciate this phase of his New Englandism. Even in the pit of the New York subway, Robinson lived spiritually in Tilbury Town. He was brought up among people uncomfortably critical of one another. Uncompromisingly harsh, but inveterately skeptical, as reserved in praise as in judgment, he always remained the ultra-New England poet: Frost seems tropical beside him. Although Frost rightly declares himself highly sensitive to the "inner weather," he has painted the outer weather of his native country with a romantic warmth and affection approached by no other man, and least of all by the chief son of Gardiner, Maine, a town significantly further "north of Boston" than Frost's dwelling places. To appreciate

Robinson's analytical style we should begin not with its literary but with its human environment. He lived as though in the center not of a roomful of books but of the tumultuous privacy of a winter storm, with nervously critical men and women face to face in wooden houses. Robinson's idiom is chilled by cold fog and melting snow. He probes his characters as though he had been accustomed to scrutinize a few housemates through a score of winters. His verse tales have few persons and little action, but what persons or action there are he analyzes relentlessly.

As a man this more poetical Thorstein Veblen loved billiards and detective stories, esteemed science, was fascinated by all qualifications, and profoundly believed in the mysterious intricacies of the human personality. Repeatedly in his poems, sometimes with quite foreign associations, he describes the style that for him constituted the essential man. He might have addressed his own Muse as Prince Jasper addressed the Queen:

> Mother, your manners are immaculate,
> Majestical, and somewhat serpentine.

One of his characters in *Amaranth* observes of the poetic mind:

> There are complexities and reservations
> Where there are poets, for they are alone,
> Wherever they are. They are like Ampersand;
> They do not like us if we harass them
> Unseasonably.

Ampersand, it will be remembered, is a mysterious black cat. Similarly in his sonnet to Zola he glances at his own style when he speaks of "the grim dominion of his art." He dedicates a poem of over three hundred lines to Rembrandt's love of shadows and the failure of the artist's public properly to appreciate their charm. Characteristically he writes of one of his mysterious figures as having his reasons hidden in a deep well. Zoe,

his personification of truth, he describes as "intricate and in-
dustrious." In the following he certainly intends a travesty on
his own verse:

> "Whenever your poet or your philosopher
> Has nothing richer for us," he resumed,
> "He burrows among remnants, like a mouse
> In a waste-basket, and with much dry noise
> Comes up again, having found Truth at the bottom
> And filled himself with its futility. . . ."

One notices his fondness for the words "inferentially" and
"dubiously." Behind all this art stirs the burrowing mole of the
Puritan conscience, much aided by the intellectual developments in English poetry during the later half of the nineteenth
century.

Some of his most involved language appears in the grandilo-
quent but slightly prosaic eloquence of *The Man against the
Sky, Dionysus in Doubt,* and other pieces modeled upon the
rhetorical style of the nineteenth-century intellectual ode or
verse essay. Here immensely long and rambling sentences, perplexing constructions, and wordiness produce something of the
obscurity but little of the characteristically dry and crisp manner
of his more representative poems. His inspiration flourishes best
in the field wherein he exercises it most, in psychological narrative ranging from tightly packed sonnets to poems as long as
novels. It is in this, the major and most distinctive section of
his work, that one chiefly looks for his analytical style. Intensely
intellectual, he grapples with the most mysterious manifestations of feeling in an almost painfully exact language, intricate
but not properly speaking elaborate or rhetorical. The intricacies
observed can be unriddled only by his correspondingly involved
language.

His ingenious search for the one exact word appears in such
instances as his imaginative use of "upheaval" to signify a hill

and "absolute" to express the exact posture of a bold man in a crisis. What he achieves in phrases he attains with an even clearer purpose in similes. As he describes an undesired crown falling over the face of a king to obscure his vision, he uses an image almost mathematically correct. The image fits neatly and perfectly. Such style follows one of the typical urges of the best nineteenth-century prose. The expression is strikingly accurate; from the Parnassian view of poetry it is hardly poetic.

The poet, who was himself worried about his dry style, aimed perhaps too often to inform and too seldom to delight. In his sonnet on Thomas Hood, for example, he tells us, "His brother was the branded man of Lynn." Although Robinson uses this information in the moving thought of his poem, his style becomes for the moment clearly didactic. Robinson attributes "stubborn skill" to his beloved George Crabbe, which led Frost to remark that Robinson's style was rather a "happy skill." But at times, as in the cases of Browning, Meredith, and Hardy, to absolve it of obstinacy is difficult. Again in his poem to Hood he refers to those who sailed "with Ines to the West." Occasionally the allusions in his verse put a heavy tax upon the reader's knowledge.

His regard for the more arduous analysis often appears in the opening lines of his poems. He enjoys plunging into the midst of a character or an action, striking the dominant spiritual note but mystifying the reader as to the merely material events. Almost all his poems, short or long, begin in this abrupt manner. *Avon's Harvest*, for example, tells us that Avon feared, but just what he feared is not clear. It is a favorite technique in the more intellectual school of poets generally.

As he begins, so he continues, one puzzle issuing from another. His inclination to rationalism leads him into perpetual doubt. The "whether-or" construction haunts him. More often than not the question remains unanswered. One of his earliest psychological poems, *Tasker Norcross*, even begins with

"Whether," his *Nicodemus* with "If." "May or may not" like-wise appeals to him. One long passage in *The Glory of the Nightingales* significantly and typically ends with the word "perhaps." The same dubiety leads him to give the atmosphere surrounding an action rather than its simple material mani-festation. He allows us to judge for ourselves whether an old maid killed herself. All he says is,

> Love, with its gift of pain, had given
> More than one heart could hold.

Similarly he masks the deaths of husband and wife in a poem called *The Mill*. He writes only of "what was hanging from a beam" and of the suicidal atmosphere surrounding the woman's death.

A lover of subtlety, this archmaster of ghost stories delights in delicate distinctions. Once, for example, he acutely contrasts the verbs "to see" and "to know." His phrases betray his mental refinement, as when he speaks of the "tinglings of inveigle-ment." Many of the somewhat archaic words that please him have a logical flavor, as "howbeit," "thereupon," "contrarywise," "residual," "dereliction," "impredictably," "negative immunity," and "contingent entertainment." He enlarges and perplexes his vocabulary with numerous old and seldom-used words, as "um-brage" and "almagest," or such rare words as "foremeasured" and "mordacious." Scientific and other technical terms attract him. He writes most unpoetically of "parallel lines," "my econ-omy," "catalepsy," "aneurism," "repetend," "architrave," "equiv-alence," and "biologists." "Bolshevists" is no burden upon his tongue. The words "New York" have an uncomonly brassy ring in a blank verse. One encounters such chilly phrases as "discredited ascendancy," "heritage of identity," "vinous in-novation," "achieving maintenance," and "unfortified assump-tion." Such was not the poetic diction of the conservative poets of the early nineteenth century and indeed it was seldom among

their predecessors. The radical innovations of Browning and
Meredith chalked out the way.

Involved syntax is a conspicuous feature of the analytical and
intellectualized style. Confusingly parenthetical phrases appear
frequently, as here, where parenthesis is further perplexed by
supposition:

> If you had lived,
> Your freaks of caution, and your hesitations,
> And your uncertainties—if once you saw
> Before you what was only yours to take,
> And hold, and say was yours—would have been clogs
> And obstacles that would have maddened me,
> And might have tempted me to tell worse lies.

It is no easy walking through such a word-jungle as this:

> Now he could see; and he could ask in vain
> If earlier sight would have seen far enough
> To read for what they were the fire and gold
> Of shining lies that opportunity
> Had held and waved until they were all true.

The ungrammatical opening sentence of *Avon's Harvest*, with
its circuitous tangle of relative clauses, epitomizes the darker
side of Robinson's style:

> Fear, like a living fire that only death
> Might one day cool, had now in Avon's eyes
> Been witness for so long of an invasion
> That made of a gay friend whom we had known
> Almost a memory, wore no other name
> As yet for us than fear.

In such passages the poet's meaning is more readily clarified by
a rapid, dramatic reading than by a slow, pensive one. Similar
lines have spawned the commentators of Browning and the
textual emendators of Shakespeare.

One cannot always be clear as to the antecedents of the poet's pronouns. Or he boldly omits pronouns altogether. And he uses an almost affected word order, as appears in the following:

> Who sees unchastened here the soul
> Triumphant has no other sight
> Than has a child . . .

As may be inferred from the above quotations, the poet's fondness for pure abstraction endangers the conventionality of his poetic diction. Such lines as the following, rich in generalization and bare in tangible statement, contribute at once to the dryness and the difficulty, the rationalistic and the "unpoetical" flavor of his verses.

> In his fear there was a numbness of defiance,
> Like a spell to foil an onslaught of illusion;
> In his pride there was a calm and overwhelming
> Recognition of irrevocable changes.

Doubtless these quotations from Robinson taken together give an impression of an even drier, cooler, and more analytical style than he really has. Extreme cases have been chosen to isolate this quality and to examine it for what it is. The poet's own avowed fears that he had overdone his austerity may or may not have been well founded; into this we need not go. Here it suffices to point out that a poet of high gifts continually adopted the analytical and proselike idiom bequeathed to him by the most experimental of the later Victorians, fused it with his own New England temperament, and turned it brilliantly to his creative purpose. He is so far a leader in this modern idiom—though it has been widely practiced with variations by countless poets—that in examining his pages we capture the gist of all and at the same time enjoy this severe idiom at its undoubted best.

INFLUENCE OF THE AUGUSTAN WITS

Modern literature owes more to the prose than to the verse of the Augustan eighteenth century; the poets of the age are less congenial to readers today than the novelists, essayists, biographers, and letter writers. The current view of the period is that its greatness lay rather in making life an art than in making the poetic art thoroughly alive. Its materialistic society excelled in arts demanding the most obvious craftsmanship. It was a brilliant period for the mechanical development of the orchestra and for orchestral compositions, as well as for architecture, landscape gardening, household furnishing, costume, and decoration generally. The freer flights of the imagination characteristic of the purest poetry tended to languish in so conventional an age. Poetry, held largely within Horatian limits, produced brilliant verse essays, satires, and epistles, but no narratives equal in power to the chief novels of the age and few lyrics or poetic dramas comparable to the products of earlier centuries. Where Augustan poetry preserves the essence of a great culture, it has been cherished. But its peculiar mannerisms and technique, its polish and detail, have not been widely imitated in this century. While its diction has sometimes been admired in its native setting, relatively few modern poets have ventured to transplant or crossbreed from it, commonly fearing that closed couplets, classical epistles, and Augustan rhetoric would seem frigid and affected when associated with the themes of the twentieth century. The highly artificial diction appears in no more than half the Augustan verse, though the genuine humanity of a great part of this poetry might profitably have been an inspiration to more modern writers than is in fact the case. A few of our contemporaries have attempted close imitations of the Augustans, with results more charitably forgotten than remembered; but a few others have utilized this tradition with happier consequences.

The Augustans have actually been better remembered than

a cursory view of modern published verse leads one to assume. This school excels, of course, in occasional poetry, vers de société, and light verse of all kinds. Such verse is even today much more often written than printed and more often printed than collected. Many dilettantes in rhyme write in honor of a birthday, a festival, a reunion, a dog, or a cat, much as Mrs. Thrale or Horace Walpole included occasional verses on such subjects in their correspondence. Much Augustan verse, then, was never designed for publication and found its way only indirectly into print. Still more verse of a similar nature today remains in private hands, with allusions too local, ephemeral, or personal even to see the light of the local newspaper. Such verse is often by men and women who are familiar with Augustan poetry and materially aided in their productions by such an acquaintance. Perhaps nine tenths of the academic verse written in America today takes this form. A colleague, for example, is about to retire. He may address his farewell to his friends in heroic couplets, and they address their good wishes to him in this inviting form. Persons interested in the practice of poetry as a lively, rather than as a fine, art naturally turn to this quiet but sparkling source.

Comparatively recent editions and critical studies of Prior, Gay, Collins, Swift, Churchill, and Cowper indicate the vitality of the tradition. The romantic prejudice against Augustan poetry as prosaic trifling is clearly wearing off. Dryden has gained immensely in prestige among the poets of today, a fact strikingly shown in essays by T. S. Eliot and Mark Van Doren, for example. It is customary in a small circle to quote Dryden, not only as a critic but as a poet. Meanwhile it has become popular among a larger group to attend and applaud the lyrics of Gay's operas, which have been revived with sensational success in England and America. Shakespeare of late has too often resembled a revered institution; Gay has been the unfeigned delight. The more sober Augustans, such as James Thomson, author of *The Seasons*, have in recent years less often been read by poets to suggest new features for their own verses than used by critics as instances of bad taste—door mats on which to wipe one's feet before entering the shrine of Donne. But if the current towards the Augustans continues to flow at the present rate, even *The Seasons* may enjoy at least a part of the popularity which it possessed a century ago; and Eliot may discover Young's *Night Thoughts*, as Wordsworth found them, a rich province for plunder and pillage.

Thus the Augustans have influenced our contemporaries more through the compelling charm of their culture than through the technique of their verse. In a later chapter we shall examine to what extent some of the modern poets, as the Sitwells and the American, Wallace Stevens, have utilized the eighteenth-century spirit. The specific verse technique, however, is another matter. Even so, there is a considerable number of contemporary writers who have leaned upon Augustan method and form. Roy Campbell's spirited *Georgiad* is, as the title implies, a conscious imitation of the slashing manner of the school of *The Dunciad* and *The Rosciad*, turned upon the field of modern life and letters, more particularly in Bloomsbury. Robert Hillyer has frequently followed the Augustan forms, as in his *Letter to Robert Frost*. This evoked a lively reply, also in emulation of eighteenth-century style, from Granville Hicks. Aldous Huxley has some baroque Augustan verse included in his novel *Crome Yellow*. The poetry of V. Sackville-West contains Augustan reminiscences. *The Land*, her chief work, is not only based on the ideas of Virgil's *Georgics* and the plan of Thomson's *Seasons*, but its utilitarian descriptions of old-fashioned agriculture suggest Thomson's poem, Cowper's *Task*, and many other didactic pieces of the eighteenth century. Much of the light verse published during the last decade in *The New Yorker*, such as Clarence Day's brilliant animal fables, would seem natural enough in style to an eighteenth-century wit, could he read it

today. But to avoid losing ourselves in a maze of frequently
vague approximations to the Augustan technique, it will be best
to focus attention upon a single poet who has more often than
any other succeeded in bringing new life to the old forms.

Hilaire Belloc is as wide and omniverous a reader, as versatile
and prolific a writer, as any Englishman now alive. Born in
France and educated there as a youth, he came most naturally
into the Augustan heritage. He has proved himself a master of
the most characteristic of all eighteenth-century forms, the essay;
has written at length on eighteenth-century history, philosophy,
and letters; has criticized the Augustan poets; and has composed at least half his own verse with a lively recollection of
their accomplishment. Belloc is the best living exemplar of the
Victorian ideal of the man of letters. For he is widely read,
highly sensitive, and hugely prolific without being technically
a scholar or philosophically profound: he is at once a professional writer and an incurable dilettante. His sensitivity appears
in his ability to assimilate his reading so that he can not only
recall the items of his learning but spontaneously imitate the
style of any books that he has read. His inveterate bookishness
makes him a singularly attractive figure for such a study as this.
He has fallen beneath the spell of French letters, which renders
him especially equipped as spokesman for the English literature
of the eighteenth century, an age in England deeply stirred if
not actually dominated by French culture. His unusually sound
and vigorous classical background likewise equips him to re-
interpret the neoclassical period. Catholic in more senses than
one, he has stood on many occasions among the ablest imitators
of medieval, Elizabethan, and Augustan poetry, while he is one
of the few living poets whose style was matured in the latter part
of the Victorian period. Belloc undoubtedly has the talent to
write much good verse; the relative brevity of his verse output
is owing to his practical concern for prose. He has written several poems of distinct merit, although by imitating the weakness

as well as the strength of Augustan verse some of his work is undoubtedly too pretentiously rhetorical, more of it too trivial, and almost all too clever to be entirely pleasing. His prose inevitably overshadows his verse; and he will hardly rank as the equal of younger men such as Wilfred Owen more austerely devoted to their craft.

His temperament illuminates both the poetry which he is most fond of imitating and the spirit of eighteenth-century verse itself. The Augustans called themselves wits, using the word with a meaning somewhat different from its present connotation but not so far different as to invalidate the statement that they were all—or virtually all—exceptionally witty. Prior, Swift, Pope, Gay, Churchill, Cowper, and beyond question even Young are all delightfully clever men. Whether in earnest or jest, their wit is likely to appear. They stand among the greatest masters of light verse, though not always of colloquial verse. Belloc always prefers a witty style. The poetry that he emulates proves almost invariably a witty poetry. With spirit and ease he parodies the sprightly ballades of Villon, the conceited sonnets of Shakespeare, and the salty poems of John Gay. The Augustans are, to use Shakespeare's phrase, his home of love. Medieval and Elizabethan poets appeal to him precisely as they exemplify qualities also found in the school of Pope. Belloc translated the *Canterbury Tales* into modern English and into a language midway between that of Chaucer and the neoclassical modernizations of the same stories by Dryden. His practice is thoroughly representative. No generalization stands out more clearly regarding the habits of modern poets roaming the past for poetical honey than the preference of one group, the realists, for medieval and Augustan verse and of the other group, the idealists, for the Elizabethans and the romantics. Whoever loves Pope is likely to love Chaucer. Whoever loves Keats is likely to love Spenser. So three quarters of what is not neoclassical in Belloc's verse is neomedieval. Prior, Pope, and Gay were all devoted to Chaucer, imitating him in occasional poems. Both schools of verse have at their best a modest and sociable theory of poetry, frequently use a colloquial tone, and express the life of a well-coördinated society. Belloc bears witness to their harmony. The depth and poignancy of Chaucer and Villon he can scarcely be expected to translate, but their sociability and wit seldom escape him.

A number of strong though largely fortuitous analogies occur between the poetry of the skeptic and archtrifler Gay and the Catholic and archenthusiast Belloc. Widely different in temperament, the two men emerge on curiously parallel lines. Each writes political satires, satirical ballads, uproarious burlesques, witty epigrams, and cautionary beast fables and other didactic poems for children; and each composes a verse essay entitled *Wine*. Each has distinct lyrical gifts, a fondness for drinking songs, and more than common skill in both octosyllabic and heroic couplets. Gay is a perfect example of a minor poet in the Augustan age, and Belloc of a minor poet in our own age who writes in studied imitation of the Augustans. It is difficult to doubt that he kept Gay's *Fables* in mind when composing his own fables for children, poems in strictly the same traditions morally and technically, in the same diction, rhythms, and meter. But generally speaking Belloc remembers the sum of the Augustan tradition, with which he is thoroughly in sympathy. Writing virtually as a poet of the age of Queen Anne might have written, he follows all the poets in general tone and none in particular. He adheres to the school; he is too genuine an artist and a man to ape individuals. Nevertheless the broad likeness to Gay (the two men resemble each other even physically) is irresistible and proves helpful in a general review of the revival of Augustan technique.

Belloc's Augustan verses easily divide themselves into groups, although some are well represented by only a single piece. One of his few poems in the grand manner is *Wine*; one of his few satires in the heroic couplet, *To Dives*. For typical political satire in the octosyllabic couplet one may turn to *Lord Lundy*. An excellent burlesque is his *Newdigate Poem . . . Submitted by Mr. Lambkin*. His epigrams constitute one of the richest modern harvests in this ancient field. Finally, his children's poems rank with his most entertaining work, having a style the closest of all to the Augustans.

Most eighteenth-century verse remaining attractive today as well as most of Belloc's own contribution to the Augustan tradition is light verse, so that his use of the grand manner proves distinctly unusual. *Heroic Poem in Praise of Wine* is an exceptional performance and such a success as to leave a reader regretful that this style is rarely revived. Not all the poem, however, is equally in debt to the same phases of that movement. In the first quarter, chiefly depicting the progressive triumph of Dionysus over Europe, Belloc uses an even freer verse form than Dryden's typical couplets. Perhaps he recalled here not only the Augustan school itself but variations played upon such verse by Keats, Dryden's warmest admirer among the romantics. As the poem progresses from the account of the Dionysian rout to more reflective or panegyrical passages, it adheres more narrowly to the highly artificial manner first perfected in English by Pope.

Well-rounded and well-studied verse paragraphs constitute as characteristic a feature of Augustan poetry as any scheme of versification. Clearly Belloc's poem is a series of these strictly planned paragraphs, ultimately a reminiscence of the effect of classical oratory on classical poetry. The paragraphs are frequently reinforced by repetitions of key words or phrases. In a passage of twelve lines, "for such" launches four sentences, being in the first three occasions yoked with "in vain." The last instance, slightly varying the pattern, reads instead, "bootless for such." This is quickly followed by a score of lines alternating emphatic contrasts between "they" and "we," an arrangement likewise four times repeated. Again, three lines in succession begin with the words "by thee." In all such cases the reëmergence of Augustan eloquence proves conspicuous.

Accumulative passages are common, with calculated sense for progression and climax. The first line exhibits this: "To exalt, enthrone, establish and defend." Belloc has not only the skill to mount to deliberated climax but the complementary art to make the bold but studied transition so much practiced by the didactic poets and perfected in Thomson's *Seasons*. Thus the mention of Orvieto in one connection leads to a sharply contrasted train of thought when the poet recalls it in another.

The technique becomes most Augustan in its most verbal aspects. Here various Latinized uses of the participle appear conspicuously, as in these phrases:

> *Stark, African, informed of burning air* . . .

> *Fullfilled, apparent, that Creator stands* . . .

The balancing of active and passive forms of the verb is thoroughly Augustan:

> *Debased, accursed I say, abhorrent and abhorred.* . . .

> *Accursed and curse-bestowing.*

Another common device occurs in the pairing of epithet and noun. In the following passage the noun usually has its attendant adjective, resembling—to use Pope's simile—the Homeric hero accompanied by his charioteer:

> *When from the waste of such long labor done*
> *I too must leave the grape-ennobling sun*
> *And like the vineyard worker take my way*
> *Down the long shadows of declining day,*
> *Bend on the sombre plain my clouded sight*
> *And leave the mountain to advancing night* . . .

The pairing of adjective and noun to balance short words and long repeats a favorite usage:

> And crown abundant age with generous ease. . . .

> To watch grey dawns and mourn indifferent skies.

Compounds are frequent, as in such words as "grape-ennobling." The calculated placing of the adjective in an unusual position has neoclassical flavor: "And, sacramental, raise me the Divine. . ." Parenthetical phrases abound, as in, "He struck, the Atlantic seethe and surge before." Needless to say, inversions are common, as in the phrases "of majesty Septembral," "though all the Gods indignant," or "hamlets Appenine." A formal pairing of such inversions occurs in this couplet:

> And, indestructible, the Arch, and, high,
> The Shaft of Stone that stands against the sky . . .

With good Augustan precedent, a noun occasionally appears between two adjectives: "We from the couch in roseate mornings gay . . ." Triple parallelism is not infrequent and is exemplified in: "Swell the rich slope or load the empurpled plain." The rhetorical question combines with parallelism in this couplet:

> On what gin-sodden Hags, what flaccid sires
> Bred these White Slugs from what exhaust desires?

Adjectives formed from proper names have the neoclassical ring, as Hipponian, Burgundian, or Ausonian. Negative epithets are frequently used, as in the line: "They pass unblest through the unfruitful light . . ." Personification is common, as in the couplet:

> When beauty sickens and a muddied robe
> Of baseness fouls the universal globe.

Or in the line, "And when we open the bronze doors of Night."
The entire subject matter, allusions, imagery, spirit, and idea of
this piece are neoclassical. Archaistic as the style is even to its
punctuation, it remains lively and sincere. Such poetry cannot
be written mechanically. Only a spontaneous enthusiasm for the
thought and form of Augustan verse makes such lines possible.

Among Belloc's lesser poems is *To Dives*, comparing himself
by inference to Lazarus. Language and versification are equally
virile and free, preserving the vigorous style of Dryden and
Churchill rather than the more artificial Popian manner. The
imagery strongly suggests a passage in Churchill's slashing poem,
The Contrast, in which his own soul is weighed in the balance
with Lord Lyttelton's and found far the heavier. Belloc's slur
at the supposed poverty of his victim's father is wholly on the
eighteenth-century plan, as also is an allusion to the dilettante's
toying with Latin and Italian verse. A comparable satire on the
futility and corruption of an aristocratic government may be
seen in *Lord Lundy*. It is in the easy, octosyllabic verse perfected by Butler, Prior, and Gay; in its mixture of tartness and
urbanity it suggests the character sketches by Pope. A brief
summary may be suggestive. The unfortunate lord was a feeble
crybaby in youth, and though later Secretary for India, the Col-
onies, and War, he remains a crybaby still. He breaks into tears
once more when his grandfather, the duke, tells him that he
has been a rank failure and must go into exile as governor of
New South Wales. Here the heroic style has properly disap-
peared, yielding to a manner equally typical of Pope, the col-
loquially witty.

Had Belloc not written *Wine* and other serious pieces, the
Newdigate Poem . . . Submitted by Mr. Lambkin might conceivably be construed as the work of a clever man wholly un-
sympathetic with the grand tradition. Since this is one of the
happiest burlesques, the quotation of a few representative lines
may be welcome;

Shall pure statistics jar upon the ear
That pants for Lyric accents loud and clear?
Shall I describe the complex Dynamo
Or write about the Commutator? No!
   To happier fields I lead my wanton pen,
The proper study of mankind is men. . . .
      Aroint thee, Muse! Inspired the poet sings!
I cannot help observing future things!
Life is a vale, its paths are dark and rough
Only because we do not know enough:
When Science has discovered something more
We shall be happier than we were before.
   Hail, Britain, Mistress of the Azure Main,
Ten thousand fleets swoop over thee in vain!

The burlesque demonstrates Belloc's close knowledge and shrewd appreciation of the bombast and banality of inferior Augustan poets and their imitators. The lines, which are in praise of the electric light, depict the conjunction of a false literacy with a shallow materialism. They waver between frigid affectations and the most flat-footed commonplaces. Dry bones of a classical dictionary are jumbled with the prosaic data of the petty mechanic. The prize poet obviously knows little about either Virgil or electricity. If the classical poet and the mechanical force are in any way to be related, certainly Lambkin has failed to establish the contact. To know the faults and inconsistencies of a poetic tradition so thoroughly as this requires a genuine understanding of the virtues as well. Actually Belloc nowhere gives better evidence of his love for the Augustans and command of their powers than in this travesty of their ideals as perverted by middle-class stupidity.

Alexander Pope, it will be recalled, wrote many epigrams, some of them pious epitaphs, others stinging witticisms. Typical of the latter is the well-known couplet:

> *I am his Highness' dog at Kew;*
> *Pray tell me, sir, whose dog are you?*

The Augustans as a whole cultivated the epigram, or shortest poem, assiduously, now in a lofty and now in a facetious style. On the sober side is Gay's own famous reflection:

> *Life is a jest; and all things show it;*
> *I thought so once; but now I know it.*

Especially on their serious occasions the poets turned for suggestions to the mellowest of poetic volumes, the Greek Anthology.

As a neoclassicist Belloc cultivated the epigram, often being witty, sometimes serious, and occasionally learned. When he writes a couplet entitled *Epitaph on the Favorite Dog of a Politician,* one rests assured that he follows in the footsteps of Pope. In a timeworn tradition he composes an excellent series of epigrams for sundials. His satirical and political epigrams are both his best and most clearly derivative. The following shows him equally conservative in art and social philosophy:

> *Lord Finchley tried to mend the Electric Light*
> *Himself: It stuck him dead: And serve him right!*
> *It is the business of the wealthy man*
> *To give employment to the artisan.*

Equally pointed and in the witty style of Whigs and Tories is the quatrain entitled *On a Great Election:*

> *The accursed power which stands on Privilege*
> *(And goes with Women, and Champagne and Bridge)*
> *Broke—and Democracy resumed her reign:*
> *(Which goes with Bridge, and Women and Champagne).*

Gay's own praise of wine is light rather than heroic. In the light and humorous vein he also wrote many fables, nominally for children and many of them cautionary in morality. These he couched in an easy, graceful octosyllabic verse. Despite the interval of time, Belloc follows suit with no great differences. His children's poems have the matter-of-fact, informational tone seen in Gay and even more clearly in the didactic children's poetry of the later eighteenth century. We read, for example, of poor Jim, who, pulling away from his nurse's hand at the zoo, was eaten by a lion, and of Henry King, who swallowed bits of string:

> His Parents stood about his Bed
> Lamenting his Untimely Death,
> When Henry, with his Latest Breath
> Cried—"Oh, my friends, be warned by me,
> That Breakfast, Dinner, Lunch and Tea
> Are all the Human Frame requires . . ."
> With that, the Wretched Child expires.

There is also the memorable case of Matilda, who told lies and was burned to death. Once she telephoned for the fire engines and had the house thoroughly soaked before it was discovered that there was no fire. When a fire really came and she was alone in the house, the firemen would do nothing about it. So much for cautionary precept. A good instance of Augustan diction used by Belloc in such tales appears in his tribute to the Gnu.

> G stands for Gnu, whose weapons of Defence
> Are long, sharp, curling Horns, and Common-sense.
> To these he adds a Name so short and strong,
> That even Hardy Boers pronounce it wrong.
> How often on a bright Autumnal day
> The Pious people of Pretoria say,
> "Come, let us hunt the—" Then no more is heard
> But sounds of Strong Men struggling with a word.
> Meanwhile, the distant Gnu with grateful eyes
> Observes his opportunity, and flies.

The epithets "distant" and "grateful" witness Belloc's happy indebtedness to Augustan idiom. In trifles such as this no less than in his most impressive writing one notes than even a fairly close following of Augustan technique may in our own times produce enjoyable verse.

SYMBOLISM OF POETRY AND RELIGION

A surprisingly large amount of modern poetry, from Francis Thompson to T. S. Eliot, contains mystical symbolism. For most readers this is not the easiest verse to understand. Its roots in the past are exceptionally deep, far deeper than appears at first glance. Such poetry demands a certain amount of study to escape the appearance of mere nonsense. Before examining the strong traditional element in particular passages and poems, it will accordingly be helpful to consider the basic relation of poetry and mysticism, the cause for the persistence and the peculiar character of mystical verse today, and the grounds for regarding its symbolism as one aspect of poetic technique. To the modern mind the concepts of the metaphysical and the poetic have, for better or worse, drawn close together.

The greater part of poetry arises from feelings too elusive for merely conventional or rational expression. Such materials become the most natural provocation of art. Faced with the ultimate value of things as disclosed by birth or death, love or achievement, men turn from prose to verse, creating idealized expressions of their dilemmas. Thus the close relationship of poetry and religion has long been known. Faith, like poetry, resorts to symbols not in the conventional language. Words are employed with more luminous and metaphorical meaning than customary, meanings of which the dictionary is unaware. Just as the mathematical sciences demand symbols outside the realm of common speech, faith and art create similar symbols, those of poetry being the more peculiar as they inspire the body of familiar words with new spiritual meanings.

Religion disturbs the depths of human nature as these are disturbed by other great manifestations of enthusiasm and liberated imagination, such as poetry and the arts. A glance at familiar religious dogmas shows this. The "four daughters of God," as the four abstractions mercy, peace, justice, and truth were called during the Middle Ages, are powers no less in tragic poetry than in religion. The more serious verse continually depicts the heart softened by tragic pity to acts of mercy or driven through austerities of idealism toward truth and justice. That most searching and comprehensive description of the human mind, the doctrine of the Seven Deadly Sins, likewise represents man's nature disturbed as the poet commonly sees it. Faith, hope, and love are concepts equally agreeable to poet and priest. Poetry and religion have thus enjoyed prosperity and adversity hand in hand. The great ages of religion have witnessed notable expressions of religious faith in poetry or in one or more of the fine arts. The aesthetic life has frequently flourished on a plane with the religious life. In recent years the waning of both religion and religious institutions has significantly been accompanied by a waning in the prestige of poetry, or in any case by a violent readjustment in poetic ideals.

Not all poetry, of course, is leagued with religion, nor all religion with poetry, but the common ground proves an expansive one. From causes already indicated, religious or mystical poetry belongs usually to the symbolical or allegorical branches of verse. And here we discover a gauge for the continually changing references and the relative permanence of experience and technique. The basic experiences alter little, resembling the relative permanence of man's physical body; the basic principles of symbolism doggedly persist; while the symbols themselves, like costumes, alter greatly. Institutional religion fosters on the one hand a group of peculiarly sacred and ancient symbols, revised as little as possible from year to year—a stubborn core of ritual and mystical doctrine; on the other hand its exponents commonly adapt themselves to a shifting world by also using new images agreeing with the popular taste of the hour. The flower in the crannied wall is succeeded by the machine. These two phases of religious life are represented in Christianity respectively by the assigned ritual and the sermon. The liturgy changes little from age to age, the homily freely from day to day. Moreover, the basic human need for religion appears from time to time in expressions of the mystical life in the language and in persons more or less detached from the institutionalism of the Church. The individual voyages in quest of his own faith, usually borrowing conventional ideas and symbols, but in proportion to his needs and the fecundity of his imagination also creating new ones.

A minority party, as it were, in the Church itself may establish a symbolism of its own, as in the case of certain schools of Christian mysticism prevalent in the later Middle Ages and the Renaissance. Along with the embarrassment of the orthodox churches in more recent times, the disintegration of the old mystical societies, and the steady advance of individualism, the stubbornness of the religious or mystical element in human nature has appeared in the number of individuals who manufacture their own faith and symbols. We play the symbolical game of writing about God without naming him. Old urges are expressed in new forms. Every religious poet is in a sense a protestant, reinterpreting an older religion in terms of his own new imagery. The freshness of much of this symbolism conceals from the hasty observer the conservative element in the thought. Inspection discloses that the poet has simply changed old images by metamorphosis. Literature abounds in the records of persons who have hidden from themselves their deep indebtedness to the doctrine and symbolism of an older church. Speaking figuratively, the most ardent Protestant is often the truest Catholic without knowing it.

The mystical tradition in European culture is even more ancient than the theological. The intellectual mystic usually recognizes a common element in divergent creeds. All religions he finds agreeing to some extent with his own, which contains the root and germ of all. His mysticism, like Blake's, assumes philosophical features. Platonism in its many guises both within and without the Christian system has for centuries been the chief stream nourishing philosophical mysticism in poets and other groups of thinkers. The conspicuous images of Platonic or neoplatonic writing, such as love myths, cyclical myths, mathematical symbolism, and astronomical imagery, have repeatedly appeared in propagandist literature of mystical cults and in individualistic outpourings of inspired poets.

The present generation has witnessed an unusual burst of activity in symbolical and metaphysical poetry. Scholarship has rescued much medieval symbolism from the oblivion which threatened it during the eighteenth and early nineteenth centuries. The study of comparative religions, seriously begun several generations ago, has been aided by the enthralling advance in anthropology. Poets such as Eliot, Pound, Aiken, and MacLeish have responded ardently to these stimuli. So far in certain cases have the enthusiasts been carried that cults of primitivism have arisen, praising the natural man, or noble savage, his life, beliefs, myths, symbols, and art. In this movement D. H. Lawrence proved a redoubtable captain. Mexico, for example, as a land of primitivism and superromance has allured scores of poets and artists, eager to read the eternal riddles of the eagle and the serpent to the shame of modern civilization and the salvation, if possible, of the modern man. Repeating one another with monotony, the myths of the primitive world have been collated and compared with their alleged survivals in Greek legend or Christian doctrine.

For the present purposes only the technique of this symbolism is of importance. The development may be regarded as a phase of the language and imagery of figurative poetry, a venerable trunk of tradition continually putting forth new shoots in verse.

The essentially religious symbolism in recent verse comprises only a part of the larger tendency to symbolism in modern poetry as a whole. In its effort to capture the nuances of a mentality and a social predicament both growing yearly more complex and incapable of simple solution, modern poetry has found itself groping in an elaborate network of imagery. It is significant that the symbolist movement arose at a time when psychology taught the importance of conscious and subconscious symbolism, when mysticism was enjoying a rebirth, when Oriental thought was becoming increasingly a part of Occidental culture, and when much fresh religious inspiration evinced itself in art and literature rather than through the mind-wearied religious institutions. Great waves of symbolic writing passed over Europe, notably in poetic drama, as in Ibsen, Hauptmann, Maeterlinck, D'Annunzio, and Yeats. An allegorical style was enjoying a vogue hardly equaled since the Middle Ages. More than ever the poets appeared as mystics and symbolists. Their revolutionary position in a materialistic society and the freshness and modernity of much of their imagery, as well as the shallowness of modern culture, sometimes obscured their fundamentally traditional position. That the mystical idealism and symbolical language of Walt Whitman and Emily Dickinson, for example, had strong ties with medieval thought was only casually realized by these poets themselves and still more imperfectly grasped by their public. Even the most adventurous voices that were lifted to proclaim some new synthesis of life necessarily borrowed more from previous syntheses and approached these more closely than was commonly understood. The community of all spirits who have sought unity in life dawned gradually upon the modern mind. This point of view, always previsioned by the great mystics, such as Blake, became a few years ago a commonplace. Lawrence popularized the belief that the primitive and myth-making man still lives beneath the skin of his superficially civilized descendant. The love of primi-

tive myth and allegory has allured critical minds as representative and yet as different as Herman Melville and Ezra Pound.
Poets have evoked their new and powerful symbols, subtly indebted to the past, as new chalices for the essence of human life.
Whitman, for instance, found in the voyages of Columbus a
symbol for the Unitarian circumnavigation of God by man: and
when the highly gifted young American poet, Hart Crane, chose
Brooklyn Bridge to signify the same consummation, he also
remembered that Whitman had before him used Brooklyn
Ferry, the Union Pacific Railroad, and the Suez Canal. It was
itself symbolical that Crane's particular bridge, a marvel of
modern engineering, is supported upon two gigantic piers
pierced with arches in the Early English Gothic style. Since
Crane is in many ways the most talented, surprising, and difficult of all modern poets in this field, the rest of this chapter will
be devoted to his work. In Crane's poem we find a recurrence
of old ideas and an old technique, with the use of old images
and some new grafted on them.

Although Crane scarcely achieved wide popularity during his
brief lifetime and is not likely to win such recognition posthumously, *The Bridge* won enthusiastic recognition from the
more discerning critics and verse-reading public on its American publication in 1930. It is the strongest mystical poem
written in America since the work of Whitman and Emily Dickinson, as well as a remarkable example of many of the characteristic features of modern poetry. Crane's symbol of the bridge is
intended to signify, among other things, the marriage of past
and present (the future, which concerned Crane so much, need
not for the moment detain us). His own central image, then,
stands, among much else, for the type of heritage in thought
and expression that we are now considering.

Like Whitman, Crane was more a dilettante and a senti-
mentalist than a historian and a scholar. How far he realized his
full debt to tradition is not easily determined. He knew the

Middle Ages and their art and literature largely in a casual, secondhand way. Although he traveled widely and read considerably, he may have failed to realize the extent to which he was building upon old foundations, dedicating a new temple where an old cathedral had stood. In the introduction to Crane's *Collected Poems*, Waldo Frank observes: "*The Bridge* is allied to the *Commedia* of Dante who also, in response to desperate need, takes a journey in the course of which his need finds consummation." The editor's analogy is not close, and he hastens to qualify it; but, as we shall see, Crane's work shares most, in its intention, at least, with the chief mystical, religious, and allegorical poems. It is of interest to trace the relation of *The Bridge* not only to the *Divine Comedy* but to two of the chief religious allegories in English, *Piers Plowman* and *Pilgrim's Progress*. Langland's *Piers Plowman* stands poetically as well as temporally between Dante and the American poem, although very naturally nearer to the Italian. On the one hand Langland retains a larger share of the scholastic and patristic imagery so dominant in Dante than does Crane; but on the other hand Langland introduces from mysticism, from colloquialism, and from his own fancy many equivalents for the churchly imagery, as Crane does even more abundantly. Dante, to be sure, incorporated imagery from the medieval romances into his religious poem; his quest of Beatrice's eyes is comparable to the amorous imagery of the erotic poems. Most of the essential images in Dante, however, are commonplaces in those profound metaphysical poets, the medieval Schoolmen. Langland, part popular preacher and part an incipient Protestant, introduces a number of unorthodox images for the Trinity itself. He develops with freedom and originality his symbol of the Plowman; uses other agrarian figures, such as the mystic tree, otherwise than Dante and more freely; and deliberately utilizes a figure of the Trinity as a family—father, mother, and child—specifically declared to be misleading by Augustine. Langland's allegory of the pilgrim-

age of this mortal life, when compared with Dante's, will therefore be seen at least a step in advance upon that march which is
to lead through Bunyan and Milton to Melville and Crane.
There is a steady secularization in the philosophical and poetic
expression of mystical experience. The Church and churchly
modes of expression lose their preëminence before the advance
of the secular mind. Like the great poets before him, hard
pressed by the confusions of mortal life, Crane seeks that
harmonious sense of unity traditionally called God. And like
them he divides his imagery between familiar figures unaltered,
old figures slightly modified, and new figures drawn from a new
society to express the long-known experiences and adventures
of the soul.

The task of detecting traditionalism in Crane proves especially
inviting because in so many ways he is the most modern of
American poets. He writes more poetically of travel by subway
and by air, of electrical machinery, and of the street life of New
York than any poet of his times. Modern architecture and engineering, chemistry, radio, and advertising fascinate him. His
difficult and subtle stylistic idiom, poetic suggestion crowding
at all times upon poetic symbolism, his meanings swift and
secreted, his expression keyed to the tempo of the machine
age—all help to make him in many ways a better spokesman for
his times than such austere and detached spirits as Frost, Robinson, or Jeffers. We may, to be sure, hesitate to say that his
metaphysical and essentially religious thought is typical of any
but a rare and sensitive minority of modern men. The core of
his experience and its guiding symbolism are ancient; but the
incidental symbolism, his variations upon the old themes, his
words and rhythms, are as strikingly new. Crane is one of the
most sensitive poets of modern America, looking at the same
time farther back and farther forward than most, if not all, of
his companions. His retrospections show the undying urge of
men to probe insistent problems. Thousands before him have

known his experiences and even much of his imagery; as many others to come will follow in the same course, equally traditional and audacious.

Man's knowing of God involves an acknowledgment and a reconciliation of difficulties. There must be a bridge between the finite and the infinite, the many and the one, the uttermost parts of the universe and its center, the beginning and the end, evil and good, matter and mind, past and future, the chaos that life appears and the harmony it is found to be. Thousands of symbols have been used to express this reconciliation of seeming contradictions. One day (or probably one night) while living at 110 Columbia Heights in a room overlooking Brooklyn Bridge and New York Harbor, in a moment of intense enthusiasm and excitement or in what sympathetic persons would call mystic vision, Crane found his answer to these paradoxes in the symbol of the most audacious and imaginative of modern bridges. But the image no less than the need was really an old one.

The last few lines of Dante's great poem contain, for example, an image of a bridge signifying the Second Person of the Trinity, his incarnation effecting the bridge between God and man or between the divine and the human nature in Christ. On this mystery all else depends. Variations on bridge imagery are common in mystical verse. Crane himself uses the Dantesque symbol of the rainbow as a bridge in an outstanding passage of his own poem.

In the first American edition of his poem there appeared as a frontispiece a photograph of Brooklyn Bridge taken from an angle indicating one of the peculiar attractions which this aesthetically and historically remarkable structure possessed for him. The unique plan of the bridge provided for a vast number of cables radiating from the towers. Especially to one who walks across the bridge this plan is striking and almost hypnotic. In several sections, notably in the closing part of his allegory, Crane shows his poetic sensitivity to this structural feature.

The most widely radiating lines meet in a single point, producing a net in which the walker is caught and happily sustained. The bridge, therefore, becomes the symbol for a focal point, like the medieval images of concentric circles, the mystic rose, scattered leaves of the universe gathered into a perfect volume—images all occurring in the last canto of Dante's *Paradiso*. Many other images for God are used by Crane in diffusing what he terms his "secular light." Like Dante, he employs the figure of the choir, an infinity of voices chanting a song in unison. Perhaps with a recollection of the alchemists and their spell over the Middle Ages, Crane evokes the power of "fresh chemistry" to "sing the canticle" of God. He writes of "Deity's young name, kinetic of white choiring wings." He makes symbolical use of an axletree, an image familiar to Dante and the Middle Ages as indicating the universe revolving about its center in God. "Then you may laugh and dance the axletree," writes Crane, as Dante wrote of the mystical dance of angels about the beatific vision or around the wheels of the celestial chariot. A startling development of this figure lies in Crane's image of mystical vision glimpsed while the mortal eye is caught in the revolutions of machinery:

> . . . but fast in whirling armatures,
> As bright as frogs' eyes, giggling in the girth
> Of steely gizzards—axle-bound, confined
> In coiled precision, bunched in mutual glee
> The bearings glint,—O murmurless and shined
> In oilrinsed circles of blind ecstasy!

Elsewhere in the poem a meditation on Columbus has a mystical imagery wholly in keeping with the medieval poet's vision of the spheres.

> Yet under tempest-lash and surfeitings
> Some inmost sob, half-heard, dissuades the abyss,
> Merges the wind in measure to the waves,

Series on series, infinite,—till eyes
Starved wide on blackened tides, accrete—enclose
This turning rondure whole, this crescent ring
Sun-cusped and zoned with modulated fire
Like pearls that whisper through the Doge's hands
—Yet no delirium of jewels! O Fernando,
Take of that eastern shore, this western sea,
Yet yield thy God's, thy Virgin's charity!

Later Columbus reflects in true mystical spirit:

This disposition that thy night relates
From Moon to Saturn in one sapphire wheel:
The orbic wake of thy once whirling feet,
Elohim, still I hear thy sounding heel!

In another section Crane uses a further sequence of mystic figures common in Dante and most visionary poets:

Within whose lariat sweep encinctured sing
In single chrysalis the many twain,—
Of stars. Thou art the stitch and stallion glow
And like an organ, Thou, with sound of doom—
Sight, sound and flesh Thou leadest from time's realm
As love strikes clear direction for the helm.

The favorite problem of the mystic, the harmonizing of permanence and motion, is expressed in unusually powerful but thoroughly traditional imagery thus:

But that star-glistered salver of infinity,
The circle, blind crucible of endless space,
Is sluiced by motion,—subjugated never.

This thought repeatedly inspires new images in Crane's poem, as it does in Dante's. The fourth line of The Bridge, for example, succinctly reads: "Over the chained bay waters Liberty" —referring to the colossal statue at the entrance to New York.

The "chained" waters signify permanence, the statue stands for freedom.

Astronomical imagery shines almost continuously in the American poet. Like Dante, he sees a cross in the sky; it is here the Southern Cross. When he writes of "Easters of speeding light," we have the mystical essence of Dante's imagery conveyed in a phrase typical of the succinctness and abruptness of modern verse at its best.

Mystical imagists are almost as devoted to streams as they are to stars. The Angel of the Apocalypse showed John "a pure river of the water of life." Rivers flow through Dante's hell, purgatory, and paradise, and more than once in his poem the outlet of a river into the sea figures the mystical union of man with God. Similarly long passages in Crane's work deal with the Mississippi or the Hudson as symbols of time merging into the ocean of infinity.

Like the Schoolmen and their poets, Crane broods over the beginning and the end. His God embraces all, as alpha and omega. In his own imagery, only slightly altering traditional usage, he writes of a state transcending time:

And saw thee dive to kiss that destiny
Like one white meteor, sacrosanct and blent
At last with all that's consummate and free
There, where the first and last gods keep thy tent.

Several parts of The Bridge are inspired by a love imagery equally reminiscent. The coarse and profligate life sketched by Crane reminds one of passages both symbolical and autobiographical commonly found in religious works. Even the sin of lust proves ultimately a lure to lead the soul upwards. At the height of his sin Augustine was struck with the fear of God. Likewise out of his mistaken loves Dante arrives at his pure and theological love, Beatrice. Like the medieval poets, Crane remembers Magdalene, using the name more than once as a symbol in connection with what to the Middle Ages would have been the sacrament of penance.

The yearning for a brotherhood of man stirs him, as it stirs all mystics, who are, theoretically at least, more occupied with the universal than with the personal man. In Crane's words he seeks "a pact, new bound, of living brotherhood." As a religious spirit, he sees the unity rather than the diversity in the human family, using familiar symbols to express his vision. Turning even to the Latin of the Church, he evokes the universal food of the spirit, "*panis angelicus.*" Images of an ideal age of innocence occur from time to time in his verses, reminding the reader of pagan myth or Christian story. He refers to Eden, the lost paradise. The cyclical imagery, so typical of all mysticism and common in all nature worship as the myth of the departure and the return, enters with surprising frequency into his lines. The cycle theory is conspicuous in the following stanza, full of other symbols well known in mystical poetry.

> *Tall Vision-of-the-Voyage, tensely spare—*
> *Bridge, lifting night to cycloramic crest*
> *Of deepest day—O Choir, translating time*
> *Into what multitudinous Verb the suns*
> *And synergy of waters ever fuse, recast*
> *In myriad syllables,—Psalm of Cathay!*
> *O Love, thy white, pervasive Paradigm . . .*

Turning at times to an imagery of even greater antiquity and primitivism, he sees the cycles of life and death figured in the snake dance of the American Indians.

> *Dance, Maquokeeta! snake that lives before,*
> *That casts his pelt, and lives beyond! . . .*

His vision of the bridge also propagates imagery neither primitive nor wholly Dantesque but in part modern, as when he expresses the old cyclical doctrine with the symbol of the migration of birds:

> O Thou steeled Cognizance whose leap commits
> The agile precincts of the lark's return . . .

But strictly liturgical imagery on this theme appears in the lines:

> Inquisitor! incognizable Word
> Of Eden and the enchained Sepulchre . . .

Platonic reminiscences occur frequently. For a motto to the last section of his poem he selects a sentence from Plato: "Music is then the knowledge of that which relates to love in harmony and system." With Platonic echoes he conceives life as a song sung on a bridge spanning two worlds of sleep, life before birth and after death. Like many a mystic, from Augustine to Blake, he is haunted with symbolic notions of a universal reality greater than memory and beyond it.

His preference, however, for strictly Christian images shows in their frequent occurrence even in passages of seemingly alien symbols. He wishes, for example, to depict the common romantic sexual urge of the sentimental modern man. His hero for the moment is a New Yorker whose Saturday-morning hours pass slowly till he is able to take a secretary in a downtown office on a Saturday-afternoon outing. Along with oyster shells and figs of Prince Street and crap-shooting gangs in Bleecker Street is an allegory of the Woolworth Tower as a five-and-ten-cent cathedral and the girl as "Cathedral Mary." In short, the Virgin, no longer of an ancient family in Palestine, becomes a sentimental office girl in New York. Haunted by biblical and sacred imagery, Crane, the seeming revolutionary, alludes in all seriousness to such biblical parables as the raising of Lazarus or unexpectedly to such acts of reverence as the kneeling waves of the sea—so thoroughly has this imagery pervaded the style of one of the most alert and experimental of American poets.

It remains true that medieval or Christian imagery and variations thereon color only a part of his thoroughly mystical allegory. He diversifies his symbols by allusions to the Vedic and the Orphic hymns, to rituals of the American Indians, and to what he regards as the native American myths, among them the story of Rip Van Winkle in Sleepy Hollow. His direct contact with poets of the most various ages merely confirms the mystic character of his art and vision. He turns backward to Seneca, beloved of the Middle Ages, who supplies a motto for one of his cantos; while in the poem itself he mentions Emily Dickinson, devotes some of his most moving lines to Poe, and writes a long and impassioned passage in praise of Whitman. He celebrates the modern poets for qualities shared with the medieval ascetics: Emily Dickinson and Poe for their contempt of "the world" and Whitman for his mystic insight. To Whitman he acknowledges the debt of pupil to master, both for his thought and his images. Whitman had chosen a ferry where he himself chose a bridge over the same waters to symbolize the same mysterious brotherhood of mankind. In *The Bridge* Crane carefully explains how one spiritual image becomes in the course of time another. Whitman's open road, symbol of spiritual freedom in terms of the pedestrian, becomes for Crane the open sky, symbolizing the same ideal in an age which echoes with the motor of the aeroplane. His debts to mystical worshippers of the sea, as Ibsen and Swinburne, and to contemporary figures such as D. H. Lawrence further enrich his mystical thought and symbolical expression. As the medieval centuries found in their cathedrals symbols of their corporate aspiration to the divine, so Crane discovered in a masterwork of modern architecture, the uniquely beautiful bridge across New York Harbor, the symbol for his own similar faith and desire. In spirit and technique he stands with Hugo of St. Victor, who pictured God in stone, and with Dante, who depicted him in words.

In spite of this underlying traditionalism, Crane's poetry never becomes academic and always remains thoroughly vital. By expressing the universal experiences of the mystic in the idiom of a mechanistic society, his religious verse grows much more alive than T. S. Eliot's wholly archaistic *Ash Wednesday* and other allegories smelling of church incense. Yet the relative infrequency of mystical visitations in modern society must render the religious symbolism of both Eliot and Crane significant only to a small minority of readers. Whatever may be the prestige of the literary or ecclesiastical tradition to which they appeal, their writing remains in modern life somewhat secretive and esoteric. Their symbolism, courting the mystical shadows of the moon, fails to emerge into broad daylight.

Allegory is not compelled to inhabit this dimness and shadow. Only a short while after the appearance of Crane's poem, the poet first by seniority and possibly by merit in America, E. A. Robinson, produced the last of his works to be published during his lifetime. *Amaranth* is closer to the *Divine Comedy* than *The Bridge* in that its allegory is more clearly mingled with realism. But here the likeness to the medieval work ceases. Robinson writes a humorous poem on the differences of human beings and the practical problem of each man in attaining social well-being through the fullest expression of his individuality. Robinson's allegory is the work of a humorist, a realist, and an individualist. Crane composes a serious poem on what he alleges to be the essential likenesses of human beings, united by their awareness of a harmonious and significant universe. His allegory is the work of a contemplative, a mystic, and a believer in God rather than in men. It is typical of the two approaches to life and thought that Crane's poem is inspirational where Robinson's is dry and critical. Crane's allegory has wings. But they are the wings of a seraph. His poem lacks the humanity of the Latinized humanist traditions focused upon the relations of man to man. Crane perfects one function of poetry and poetic symbolism. But poetry and allegory have other uses, better exemplified and more fully attuned to modern life in the quieter and less rhetorical beauty of *Amaranth*.

Whatever may be the merits of Crane's theory or technique, the importance of an acquaintance with other mystical poetry for an understanding of *The Bridge* can hardly be exaggerated. Crane not only uses old ideas and old or modified symbols—from Brooklyn Bridge all roads to mysticism radiate. The bridge is to Crane what the blade of grass was to Whitman. It spans the gulf between God and man, city and city, land and land, continent and continent, past and future, night and day, good and evil, art and morality. Because macadam paves it and makes it a roadway, it suggests all roadways of the nation, or the open road of Whitman. Because ships of all lands and seas pass beneath it, it suggests the globe and the universality signified by the sea. Because of its unique network of cables, it points to a union of the many and the one. Because it links space, it suggests Columbus. Because it links time, it hints of the American Indians. Since it carries all kinds of men, it suggests another symbol for civilization: the modern hotel. Since it is a masterpiece of mechanical engineering flung across the waters, it suggests aviation. It sings to its lover the song of sailors, whom Crane regards as the waifs and strays of infinity. Joining two lands at the mouth of a great river, it sings of the union of a river with the sea and of a people with their Creator. It whispers to its lover also of the union of men and women in love. As it spans two islands, it tells of Whitman, the great poet, whose vision and charity embraced equally both contestants in a cruel civil war. There is seemingly no end to its meanings; but all, in one word, to Crane signify God. Such multiple meanings in allegory occur in many poems, from Dante's *Commedia* to Blake's *Jerusalem* and to Whitman's dirge on the death of Lincoln. Here, then, is a traditional treatment of poetic imagery as well as a traditional subject matter. Such symbolism is the shorthand of poetry—the shorthand extended to such amazing lengths by James Joyce. From the standpoint of the technical development of poetic symbolism, Crane's poem affords an admirable model for any author, whether his theme is secular or religious, his temperament realistic or platonic. The eminence of *The Bridge* is owing to Crane's thorough assimilation of the still vital allegorical tradition.

III: THE HERITAGE OF FORM

POETIC SYMBOLISM IN ITS FULLEST DEVELOPMENTS, as shown in the immediately preceding pages, not only is a phase of the texture and language of a poem but enters directly into its architecture. The arrangement of the symbols becomes also the plan of the poem, the unfolding of its allegory becomes the plot of the story. So by virtually undefinable steps the critic is led from the view of style or technique to a view of the larger phases of composition, from a consideration of language to an analysis of general design.

Although the form of a poem is properly determined by the urgency of its spirit, or, in other words, its verbal embodiment is determined by its significance or meaning, form still holds a conspicuous place in any detached or intellectual view of the whole. Monsieur Jourdain may not know when he is reciting verse, but the intelligent reader does know. Moreover, he easily perceives that the rhythms constitute a highly important part of the structure of the whole and of its ultimate value. And such a reader similarly recognizes the formal significance of certain genres or types of poetry. Properly speaking, too, the meaning also molds the enveloping form and contributes largely to the definition of any particular genre or type of poetry into which a work falls. But sooner or later the critic almost inevitably finds himself examining the versification and the forms imposed from within or without by traditional themes. For tradition appears no less in the development of versification and of genres than in language patterns or in the more widely embracing cultural heritage. These larger contours of form are themselves transitional. Versification leans backward upon style and the natural rhythms of language, traditional poetic types look forward to wider meanings and fuller cultural implications. Thus the first part of the present chapter deals with versification, while the second part considers the broader and more liberal subject of the familiar types of poetry.

HEREDITARY RHYTHMS

Versification gives the clearest though not the most important evidence of poetic tradition. Feelings, ideas, and images, being more elusive than metrical systems, resemble the ultimately undefinable rhythms of individual poems and poets rather than the skeleton forms of prosody. Nothing about verse is clearer than its metrical patterns foreign to prose, nothing so baffling as the variations which true poets play upon them. Thus the formal study of versification proves in some respects the most satisfactory type of literary research, since it remains uncommonly definite; but it also is comparatively prosaic. It too easily deals with facts and not with meanings. Beyond the literal account of metrical schemes lie their virtually undefinable relations to subject matter and the nuances in rhythm which make a work a living poem, not a cold mechanism. Certain limitations to the study of rhythms are inescapable.

English versification shows the accumulated growth of ten centuries. Although a few verse forms of early times are temporarily or permanently out of fashion, poets are now under obligation to each of the centuries of uninterrupted production. The greatly augmented publication of the verse of all epochs gives the modern poet a more intimate contact with predecessors than poets of earlier periods have enjoyed. As a result our versification is highly eclectic. Only about a tenth of it is truly original; nine tenths is deeply indebted to other periods. Since the Chaucerian age there has, perhaps, been a slightly diminishing rate of sheer innovation, for which modern eclecticism amply compensates.

Versification is the only aspect of poetry resembling in its development the history of natural science. In the art of poetry as a whole no progress is observable since the first English poems known to us, the moving and beautiful literature, pagan or Christian, of the Anglo-Saxon period. But there has been a steady, accumulative progress in the mechanics of verse comparable to that in scientific fields or in the invention of new musical instruments. In the course of time relatively little that has been discovered has been forgotten; what has been learned has been gathered into a vast treasure of practical, working knowledge. The advance is, of course, merely quantitative, not qualitative. Because we command more verse forms than ever before, we write more variously than the Anglo-Saxons: more variously but certainly not better.

A few characteristic forms of earlier epochs, then, are rarely if ever used today. Although alliterative verse has returned as a notable influence on modern verse, the precise alliterative patterns dominating several centuries of English poetry are hardly ever reproduced in their integrity. The long line based on the Latin septenary, a stately and powerful verse form highly popular for three centuries preceding Chaucer, has unhappily been lost sight of. The leisurely Elizabethan "fourteener" might seem distinctly quaint in our own times. Although the romantic poets wrote brilliantly in the Spenserian stanza, no major poem in this meter has recently been composed. The polish of the Popian couplets seems today irrecoverable, notwithstanding such near triumphs as we have examined in Belloc. These and similar types once highly popular appear at present virtually obsolete. On the other hand the ten-syllable couplet perfected by Chaucer, his octosyllabic couplet, Skeltonic verse, ballad poetry, dipodic verse generally, and even some of the elaborate stanzaic forms and adaptations from the French are a living heritage from the Middle Ages. Whatever may have been the originality or imitativeness of his own work, Chaucer to the retrospective eye appears the main stem of English versification. The great

Tudors put forth flourishing branches, such as blank verse, the sonnet, dactylic verse, Sapphics, and many new subtleties in the verse foot and stanza. The Cavalier poets contribute still further elaborations of the lyric stanza, with a new ruggedness and freedom; they rework octosyllabic verse, especially by a delicate use of trochaic feet and by Hudibrastic rhyming; and Milton creates a radically new type of the sonnet. The school of Dryden gives new energy to the couplet, while the racy poets of the eighteenth century invigorate their lyrics with popular rhythms still ringing in the ears of modern poets. Blake, Coleridge, and Southey introduce freer verse forms dispensing with rhyme, thus opening the way for the so-called free verse of Whitman and the twentieth-century Americans. Anapaestic verse grows orthodox, lively syncopation becomes a common practice, the limerick is perfected, and the acceleration of literary scholarship promotes the perennial revival of old forms and the restless experimentation reaching their highest development in recent years. So the tree rooted in tradition has grown to its present magnitude, with few of its branches swept away with the wind.

In viewing the roles of imitation and creation in versification, some biographical data may occasionally prove helpful, since it is theoretically quite possible that a poet wholly ignorant of the work of his predecessors may rediscover an important metrical form. Blake, apparently little read in medieval literature with the exception of Chaucer, created verse in vital respects very like the earliest English poetry, while Coleridge, a scholar in these fields, also became a radical, but more through reading than through sheer invention. Probably no Englishman rivals Blake in metrical inventiveness. Where an old path is retraced, the presumption is usually that the newcomer has observed the footsteps of his forerunners. In the case of complicated stanzas there can be practically no doubt; with the subtler cadence of the verse foot the literal indebtedness becomes questionable. As a general rule innocence in metrics is hardly characteristic of

the chief poets writing today. A few, not themselves familiar
with medieval verse, doubtless borrow patterns from secondary
sources. But if one can only occasionally trace the metrical
movement of a modern work to specific poem or poet of older
times, there is seldom a question what group of poets the modern writer has been reading. Hence it is possible to describe
some outstanding characteristics of each of the chief epochs of
English versification, to cite in turn a few examples, and at the
same time to consider passages or authors in the contemporary
field where indebtedness to the earlier tradition becomes indis-
putable.

A few definitions may prove useful. It is a basic fact that in
the Germanic languages some syllables are decidedly more
stressed than others. In these languages verse is distinguished
from prose by the comparatively regular recurrence in the
former of stressed syllables. In short, verse has a basic, underlying rhythm strictly analogous to that of music or dancing.
Another fact is that the speaker, whether of verse or prose,
speaks in phrases determined by the sense. The verse foot is
a phrase comprised of a stressed syllable and any secondary
syllables or pauses naturally associated with it by the speaking
voice. Now, according to the system of verse adopted by Chaucer and made the basis of most English verse thereafter, the
design of the foot becomes of considerable importance in versification. So poems often tend to be written in one type of foot,
such as a stressed syllable followed by a light one (trochaic), an
unstressed followed by a stressed syllable (iambic), two light
syllables followed by a stress (anapaestic), a stress followed by
two light syllables (dactylic), and so on. Complete regularity
in stress is rarely found and to most ears produces an intolerable
monotony. Sometimes one type of foot tends to dominate
certain groups of lines, while another type dominates other
more or less regularly alternating groups, as, for example, groups
of iambs and trochees. Since the phrase may be expanded to

several syllables with pauses or rests included, the number of possible varieties of feet becomes exceedingly large. Moreover, secondary stresses occur, these too, treated at times rhythmically, creating what is termed dipodic verse. A good example is afforded by Masefield's line, "Spanish waters, Spanish waters, you are ringing in my ears." All these types of meter have definite meaning for English versification from the beginning of the Middle English period. Historically the system is heir of medieval Latin prosody. But English poetry has tended also to very loose patterns of the foot. The most regular use of the foot as we find it commonly in Orm of the twelfth century, Scott of the nineteenth, and Robert Service of the twentieth hardly lasts in favor. The most esteemed poetry, whether appealing to the minority, the majority, or both, shows great liberty with underlying patterns. And Anglo-Saxon poetry had in the opinion of most scholars no real pattern for the foot whatsoever. Its only accentual principle seems to be the regular recurrence of accents, the ear recognizing no patterns wrought with the aid of unstressed syllables. A high degree of metrical freedom is cherished as an aid to expressiveness. A few students trace a dipodic principle in early alliterative verse, but even this view is not generally held. Whether historically correct or not, almost all imitations of Old English versification by twentieth-century poets show they at least take the conservative position that the verse shows a maximum of freedom; and this fact is of outstanding importance in our review of poetic heritage. From our standpoint a bastard theory would be as true a descendant as the legitimate heir.

The lively interest of modern poets in medieval versification invites a somewhat detailed statement of the old principles. The loose accentual principle of Old English verse received hardening and support from the additional strength given accented syllables by alliteration. This alliteration in a simplified and debased form persisted till the close of the Middle Ages, outlasting by several generations the innovations of Chaucer. In short, through the Middle English period two traditions of versification flourished together and to some extent combined. Poets who, like Langland, use alliteration rigidly in the structure of their verses dispense with rhyme. Those who use alliteration decoratively, as the author of the brilliant devotional poem *Pearl*, employ rhyme even with uncommon virtuosity. Many of the structurally alliterative pieces, as *Piers Plowman*, are virtually without systematic treatment of the verse foot. And while Chaucer and the more literary school used lines fairly regular in the number of their syllables and even in the cadence of their feet, the most popular poetry of the age, as the ballad verse, remained extremely licentious. Using rhyme, it nevertheless failed to accept the metrical discipline imposed by literary London. The example of the popular ballads in the free treatment of the foot early attracted the sympathetic attention of the romantic poets, especially Coleridge, and even more than the metrical study of Anglo-Saxon verse or of Shakespeare aided the rise in modern poetry of a renewed license and in time of free verse.

The Anglo-Saxons and their alliterative school generally, to repeat, use a versification without rhyme and without any readily perceptible regularity in the verse feet. The line, however, as in Shakespeare's early blank verse, has a certain integrity as a verse phrase or unit of meaning, further defined, of course, by the alliteration. For the line is also the unit of alliteration. There are various patterns of alliteration, the commonest one at first and virtually the sole one at last being alliteration on the first three stresses in the line, a fourth and final stress being without alliteration. Thus the metrical pattern is a four-stress line, or tetrameter, with no metrical pattern for the feet as such. Now a large number of lines in the blank verse of Marlowe or Shakespeare are extremely free in their foot structure and strongly tetrameter, thus recalling the old alliterative line. These free and vigorous English verses read like an ancestral memory. Anglo-Saxon was just beginning to be read by such Elizabethan scholars as Archbishop Parker, one of whose scholarships sent Marlowe to Cambridge. But it would be fantastic to hold so casual a phase of Elizabethan verse indebted to Old English. For our present purposes this episode in Elizabethan verse has interest only as it complicates the question of the literary indebtedness of the modern poets who write unrhymed tetrameters without scruples regarding the verse feet. The following lines by Archibald MacLeish may be considered echoes of Elizabethan verse, of Anglo-Saxon verse, or merely independent creations. The case for the Anglo-Saxon is, however, the strongest. MacLeish's rhetoric, as we have seen, shows conclusively his relationship to the Anglo-Saxon. Mere accidental similarity in so scholarly a writer seems unlikely. And the lines stand far closer to the medieval than to the Renaissance poetry, since they have a greater irregularity and redundance of syllables than even the Elizabethan blank verse, especially in its tetrameter forms, admits.

This is The Making of America in Five Panels:

This is Mister Harriman making America:
Mister-Harriman-is-buying-the-Union-Pacific-at-Seventy:
The Sante Fe is shining in his hair:

This is Commodore Vanderbilt making America:
Mister-Vanderbilt-is-eliminating-the-short-interest-in-Hudson:
Observe the carving on the rocking chair:

This is J. P. Morgan making America:
(The Tennessee Coal is behind to the left of the Steel Company:)
Those in mauve are braces he is wearing:

This is Mister Mellon making America:
Mister-Mellon-is-represented-as-a-symbolical-figure-in-aluminum-
Strewing-bank-stocks-on-a-burnished-stair:

This is the Bruce is the Barton making America:
Mister-Barton-is-selling-us-Doctor's-Deliciousest-Dentifrice:
This is he in beige with the canary:

You have just beheld the Makers making America. . .

A metrically similar passage from T. S. Eliot's *Rock* indicates
the same relationship:

> The Word of the Lord came unto me, saying:
> O miserable cities of designing men,
> O wretched generation of enlightened men,
> Betrayed in the mazes of your ingenuities,
> Sold by the proceeds of your proper inventions:
> I have given you hands which you turn from worship,
> I have given you speech, for endless palaver,
> I have given you my Law, and you set up commissions,
> I have given you lips, to express friendly sentiments,
> I have given you hearts, for reciprocal distrust.

Ezra Pound, who has made a striking translation of the Anglo-
Saxon poem *The Seafarer*, blends an old rhythm and an ancient
theme in these typical lines in his *Cantos*:

And then went down to the ship,
Set keel to breakers, forth on the godly sea, and
We set up mast and sail on that swart ship,
Bore sheep aboard her, and our bodies also
Heavy with weeping, and winds from sternward
Bore us out onward with bellying canvas,
Circe's this craft, the trim-coifed goddess.
Then sat we amidships, wind jamming the tiller,
Thus with stretched sail, we went over sea till day's end.
Sun to his slumber, shadows o'er all the ocean,
Came we then to the bounds of deepest water,
To the Kimmerian lands, and peopled cities
Covered with close-webbed mist, unpierced ever

With glitter of sun-rays
Nor with stars stretched, nor looking back from heaven
Swartest night stretched over wretched men there.
The ocean flowing backward, came we then to the place
Aforesaid by Circe.

There have been few stronger influences on modern versification than Pound's early interest in medieval literature. His *Personæ* and *Exultations* (1909), *Canzoni* (1911), and *Ripostes* (1912) showed renewed interest in old forms and ideas.

As indicated by these citations, the recurrence of the beat is more important than the recurrence of the line. Hence not only tetrameters but lines of all lengths in modern verse enjoy the freedom inherited from the Old English. MacLeish, for example, uses many more pentameter than tetrameter lines. In Robinson Jeffers the line becomes longer still and so often is run on to the succeeding line as to be reduced almost to nonentity. Only in *At the Birth of an Age*, an adaptation from the Volsung Saga, does he imitate to any extent the four-beat alliterative line of early Germanic verse. The important thing is therefore the freedom of the verse foot, a usage best exhibited in the Old English, intuitively discovered by Blake, dignified on historical principles by Coleridge, approached by Whitman and the early writers of free verse, but thoroughly reëstablished as orthodox versification only by outstanding writers of the present day, familiar with springs of English undefiled.

The younger and more vigorous stock of romance forms, with syllabic and metrical regularity, rhyme, and new stanzaic structure, introduced about the time of the Norman Conquest, assimilated and finally effaced the native versification. While the French spirit compromised with the English, the French technique won a prolonged victory. The later Middle Ages proved especially fertile in the development of rhyme schemes and regularized verse feet, so much so that this period is probably the most productive of all in this respect. Succeeding centuries forgot something, added much, but inherited much more— more than they ever generally acknowledged. The iambic foot has been the favorite with English poets since Chaucer or earlier, only to be seriously challenged in its supremacy in recent years. The larger part of Chaucer's poetry is divided between pieces in ten- or eight-syllable lines, two of the most popular verse forms to the present day. His couplet rhymes are again the commonest of all patterns in rhymed verse. Shakespeare and Milton omit the rhyme from Chaucer's pentameters, thus producing blank verse; Dryden and Pope merely add new patterns to the inner phrasing of the lines, so producing heroic couplets. Milton and Butler again add only secondary features to Chaucer's octosyllabic verse. His mastery of the narrative stanza afforded a basis for the no more remarkable achievements of Spenser and Byron, the former adding an Alexandrine to the stanza of *The Monk's Tale* to produce the languorous and aristocratic Spenserian stanza, the latter speeding it up and vulgarizing it by modifications afforded by the Italian ottava rima. Only in the field of lyrical poetry Chaucer apparently wrote so little and clung so timidly to foreign models as to leave a minor mark on English verse. For this inactivity the work of his contemporaries fully compensates. Popular, non-literary poetry has never forgotten the popular lyrical versification of the Middle Ages. The ballad meter lives on, employed also in innumerable hymns and secular songs. So the American folksong *Rye Whiskey* has a versification identical with that of such a medieval ballad as *I Have a Young Sister*, as typical verses from each will show:

> *How shulde ony cherye*
> *be withoute ston?*
> *And how shulde ony dowe*
> *ben withoute bon*

> *Sometimes I drink whiskey*
> *Sometimes I drink rum,*
> *Sometimes I drink brandy*
> *At other times none.*

This popular dipodic verse of the medieval ballads and mystery plays came into renewed literary attention through brilliant songs by Kipling. Dipodic verse, which has many forms, is easily detected by the lilt or swing resulting from the alternation of strong and secondary stresses. Three types of syllables rather than two enter into the verse pattern. A line from Masefield has already been quoted to illustrate the form: "Spanish waters, Spanish waters, you are ringing in my ears." The heavy stresses here fall twice on the first syllable of "waters" and on "ring" and "ears," the light stresses twice on the first syllable of "Spanish" and on "you" and "in." Much popular modern dipodic verse is too widely known to require quotation, as, for example, Kipling's familiar *Danny Deever*. *Saint Stephen and Herod*, a medieval ballad likewise in dipodic form, shows that Kipling fell back upon a long tradition in English verse.

> *"Lakyt me neyther gold ne fe, ne non ryche wede;*
> *Ther is a chyld in Bedlem born schal helpyn us at our nede."*

> *"That is al so soth, Stevyn, al so soth, iwys,*
> *As this capoun crowe schal that lyth here in myn dysh."*

> *That word was not so sone seyd, that word in that halle,*
> *The capoun crew Cristus natus est! among the lordes alle.*

> *"Rysyt up, myn turmentoures, be to and als be on*
> *And ledyt Stevyn out of this town, and stonyt hym with ston!"*

> *Tokyn he Stevene, and stonyd hym in the way,*
> *And therefore is his evyn on Crystes owyn day.*

Chaucerian versification is basically French. In the Tudor Renaissance various patterns well recognized as classical, such as

Sapphics, were imported into English verse, swelling further the bulk of distinctly literary meters. There is accordingly a temptation to group all nonliterary forms together as more indigenous and more ancient in English poetry than their more dignified rivals. But popular verse has itself gone through many changes, and no close analogues to many popular forms today can be found in Middle English. Vachel Lindsay built the greater part of his most vigorous verse around the rhythms of certain American folk songs, the rhythm rather than the words ringing in his head. If there had been no ballads like the famous *Darky Sunday School* ("Young folks, old folks, everybody come"), his own poetry would have taken a form radically unlike that which it now has. No real parallels to the meter of that song or of many of Lindsay's pieces can be found in Middle English.

The rediscovery of the Anglo-French lyrical forms, such as the ballade, rondeau, and triolet, by Swinburne and his associates is a well-known episode in the history of versification. What may not be so obvious is the continued if not ardent interest of the poets in this domain. A number of much-admired poems of this kind have been written in the present century. It ballade, rondeau, and triolet are less popular than a generation ago, they have by no means sunk again into obsolescence. At various stages of his life Hardy practiced the briefer forms, as in his well-known *When I Set Out for Lyonnesse* and in those exquisite bird-notes, *Birds at Winter Nightfall* and *Winter in Durnover Field*. True ballades have been written with much ease and gusto by G. K. Chesterton and Hilaire Belloc. Even the irrepressible lover of slang and Americanism, E. E. Cummings, includes an exuberant ballade in his volume W.

To medieval poets we are largely indebted for the refrain, still occasionally encountered in stanzaic verse. Modern lyrical poetry has doubtless a few obligations to the Middle English poems written in short lines, as trimeter and dimeter. The almost infinite wealth of metrical variety in medieval stanzaic

verse may have suggested some of the daring experiments by
Edith Sitwell. Thus her delightful *Trio for Two Cats and a
Trombone*, for example, recalls lines in a mystery play spoken
by one of the guardsmen at the sepulchre of Christ:

> *I wyl have this syd*
> *What so betyde.*
> *If any man ryde*
> > *To steel the cors,*
> *I xal hym chyde*
> *With woundys wyde*
> *Amonge hem glyde*
> > *With fyne fors.*

What the later Middle Ages called "tumbling verse" has occasionally been revived with success by enthusiasts for the old
poetry such as C. Day Lewis. In this meter he writes:

> *Make no mistake, this is where you get off,*
> *Sue with her suckling, Cyril with his cough,*
> *Bert with a blazer and a safety-razor,*
> *Old John Braddleum and Terence the toff.*
> *And now, may I ask, have you made any plans?*
> *You can't go further along these lines;*
> *Positively this is the end of the track;*
> *It's rather late and there's no train back.*

The poet seems to have recalled the very fetching rhythms of
a passage from the *Play of Coventry* or some similar satirical
lines.

> *Cok Crane and Davy Drydust,*
> *Luce Lyere and Letyce Lytyle Trust,*
> *Miles the Myllere and Colle Crake crust*
> > *Both Bette the Baker and Robyn Rede.*

And loke ye rynge wele in your purs
For elles your cause may spede the wurs.
Though that ye slynge goddys curs
Evyn at myn hede, fast com away.

John Skelton, the most gifted English poet at the beginning of the sixteenth century, is one of the happiest innovators in verse form. He has of late become, as he remained for a century after his death, a notable force in English poetry. New editions and biographies have appeared; his works have been freely anthologized and criticized. The excellent Welsh poet, Richard Hughes, edited Skelton; the better-known poet and critic, Robert Graves, helped to popularize him. As already noted, W. H. Auden has written an essay on him. Although he was deft in many forms, he became celebrated for the "Skeltonic" meter, which is a dipodic dimeter with rhymes running in sequences from two to a dozen lines. The effect is, of course, dashing in the extreme, and it is not unfair to say that many young poets in England of radical political views have sought to harry conservative ministers in verse at least vaguely Skeltonic, as their master once tormented the king's favorite, Cardinal Wolsey. The last poem in Lewis's *Magnetic Mountain* affords an instance:

> *Let us be off! Our steam*
> *Is deafening the dome.*
> *The needle in the gauge*
> *Points to a long-banked rage,*
> *And trembles there to show*
> *What a pressure's below.*
> *Valve cannot vent the strain*
> *Nor iron ribs refrain*
> *That furnace in the heart.*
> *Come on, make haste and start*
> *Coupling-rod and wheel*

Welded of patient steel,
Piston that will not stir
Beyond the cylinder
To take in its stride
A teeming countryside.

Skelton's unique verse form as he wrote it befitted a wide range of subject matter, from the fierce profanity of his diatribes against vile Scotchmen and rival poets to the serious social satire of *Colin Clout*. It nowhere becomes more at home than in animated passages depicting the fury of birds and animals and the passions and griefs of children. His *Ware Hawk*, an invective against a hateful priest who carried a hunt into the choir of Skelton's church and caused the birds to mute upon the altar, is sped to its climax on the wings of an amazingly nervous versification. The poem usually regarded as his masterpiece is a quieter cousin of the foregoing. *Phyllyp Sparowe*, a vast expansion of Catullus's lines, depicts the grief of a pious young novice who has lost her pet bird through the villainy of a cat. The lines on the cat, spoken by the injured girl, give a favorable view of the verse form.

O cat of carlyshe kynde,
The fynde was in thy mynde
When thou my byrde untwynde!
I wold thou haddest ben blynde!
The leopardes savage,
The lyons in theyr rage,
Myght catche the in theyr pawes,
And gnawe the in theyr jawes!
The serpentes of Lybany
Myght stynge the venymously!
The dragones with their tonges
Might poyson thy lyver and longes!
The mantycors of the montaynes
Myght fede them on thy braynes!

This passage and its context have been recalled by John Crowe Ransom, one of the most graceful, witty, and learned of contemporary poets in America. The situations are parallel in the two poems. *In Mr. Minnet's House* tells of a little girl with a pet canary and her small brother with his pet cat. One morning when bad weather kept all the family indoors, sister and brother fell to quarreling, and the cat jumped at the canary:

> *Old Tom was too loyal,*
> *With white whiskers and blood royal,*
> *Eyeing the yellow bird*
> *That twittered and stirred,*
> *And his master with his hands*
> *In his sister's yellow strands;*
> *He leaped up on the table*
> *As only a cat is able*
> *And swung from the cage*
> *To accomplish an outrage;*
> *Seized that bird in his paws*
> *And with teeth and sharp claws*
> *Made her to sing no more*
> *But to lie upon the floor*
> *With her yellow feathers spattered*
> *And her little pieces scattered.*

This verse would hardly have been written but for Skelton's work. Another fine example of Ransom's effective use of free, Middle English rhythms is his poem *Captain Carpenter*.

The greatest of the Elizabethan discoveries in versification was blank verse, resembling Chaucer's couplets of ten syllables minus the rhyme. At first borrowed from Italian and used in translation to imitate the unrhymed verse of Virgil, its role soon became confined to the drama, whence it was lifted and once more employed in epic poetry by Milton. Every true poet who used it bent it to his own personal rhythms. Blank verse is employed with marked individuality by Marlowe, Shakespeare,

Jonson, Middleton, Beaumont, Fletcher, Ford, and Milton. In Marlowe it becomes almost lyrical; in Shakespeare it is used with a maximum of flexibility. The modern tendency to recover a more colloquial idiom than commonly used by the Victorians has made the blank verse represented by Jonson and Middleton more influential in recent years. A few lines from Middleton will indicate his typical style:

> *I bought a jade at Cambridge;*
> *I'll let her out to execution, tutor,*
> *For eighteenpence a-day, or Brainford horse-races;*
> *She'll serve to carry seven miles out of town well.*
> *Where be these mountains? I was promised mountains*
> *But there's such a mist, I can see none of 'em.*
> *What are become of those two thousand runts?*
> *Let's have a bout with them in the meantime;*
> *A vengeance runt thee!*

In such verse the movement of the feet proves unusually free, so that the meter approaches the license of the earlier alliterative poets. The following lines by T. S. Eliot are rugged in the manner of the more realistic of the Elizabethans, as, for instance, Middleton or Tourneur:

> *. . . Words strain,*
> *Crack and sometimes break, under the burden,*
> *Under the tension, slip, slide, perish,*
> *Decay with imprecision, will not stay in place,*
> *Will not stay still. Shrieking voices*
> *Scolding, mocking, or merely chattering,*
> *Always assail them. The Word in the desert*
> *Is most attacked by voices of temptation,*
> *To crying shadow in the funeral dance,*
> *The loud lament of the disconsolate chimera.*

The alternation of passages inspired by Elizabethan blank verse with passages inspired by Old English alliterative verse affords in *The Hamlet of A. MacLeish* one of the most fascinating verse patterns in modern poetry. Blank verse has seldom been more effectively used than by Robert Frost in his New England eclogues, comprising half of his poetry, and by E. A. Robinson in nine tenths of his work, including all his narratives, longer dialogues, and monologues. These moderns resemble the Elizabethans in employing the measure with individuality. Frost's blank verse abounds in Jonsonian ruggedness and Shakespearean surprises, Robinson's in an elasticity and a flexibility even closer to the latter dramatist. The irregularities in Frost are exaggerated almost to the degree of the grotesque, those of Robinson softened so that, while the verse is intellectually stimulating, it remains emotionally grave. Frost's style is rough and democratic, Robinson's smooth and aristocratic. Both men unquestionably profit from Elizabethan poetry without actually imitating it. The Shakespearean echoes in the blank verse of Hardy's *Dynasts*, on the contrary, vigorous as Hardy's masterpiece becomes, seem too openly derivative. From the work of all these men it is evident that recent blank verse is more vital and closer to the Elizabethan than most Victorian writing in that form. Modern poets have dispensed with the vain task of recovering Milton's profound harmony and have become far more sensitive to the freer and franker movement of Shakespeare. With recent accomplishments in view there seems no reason to suppose that blank verse has come to the end of its usefulness, although younger poets turn more commonly elsewhere. Evidence of its vitality may be seen, for instance, in recent volumes by Conrad Aiken, which give us once again the superb music of the Elizabethan tragic soliloquy.

Quite as vigorous as the tradition of blank verse is that of the sonnet. Although a doubtless fortuitous sonnet or two exists in Middle English, this form failed to reach England as a poetic type until the sixteenth century. Its general characteristics are almost too well known to bear restatement. The most common variety is that first practiced in Italian, consisting of eight decasyllabic iambic lines rhymed *abbaabba*, followed by six similar lines for which no fixed rhyme scheme is required. This plan was modified by Shakespeare and others to three quatrains each rhymed *abab* and a final couplet. Since many poems of the same rhyme schemes, the same number of lines, and similar effect have been written in other types of line than iambic decasyllables, there is good reason to consider as sonnets poems of a great variety of meters. Many of these heterodox sonnets have been composed by modern poets, from Gerard Manley Hopkins to the amazingly vigorous American sonneteer, Merrill Moore. The use of an increasing variety of rhythms and meters has helped to preserve vitality. Of all metrical patterns for entire poems the sonnet has proved by far the most popular. From time to time it has gone briefly out of vogue but always recovered greater favor than before. At the close of the last century the vast number of trite sonnets aroused suspicion that the form was exhausted. E. A. Robinson mocked the host of trifling sonneteers and then proceeded to write the finest sonnets which had as yet been seen in America. Much as in the case of blank verse—and indeed even more clearly—the pattern has survived because it has proved a magnificent instrument for the expression of diverse personalities.

The long continuance of the sonnet tradition makes it an ideal unit of measurement or comparison in the historical study of poetry. Writers in widely severed lands and centuries thus appear side by side, each furnishing the same room to please his own taste. Great variations in rhythmical structure are wrought by the more imaginative. We find good evidence of this in five works by poets within the scope of the present study. Wilfred Owen, at once conservative and imaginative, fuses the romance tradition in which the sonnet was born with the ro-

mantic tradition in which it flourished anew; Robinson's deep
and tender harmony is so fluent as to conceal every trace of the
subtle thinking that creates it; Elinor Wylie finds the discipline
of the sonnet an aid and not a barrier in the expression of her
passionate integrity—to her a sonnet is less a poem than a flash
of lightning; Cummings wields it with perfect ease as a keen
whip to chastise the vulgarities of military jingoism; and Hopkins, departing farthest from the inherited rhythms, proves the
most creative and moving of all. The following review aims to
examine the significant rhythmical variations in modern sonnets
and whatever notable analogues an earlier poetry affords.

Shortly before his own death in 1918 Owen wrote his *Anthem
for Doomed Youth:*

> *What passing-bells for these who die as cattle?*
>   *Only the monstrous anger of the guns.*
>   *Only the stuttering rifles' rapid rattle*
> *Can patter out their hasty orisons.*
> *No mockeries for them from prayers or bells,*
>   *Nor any voice of mourning save the choirs,—*
> *The shrill, demented choirs of wailing shells;*
>   *And bugles calling for them from sad shires.*
>
> *What candles may be held to speed them all?*
>   *Not in the hands of boys, but in their eyes*
> *Shall shine the holy glimmers of good-byes.*
>   *The pallor of girls' brows shall be their pall;*
> *Their flowers the tenderness of silent minds,*
> *And each slow dusk a drawing-down of blinds.*

Here is the conventional contrast of octave and sestet, the strict
preservation of the integrity of the line, the change in tempo
given to the highly significant last line—all in the Italianate
manner. This final line is a slow pentameter, tetrameters are the
most frequent, and even trimeter is used. All these details, as

well as the forthright movement of the whole, suggest Keats's imitation of the Elizabethan school rather than the Miltonic manner. Owen, whose tragic death occurred at the age of twenty-five, was in art no less than in destiny a legitimate successor of the young romantic poet. Yet the peculiar beauty of the sound and rhythm of his sonnet owes more to unchanging standards than to the survival of one or another fashion. Sound perfectly echoes and defines the sense. "Stuttering rifles' rapid rattle Can patter" is not only metrically just but beautifully contrasted with "hasty orisons." The tone of the word "wailing" is as true as its implications; the spondaic foot, "sad shires," expresses exactly the sense; and finally we have the calm rhythm and full euphony of the conclusion as signature of complete mastery.

Robinson's well-known and representative poem, *The Clerks*, combines in its movement the colloquial and the eloquent: a personal idiom with an impersonal gravity.

> *I did not think that I should find them there*
> *When I came back again; but there they stood,*
> *As in the days they dreamed of when young blood*
> *Was in their cheeks and women called them fair.*
> *Be sure, they met me with an ancient air,—*
> *And yes, there was a shop-worn brotherhood*
> *About them; but the men were just as good,*
> *And just as human as they ever were.*
>
> *And you that ache so much to be sublime,*
> *And you that feed yourselves with your descent,*
> *What comes of all your visions and your fears?*
> *Poets and kings are but the clerks of Time,*
> *Tiering the same dull webs of discontent,*
> *Clipping the same sad alnage of the years.*

Robinson's methods, which are more modern than Owen's, are the opposite of the sensational. As he remarks in an equally striking sonnet, "the loudest are outside." The most palpable devices are the colloquial phrases of the fifth, sixth, and seventh lines; the movement of the poem, both in its individual lines and its total composition, shows a singularly inobtrusive mastery of poetic form. Phrasing itself is smooth and rapid; and if we read slowly, this is not from any external difficulties of the language, which is transparent, but from Robinson's quiet skill in weighting his lines with thought. The Italian sonnet, with its octave and sestet, is a strictly balanced form, expressing the classical equilibrium of Robinson's philosophy: his purpose is never to praise or to condemn, but to speak truth.

Strange that a form which in one poet becomes marble in another bursts into flame. Elinor Wylie's celebrated last sonnet is controlled lightning.

> *Take home Thy prodigal child, O Lord of Hosts!*
> *Protect the sacred from the secular danger;*
> *Advise her, that Thou never needst avenge her;*
> *Marry her mind neither to man's nor ghost's*
> *Nor holier domination's, if the costs*
> *Of such commingling should transport or change her;*
> *Defend her from familiar and stranger*
> *And earth's and air's contagions and rusts.*
>
> *Instruct her strictly to preserve Thy gift*
> *And alter not its grain in atom sort;*
> *Angles may wed her to their ultimate hurt*
> *And men embrace a spectre in a shift*
> *So that no drop of the pure spirit fall*
> *Into the dust: defend Thy prodigal.*

Despite the original and highly effective rhymes, the poet gives just the necessary minimum of attention to the division between octave and sestet. It is her will to have her sonnet no less than her life fused into unity. And the poem, in any case, stands the strain. A single emotion can hardly be expressed with a clearer tongue. The reduction of the sonnet to one mental action suggests the manner of Spenser. Although this is undoubtedly one of the most perfect sonnets, so passionate is the mastery that in admiration of her original art one easily forgets that the poet has chosen a strictly conventional pattern. The subtleties of form are the more perfect because the external pattern was essentially unconscious. By long reading and practice Elinor Wylie thought in sonnets spontaneously.

Cummings records rhythms of speech less creditable:

> "next to of course god america i
> love you land of pilgrims' and so forth oh
> say can you see by the dawn's early my
> country 'tis of centuries come and go
> and are no more what of it we should worry
> in every language even deafanddumb
> thy sons acclaim your glorious name by gorry
> by jingo by gee by gosh by gum
> why talk of beauty what could be more beaut-
> iful than these heroic happy dead
> who rushed like lions to the roaring slaughter
> they did not stop to think they died instead
> then shall the voice of liberty be mute?"

He spoke. And drank rapidly a glass of water.

One has to know the rarer beauties of the American tongue to appreciate the full pointedness of the rhyme on "beaut," which should, of course, be pronounced as two syllables to be understood properly. The broken rhythms of this sonnet accord with the broken phrases—fragments of a public oration heard in snatches. One fairly hears the orator gulp between the second and third syllables of the last line. The voice of liberty is neither mute nor muted. Whatever may be said of the absence of punctuation in Cummings's other poems, it is here an obvious gain, especially in the sestet, where man's alacrity in not thinking receives vigorous expression. The freedom in the structure of the verse foot, the internal rhyme, and general license in construction by no means conceal the essential sonnet structure. For this Cummings's strong lyrical feeling accounts. He follows Renaissance models not only in many other sonnets but even in the use of one of the most artificial of all Renaissance forms, the sestina, cultivated no less paradoxically by W. H. Auden and Rudyard Kipling.

Cummings has obviously modernized the form in which Dante first excelled, but he has neither the imagination nor the audacity of a still more radical experimenter in verse, Gerard Manley Hopkins. Hopkins also wrote many sonnets, some barely unconventional and others so cryptic as to be virtually in a rhythm and a language of his own. The following specimen is interesting for its originality but not so original as to be actually obscure:

Not, I'll not, carrion comfort, Despair, nor feast on thee;
Not untwist—slack they may be—these last strands of man
In me or, most weary, cry I can no more. I can;
Can something, hope, wish day come, not choose not to be.
But ah, but O thou terrible, why wouldst thou rude on me
Thy wring-world right foot rock? lay a lionlimb against me? scan
With darksome devouring eyes my bruisèd bones? and fan,
O in turns of tempest, me heaped there; me frantic to avoid
    thee and flee?
Why? That my chaff might fly; my grain lie, sheer and clear.
Nay in all that toil, that coil, since (seems) I kissed the rod,
Hand rather, my heart lo! lapped strength, stole joy, would
    laugh, cheer.
Cheer whom though? the hero whose heaven-handling flung
    me, foot trod
Me? or me that fought him? O which one? is it each one? That
    night, that year
Of now done darkness I wretch lay wrestling with (my God!)
    my God.

Although in this poem Hopkins retains little of the more usual Elizabethan meter, he remains in debt to Elizabethan prosody for much more than the rhyme scheme of the sonnet. An echo of Hamlet's most famous soliloquy appears, for example, in line four. The repetition of a word with different shades of accent and meaning he could have found nowhere better exhibited before him than in the sacred poems of John Donne. It will be recalled that Hopkins is author of two remarkable "echo poems," almost the only examples of their kind since the great vogue of this "conceit" passed away with the age of Shakespeare. It may truly be said that the last line contains one of the most surprising of repetitions and parentheses anywhere in verse. This refinement is, however, even more a matter of tone-coloring than of actual time measure or accent. The words "my God" have a totally different meaning—and punctuation—as they twice occur. One occurrence expresses the vividness of a great and surprising spiritual experience, the sudden, violent meeting of man with God; the other brings the poem to its quiet, intellectual period.

Hopkins's alterations and additions to the rhythm of the Elizabethan sonnet are much more obvious than his heritage. The ruggedness is not mere eccentricity or disorder, but a systematic abruptness in detail worked into a staccato pattern for the whole. The passionate compression of image, thought, and feeling becomes a dominating phase of Hopkins's high-strung and ascetic character. It becomes also the beat of his pulse and heart. Within their beautiful and conservative contours his sonnets contain a wholly fresh rhythm and spirit. Seeds sufficient for the sonnets and the poetry of a whole new century were cast forth in his sowings. Like the poems by Hopkins, the four superb sonnets in Edward Weismiller's *The Deer Come Down*, published in 1936, combine new strength with old.

Apart from blank verse and the sonnet, the many notable

Elizabethan verse forms have left relatively small impression on modern poetry. As previously noted, the Spenserian stanza, long an important medium, has at least temporarily sunk into neglect. A widespread and successful revival of the most characteristic Elizabethan lyrical forms would be as surprising as a flock of nightingales in Greenland. For the conjunction of spontaneous spirit and intricate design in poems by Sidney, Vaux, Raleigh, Greene, Lodge, Campion, Daniel, Browne, and Herrick and in lyrics in the plays, madrigal collections, and miscellaneous songbooks of the times was lost and never fully recovered. The happiest lyrical poet still fundamentally of the Elizabethan tradition is W. H. Davies; and to this success his metrical and rhythmical skill contributes as much as any phase of his art. Nevertheless the taste and enthusiasm of the Elizabethan lyric poets was such that in their own kind they not only bear no real rivals but make most comparisons absurd. Davies falls heir to only a portion of Sidney's estate, philosophically accepting his small share of Elizabethan charity.

While our own self-conscious age has found it all but impossible to imitate the clarity and spontaneity of the emotional Elizabethan lyrics, the intellectual lyrics as written by Donne, the Puritans, and the Cavaliers, or chief poets under Charles I, have been widely used. It is not that the Cavaliers are always less emotional than the earlier Elizabethans or that the Elizabethans are always less philosophical than their successors, but the tone of the two schools in lyric verse is on the whole sharply distinguished by the rival claims of head and heart. From the formal point of view the difference is primarily that the Elizabethan verse, whether such is the case or not, seems spontaneous where the Cavalier verse vaunts its wit and intellectualism. Important changes in rhythm followed inevitably upon the changes in spirit. Moreover, the waning of the really great age in English musical culture, the age of Byrd and Campion, resulted in a poetry more attuned to the rhythms of a vigorous prose than of an ethereal music. A comparison between the musical hymns of Campion and the literary hymns of Herbert shows the change. The tone of the Elizabethans is smooth and euphonious; that of the Cavaliers, colloquial and dramatic. Roughness, at least within controlled limits, is the aim of the most popular mid-seventeenth-century style. This appears in the waning of the iambic supremacy, the free mixture of trochees with iambs, and the general irregularity of the verses. The fondness for terse expression leads to a multitude of short lines. And we find a strong tendency to arrest the flow of the feeling and of the verse by an abrupt use of short lines among long. These tendencies converge and reach a height in the choruses of *Samson Agonistes*, which have influenced modern versification as much as any passages in English poetry. Allied to the free treatment of rhythm in these choruses is the freedom shown in the ode and in many lyrics throughout the period. As the seventeenth century advances, poets at times drop the stricter rules of stanzaic structure inherited from the Middle Ages and write with lines of varying lengths dictated less by the demand of the poem as a whole than by particular passages. In this fashion Cowley writes his so-called Pindaric Odes, comprised of stanzas no two of which are alike. Crashaw follows suit. And even the fastidious Marvell in such a poem as *The Drop of Dew* writes without any symmetrical pattern for the length of his lines or for the scheme of his rhymes.

This licentious form of the ode has retained popularity from Cowley to the present day. Collins and Gray practiced it learnedly, Wordsworth and Coleridge romantically. It received additional support from the esteem in which Milton's *Lycidas* was held. But much of the technique of its founders dropped from sight because of the disfavor and neglect long attending the seventeenth-century metaphysical school. The discipline hidden beneath the vaunted freedom of the Cavalier poems was unknown, for example, to Coventry Patmore and James Russell

Lowell when writing their heroic odes. This discipline was partially recovered by close students of Cavailer poetry, such as Francis Thompson, perhaps the most assiduous imitator in the field. Many of Thompson's best poems, both religious and secular, are in this form, such as his *Hound of Heaven*, *Ode to the Setting Sun*, *Ode to the Nineteenth Century*, and *Ode to Cecil Rhodes*. Following this conservative tradition, E. A. Robinson composed his metrically comparable poem, *The Man against the Sky*. A decade later he wrote *Dionysus in Doubt*, a similar piece occasioned by the Prohibition Amendment to the Constitution of the United States. Just as with Cowley in his ode in praise of the Royal Academy, such poetry tends to become prosaic, didactic, and pretentious, losing lyrical purity and sincerity. The poet means well enough but does not feel finely enough. In recent years the more pretentious forms of the ode have lost favor, while the vogue for irregular verse has, on the other hand, increased. If the versification of Robinson's *Man against the Sky* was typical of poetry just before 1914, that of Sacheverell Sitwell's odes is typical of subsequent versions of the same tradition. Robinson played Cowley's unpromising cards and played them much better; Sitwell plays Milton's, but not so well.

The characteristics so apparent in the odes may be seen as clearly, if not so imposingly, in the less aspiring lyrical forms. Thus on Waller's *Go, Lovely Rose*, Ezra Pound writes a variation which begins, "Go, dumb-born book." (Pound has no intention of satirizing either himself or Waller; it is a pleasant poem and quite serious, despite the first line.) Significantly for the variations which the Cavalier versification undergoes in more audacious or more careless modern hands, whereas Waller's poem is regular as regards both line length and rhyme scheme Pound's is irregular in both respects. Waller's poem consists of four- and eight-syllable lines; Pound's of lines of four, six, and ten syllables. The latter, in fact imitates a school rather than a single poem, showing a fine metrical appreciation of the spirit of Cavalier versification.

Many other poets of our time owe much to the technique of the Cavaliers, as Léonie Adams, Melville Cane, and David Mc-Cord. In this respect Genevieve Taggard is typical. She has propounded a somewhat obscure theory of poetry largely based on the achievements of the school of Donne. Like Pound's lyric just cited, her fine poem, *Try Tropic*, is in irregular verse highly reminiscent of the work of Jonson, Donne, Herbert, Vaughan, and even Waller. Probably Ben Jonson's ode beginning with the line, "High-spirited friend," was somewhere in her mind when Miss Taggard wrote as follows:

> *Try tropic for your balm,*
> *Try storm,*
> *And after storm, calm.*
> *Try snow of heaven, heavy, soft and slow,*
> *Brilliant and warm.*
> *Nothing will help, and nothing do much harm.*

Of the many women who have pursued the genius of Cavalier poetry, none has achieved higher recognition than Elinor Wylie, who had both the wisdom to learn and the genius to create. Her technique is ultimately her own, though usually much indebted to the seventeenth century. She is a less licentious versifier than the modern poets just mentioned. Thus the capriciousness which she allows herself in *A Courtesy* proves exceptional. The greater part of this poem is composed of rhymes in couplets, the lines alternating between ten and six syllables. But not all the rhymes are couplets nor all the lines alternating in length. The poet is nearer her usual ground in her effective piece, *Absent Thee from Felicity Awhile*, which has a regular stanzaic rhyme scheme but a few slight irregularities in the line pattern. Virtually all lines, however, are of ten or six syllables. Thoroughly typical are poems in regular stanzas of different line lengths, such as the magnificent heir of the metaphysical tradition, *Hymn to Earth*, with lines of ten and six syllables, and *This Corruptible*, in lines of six and eleven syllables with a verse pattern suggested by Milton's *Hymn to Christ's Nativity*. Such a piece as *Hughie at the Inn*, with lines alternating between ten and six syllables, is distinctly akin to Cavalier poetry. *Confession of Faith*, written in a three-line stanza of six, four, and six syllables, has a movement reminding one of Herbert's *Discipline*.

The Cavalier poets delighted in terse lines and terse stanzas. In both of these Elinor Wylie excels and with a definite indebtedness to the seventeenth century. Thus among her more memorable poems are: *O Virtuous Light*, in octosyllabic tetrameter quatrains rhymed *abab*; *This Hand*, in the same form; *The Eagle and the Mole* and *Address to My Soul*, in six-syllable trimeter quatrains, similarly rhymed. *Minotaur* is in trimeter rhyming triplets also of six syllables. Her many poems in the octosyllabic couplet, as *The Pebble*, contain the strongest reminiscences of the similarly impeccable art of Milton, Marvell, and Vaughan. Even her few poems in long lines and trisyllabic feet have echoes of the older masters. *"Desolation Is a Delicate Thing"* suggests the beautiful hymn by Campion, *Never Weather-beaten Sail More Willingly Bent to Shore*.

Most of Elinor Wylie's lyrical versification can be traced to the inspiration of such poems as Herbert's *Lent*, *The Collar*, *To All Angels*, and *Discipline*; Vaughan's *World*, *Unprofitableness*, and *The Search*; Donne's *Love's Alchemy*; Raleigh's *Lie*; Campion's *Man of Upright Life*; Herrick's *To Live Merrily and Trust to Good Verses*; Waller's *Go, Lovely Rose*; and that anonymous meditation from a Christ Church manuscript which begins, "Yet if his majesty, our sovereign Lord." Elinor Wylie's remarkable metrical invention in her *Peregrine*, though scorning actual models, is her own contribution to the Cavalier tradition.

When Edith Sitwell in her introduction to her brother Sacheverell's *Collected Poems* lays stress upon his likeness to Milton and to Marvell, she points to those poets whom her brother emulates if not imitates. *Snowflakes*, for example, has the true ring of Marvell's octosyllabic couplets. But the Sitwells are more indebted to Marvell's spirit and visual imagery than to his verse technique.

In conclusion, one notes how much definite aid modern poets have accepted from the minor poems of the seventeenth century and from *Samson Agonistes*, and how little from the blank verse of *Paradise Lost*. For well over a century after Milton's death poets strutted pompously in futile imitation of Milton's elusive and incomparable technique. Milton is still a powerful force in the creative minds of poets; but the wisest have learned to hold their distance from the mysteries and miracles which his inner ear achieved in his masterpiece.

Meters and rhythms of medieval, Elizabethan, and Cavalier poetry have exercised a stronger influence on modern verse than those of Augustan, romantic, and Victorian times, for modern verse in quest of new vigor has turned its face more often to the more distant than to the nearer past. All periods make some contribution to the modern poets—but in varying measures.

Augustan and Victorian versifications, both of some importance to our contemporaries, are the most strikingly contrasted, the former highly conservative, the latter often highly explorative. No inferiority in the eighteenth-century verse need, of course, be assumed because fewer meters are there used. The nineteenth-century piano is a more advanced instrument than the eighteenth-century harpsichord, but the music written for it or produced on it is not on that account the finer. The conservatism of the Augustans in the meters which they employ is often more than offset by the subtlety of the variations within the outstanding metrical patterns. Superficially considered, Pope's verse looks depressingly simple; actually it proves delicately complex. Pope and his age polished and repolished familiar patterns. Our own poets care more for bold experiment and wide variety than for patient refinement within definite limitations. Versification is one of the clearest mirrors of the social consciousness. The intensive cultivation of well-established standards of taste and conduct became in all spheres typical of Augustan life, whereas we are, on the contrary, more rashly enterprising and individualistic.

Although the heroic couplet is neither so fixed a quantity nor so pervasive as some accounts of Augustan verse lead one to suppose, it is undoubtedly the most characteristic verse form of the age. Its two chief phases are represented by the two leading poets, Dryden and his followers treating it more informally, Pope and his imitators more punctiliously. Technically, Dryden differs from his successors in using more run-on lines, more run-on couplets, fewer metrical tricks, and a less pointed caesura. As the more mannered writer, Pope has always been the more tempting to imitate; but imitations only emphasize the gulf between a true genius and mediocrity. The better writers of the couplet in Pope's century, such as Young, Churchill, and Cowper, with their naturalness and vigor suggest Dryden, while the deliberate copying of Pope, although a notorious practice, at once became a mark of imperfect growth or ill-advised ambition. Time has winnowed the two schools. Between the two leaders, as Doctor Johnson observed, criticism knows no choice; but even more clearly today than in the eighteenth century, the majority of true poets stand closer to Dryden than to Pope.

The Augustan age preferred modification and imitation in verse to invention and imagination. Dryden is by no means an audacious metrist, since his rhythms are but a slight refinement upon poetry written by Daniel and Drayton three quarters of a century before him. Indeed, the seeds of the couplet as matured by Waller and Dryden had rested in the hands of Chaucer. Pope merely carried the smoothing-out process to its highest perfection. None of the Augustan authors could possibly envisage himself as a really radical figure in the development of versification. Mark Akenside's stanzaic odes may seem original till we note how regularly the iambic foot is used in the lines of varying lengths. Thomson, Young, and Cowper do their best work in conservative blank verse; Gray at times carries on the Cowlian tradition of the Pindaric Ode, also using long-familiar quatrains and ballad meters. Smart's superb *Song to David* is in a time-honored hymn meter of the Middle Ages. Swift and the robust Churchill among other conservative types produce minor variations within Hudibrastic verse. All of Burns's meters derive from the sixteenth century or earlier. These men had little fundamentally new to hand down to the future.

It is true that a considerable amount of verse vaguely related to the freer idiom of Dryden and Churchill is being written today. It is even true that Belloc, Aldous Huxley, Robert Hillyer, the three Sitwells, and other poets occasionally imitate even the refinements of Pope. But such writing usually has an antiquarian flavor. The Augustan poets best known for work outside the heroic couplet enter the most powerfully into the stream of influence affecting modern versification. Although such writers are often poets' poets, men not widely popular today, they may well be the more warmly cherished by the modern poets themselves. Although Matthew Prior, for example, is scarcely regarded by conservative critics or the general public as a major poet, it is difficult to believe that all of our many writers of creditable light verse fail to recall the happiest master of this type of writing which England has produced. *Jinny the Just*, one of Prior's jaunty trifles, was first printed in 1907. One can hardly think that its publication has been in vain so far as creative verse today is concerned. Edmund Blunden, equally representative as poet and critic, has acclaimed the art of Collins. In its rhythms of line, phrase, and sentence Collins's *Ode to Evening* has been and still is one of the ponderable arguments for a bold and free English versification. The ear of the present day is peculiarly attuned to its music. New editions of Swift's poetry and appreciative studies of his art make it probable that we shall at last correct the error ascribed to Dryden, who is said to have remarked that Cousin Swift would never be a poet. An age like our own, given to realistic portraiture of dialect, speech, and manners, to violent political satire and reforming zeal, can hardly remain oblivious of the fact that no poet, not even Langland or Byron, has turned verse in these channels to better account than Swift, the perfect master of the rhymed political lampoon. His Hudibrastic rhythms are the very genius of his theme. The ruggedness of Swift's versification and imagery is paralleled in the grotesque passages of Conrad Aiken's *John Deth* and *Punch, the Immortal Liar*.

Of all poets who flourished principally in the eighteenth century none is today so influential on verse technique as Blake. His advance was first of all in his habitual departures from the iambic rhythm, which had become by his own times the dominating form for English verse. Blake not only writes anapaestic poetry, as Gay, Prior, and Swift had done before him. Within the same line or poem he uses a great variety of feet, both in length and pattern, shows new sensitivity to the rhythmical value of the pause, and attains extreme flexibility in the length and structure of his lines. Sometimes he writes rhythmical prose resembling Ossian; but for the most part a verse form is unmistakable. Blake's radicalism is already apparent in rhymed lyrics such as *Night, Hear the Voice of the Bard*, and *Cradle Song* ("Sleep! sleep! beauty bright"), but it is, of course, in his later Prophetic Books that he goes far beyond Coleridge and Southey and virtually anticipates the rhythmical style of such a representative modern poet as Robinson Jeffers. The following lines are representative of Blake's mature style:

Thou hearest the Nightingale begin the Song of Spring.
The Lark, sitting upon his earthy bed, just as the morn
Appears, listens silent; then, springing from the waving corn-
*   field, loud*
He leads the Choir of Day, trill! trill! trill! trill!
Mounting upon the wings of light into the Great Expanse,
Re-echoing against the lovely blue and shining heavenly Shell.
His little throat labors with inspiration, every feather
On throat and breast and wings vibrates with the effluence
*   Divine.*
All Nature listens silent to him, and the awful Sun
Stands still upon the Mountain, looking on the little Bird
With eyes of soft humility and wonder, love and awe.
Then loud from their green covert all the Birds begin their song;
The Thrush, the Linnet and the Goldfinch, Robin and the
*   Wren*
Awake the Sun from his sweet reverie upon the Mountain.
The Nightingale again assays his song, and thro' the day
And thro' the night warbles luxuriant, every Bird of Song
Attending his loud harmony with admiration and love.
This is the Vision of the lamentation of Beulah over Ololon.

It is difficult to estimate the influence of Blake on modern versification. At a hasty glance it may seem that he created without models and died without disciples. But his posthumous admirers, once confined to the choicest group of English poets and men of letters, now includes a considerable public genuinely appreciative of his metrical art. The poet and critic, Foster Damon, in his volume on Blake has an interesting discussion on his importance as a metrist.

The chief romantic poets have contributed less to the versification of modern poetry than to its imagery and spirit. Illustrious in personality and spirit as many of these romanticists are, their imaginative reach frequently surpasses their technical grasp. And even where their achievements have high technical merits, more often than commonly realized their art is inherited from Augustan, Elizabethan, or even Chaucerian fields. The first of the true romantics shows this the most strikingly. In his Rowley Poems, Chatterton, the forerunner, obviously laid no claim to any nuances later than those of the Middle Ages.

Wordsworth is not especially felicitous in blank verse, the medium of the greater part of his work, and is scarcely inventive elsewhere. He works almost arbitrarily in Spenserian stanzas, octosyllabic verse, Burns's stanza, ballad meters, and sonnets, seldom owing a great part of his success to metrical skill and rarely contributing a clear, new metrical note. His spiritual power easily leads us to overlook this unimaginative imitativeness in versification. His famous Ode to Duty, for instance, is in the metrical structure of its stanzas an unadorned copy of Gray's Hymn to Adversity. His verses, nevertheless, have suggested the technique for many nineteenth-century poems and for a few of the twentieth century. E. A. Robinson's Isaac and Archibald is stylistically in all respects, notably in the leisurely blank verse and bucolic style, an imitation of Wordsworth's Michael, and many of Robinson's sonnets and stanzaic poems follow Wordsworth's use of feminine rhyme and other metrical features. Nevertheless Wordsworth as a whole has hardly been a happy influence on English versification, which he too often has helped to render conventional, sentimental, and effeminate.

Though a subtler artist in rhythm, Keats is even more conservative, neoclassical, and alien to the verse rhythms of modern times. He follows in turn Spenser, Dryden, Milton, and Chaucer, bowing to the iambic supremacy and to the ten-syllable line. On the one hand his most exquisite rhythms within these well-established patterns forbid imitation; on the other hand his favorite meters hark back to the more conservative phases of Renaissance verse rather than to elements now found most dynamic.

The case of Byron is essentially similar, their differences in temperament and sensitivity notwithstanding. Byron is even more conservative than Keats. He makes only vague modifications in the heroic couplet of the Drydenesque school, in the Spenserian stanza, blank verse, ballad and lyrical forms, and in ottava rima, which he himself imitates chiefly from Pulci and Ariosto. Perhaps the only verse movement distinctive enough in Byron to be recognizably imitated is his English ottava rima, effectively used in modern verse by W. H. Auden and Leonard Bacon.

Most of Scott's poetry is rhythmically monotonous, representing a smoothing out of ballad meters to accommodate the taste of the Regency period. Although a few of his more delicate pieces, such as *Proud Maisie*, may have aided the cause of modern verse, his prosody is on the whole uninteresting and ominous of the banality of much nineteenth-century style. Here are precisely the harsh, hard accents and wooden feet from which writers of our own time have violently revolted.

Something more positive was contributed by Shelley, more by Southey, and most by Coleridge. Shelley's versification has two phases: first, he gives his own coloring to Renaissance versification, as in his fresh and fluid treatment of the Spenserian stanza in *Adonais*, in the almost lyrical blank verse of his dramas, in the impetuous terza rima of his *Triumph of Life*, in his imitation of Dryden's manner in his charming *Letter to Maria Gisborne*, and in several of his choral odes; and secondly, he is author of poems in which his personality and imagination redeem what might in another be a specious metrical virtuosity. In such poems as *The Cloud* he popularized anapaestic measures with a dangerous fascination to writers later in his own century but with the stimulating value of new and vigorous work. The similar choruses in *Prometheus Unbound* have a vitality certain to outlast the variations played upon them by Francis Thompson, or by the still more expansive Swinburne. They have the magic swiftness and fire of the allegro finales of Beethoven's quartets. The highly complex rhythms of *To Night* possess a haunting delicacy seldom if ever imitated successfully.

Although the unfortunate Southey exercises little beyond an indirect influence on modern verse, his role in the march of prosody is too often slighted. Lacking both the taste and the discipline necessary for technical achievements of a high order, he possessed an experimental curiosity worthy of his age and friendships. His early excursions into dactyls and Sapphics at least show his explorative temper. His romantic narrative, *Thalaba*, goes much further. On a rough iambic foundation he builds an elaborate structure generally without rhyme or conventional stanzaic patterns. The following passage is representative.

> A desert Pelican had built her nest
> In that deep solitude,
> And now, returned from distant flight,
> Fraught with the river-stream,
> Her load of water had disburthened there.
> Her young in the refreshing bath
> Dipped down their callow heads,
> Filled the swoln membrane from the plumeless throat
> Pendent, and bills yet soft;
> And, buoyant with arched breast,
> Plied in unpractised stroke
> The oars of their broad feet.
> They, as the spotted prowler of the wild
> Laps the cool wave, around their mother crowd,
> And nestle underneath her outspread wings.
> The spotted prowler of the wild
> Lapped the cool wave, and satiate, from the nest,
> Guiltless of blood, withdrew.

Even if seldom read a century afterwards, writing of this sort prepared the way for the revolutionary course which English versification was to follow.

Coleridge is a far subtler and more influential metrist. Some of his typical effects were recaptured by Poe and indirectly transmitted through numerous channels. So clearly do his best-known poems evince the desire for renewed freedom in versification that they remain even today the poet's most dramatic declaration of independence. Sometimes, to be sure, he merely reverts to the metrical license of the medieval ballads; more often he discovers new idioms highly fruitful for modern verse. His *Ancient Mariner* is as far from Gray's *Elegy* as modern interpretative dancing is from the minuet. His treatment of the couplet in most of *Christabel* stands closer to the resilience of the best modern verse than to the modest license of *L'Allegro*; while his *Kubla Khan*, with its successive passages in iambic, trisyllabic, and simple dipodic verse, brilliantly displays the charms of metrical liberty. It would be hard to exaggerate the role played by the metrical element in this popular fragment.

The prolific Victorian era produced much on which modern poets have built and much on which they decisively have turned their backs. Swinburne, Rossetti, Morris, and Longfellow constructed highways little in use today. It will be noted that such important liberators of verse as Whitman, Emily Dickinson, and Bridges were not generally well received in their own times. Modern verse tends to avoid obvious patterns of all sorts, to give new freedom to the foot, the line, the verse paragraph, and the poem. This does not mean that free verse is the logical goal as it seemed in America a few years past, although Robinson Jeffers's verse is better entitled to be called free verse than Whitman's. The essential point is that modern verse at its acknowledged best revolts from the more conservative patterns formulated by the most popular poets of the eighteenth and nineteenth centuries. The tendency has been to increase such irregularities as occur in the significant word "difficult" in Alice Meynell's well-known sonnet, *Renouncement:* "But when sleep comes to close each difficult day."

Even from the more representative poets of the last century, however, those of the present have sometimes been learners. Although they have as a whole revolted from the strongly marked, strongly stressed, and ready-made patterns mechanically imposed on verse by such poets as Swinburne, they have occasionally made use of Swinburne's researches into medieval verse forms. Especially before the reading of Middle English became widespread, Swinburne served as an intermediary. Morris, too, imitated Old English meters in such poems as *Love Is Enough.* While Tennyson's verse often seems banal or flat today, he unquestionably composed some inspired and inspiring pieces in flexible meter, especially in his briefer poems, as the song, *Tears, Idle Tears,* and his dipodic verse, *In the Valley of Cauteretz.* Although much of Arnold's best verse is metrically conservative, a number of his pieces show an inventive and forward-looking mind in matters of prosody. The free and beautiful iambs of *Dover Beach,* for example, led MacLeish to write his sequel, *Dover Beach: a Note to That Poem,* on the same metrical plan. Ernest Dowson's well-known "I have been faithful to thee, Cynara! in my fashion," has an extremely free and sinuous metrical pattern. The more conservative of recent poets stand, of course, most in debt to their like-minded predecessors. Kingsley's *Old Song,* for instance, is both an old song and a new; in simple ballad meter, it strongly suggests the movement of Housman's lyrics. Kingsley and not Housman wrote thus:

> *When all the world is young, lad,*
> *And all the trees are green;*
> *And every goose a swan, lad,*
> *And every lass a queen . . .*

With the senescence overtaking the iambic pentameter at the beginning of the last century, other metrical types became increasingly popular, especially trisyllabic forms, of which the anapaest is the most practical. A large number of measures were invented or rediscovered by the more alert and experimental writers of the Victorian age, especially the masters of light verse, as Edward Lear and Lewis Carroll. The great vogue of the limerick is representative. As the simple anapaests of Swinburne and his admirers grew tedious or ridiculous, new paths in dipodic verse were explored. This quest begot some of the most admired pieces by George Meredith, as *Love in a Valley*, *Melampus*, and *Dirge in Woods*. William Johnson Cory's delicate *Anteros* is dipodic. And above all in prominence were the songs and poems of one of the chief masters of metrical virtuosity in the language, Rudyard Kipling. Chiefly to him we owe the rapid rise not only of dipodic but of syncopated verse, the vogue of syncopation in poetry slightly anticipating that in popular music. In so far as Kipling's verses represent a high degree of regularity amounting almost to doggerel, they are the antithesis of what is generally conceded to be the best in modern practice. But in so far as Kipling, Meredith, Masefield, and others enlarged the possibilities of modern verse through their numerous experiments, they made important contributions to its development. Although our poets generally decline to write poems or passages wholly in these newly available meters, such as the more elaborate forms of dipodic verse, feeling that to a sensitive ear they become singsong, the development of the foot as such in modern poetry has been enriched by the practice of these men.

In concluding this analysis we may turn to the four chief poets of the last century who have been the direct early guides to modern versification. Whitman has really had less influence than might be assumed, not because of the slight waning during the last few years of the vogue of free verse, but because much of his poetry has marked conventional rhythms. Such a typical piece as *Crossing Brooklyn Ferry*, the chief literary source for Hart Crane's *Bridge*, in many passages resembles the dactylic hexameters of Longfellow's *Evangeline*. Less frequently, as in *The Prayer of Columbus*, also used by Crane, he slips into conventional blank verse. And even he occasionally falls into singsong. But this is a relative matter; and the historical importance no less than the beauty of all the phases of Whitman's colossal verse rhetoric cannot well be denied. Precisely because Emily Dickinson shunned all banality in rhythm, she has been the greatest single force on modern American versification, especially on verse whose patterns are too clear to be called "free." Robert Bridges is distinctly a poet's poet, largely because his technical achievements are so much more imaginative than other aspects of his work. A lifelong student of metrics, he creates far more arresting rhythms than images, feelings, or ideas. His verse is a world of chilled perfection. Yet no literature can have its poetry augmented by the "loose Alexandrines" of Bridge's *Testament of Beauty* and such exquisite examples of hovering accents and pauses as in *A Passer-by* (his poem on a sailing ship), *Awake, My Heart*, and *London Snow*, without permanent effect. With the mention of Bridges and his friend Hopkins the present survey of the genetics of modern versification ends as it began. It is only in part to these two friends that Pound, Eliot, MacLeish, Jeffers, and the most representative of modern poets are indebted. Their primary debt is through Hopkins and Bridges back to *Piers Plowman* itself and to *Beowulf*.

TYPES OF POETRY

The view that society was once orderly and is at present chaotic has obsessed mankind in almost every age. Order in the world of books has long been described as the observance of strictly defined types or genres. This view, to be sure, has of late been questioned by thinkers such as Croce, who finds all definitions of types superficial and unsatisfying and prefers a more fluid theory of art. Such classifications, however, are not made to please the philosophers but employed because of their utility as a ready introduction to orderly discussion.

Poetry has been typified in many ways, by its social function, its subject matter, general form, imagery, style, and versification, for example. Since versification has just been considered in the foregoing pages, it will be wholly excluded here. Generally speaking a type is defined by its basic form, but by form as determined by subject and meaning. The types presently to be examined have all been recognized in literary criticism, although some are ancient and familiar classifications and others relatively new and unfamiliar. Not all poems fall within these categories nor are the categories always mutually exclusive. But they cover the vast majority of compositions in this or any century between Chaucer and ourselves. We shall find that in spite of the seemingly chaotic state of modern poetry, a surprising amount of it is consciously built along established and traditional pathways. The types which we shall consider are: the epic, the major philosophical poem, the verse novel, the verse tale, the ballad, the dialogue between three or more speakers, the dialogue between two speakers, the objective monologue, where the speaker is either of the first or the third person, the epistle, the interior monologue, soliloquy, or lonely debate, the elegy, the epitaph, the epigram, the satire, the verse essay, the character sketch, the myth, the allegory, the poem built upon a single dominant metaphor, the poem built upon an abstract idea, the poem built upon a simple act, the brief impressionistic sketch, and, lastly, the song.

Readers acquainted with the earliest and the latest periods of English poetry are forced to acknowledge a partial emancipation from conventional genres as an outstanding aspect of modern literature. We are doubtless right in thinking ourselves fond of free verse, the open road, and an imagination untrammeled by traditions gladly accepted by our predecessors. All earlier centuries have recognized types of poetry more willingly than our own; none has so idolized the notion of the poet as a totally free agent. And no period offers so marked a contrast with ours as Chaucer's. Idealistically striving to bring order into all phases of life, the Middle Ages to a certain extent succeeded in achieving this ideal in purely intellectual realms. The Christian world set about the writing and distribution of poetry on a wholesale basis. Topics were assigned, with appropriate forms allocated to them. Poetry, like the other arts, became ritualized. The author writing a saint's life, a fabliau, a hymn, a love song, or an elegy invariably found a definite formula prepared for him. It behooved him merely to fill in an old pattern with new detail. The medieval conventionality in genres can hardly be exaggerated. The heretic in art or poetry was once as rare as the heretic in ritual or theology. Few poems contain lines not interchangeable with lines of other poems. This is merely a phase of the communal strength and conservatism of the Middle Ages. Although some progress was achieved by the march of the fashions from year to year, rarely if ever did anyone deliberately breaks ranks. By an extraordinary communal telepathy art moved forward. But the progress, especially in verse, was slow. And the literary types were piously observed. So a modern bibliographer of medieval literature, as John Edwin Wells, finds his material arranging itself almost without an effort on his part. In medieval poetry the types, then, are the most obvious, as in our own poetry they are the most concealed.

The dynamic English Renaissance plays more freely with literary genres than the medieval period, yet not nearly so boldly as might be supposed nor so freely as our own age. The eclecticism of the times led authors to mix their genres, as tragical, pastoral, comical, or historical, but seldom to lose sight of them altogether. When John Fletcher first popularized tragicomedy in English, he had Italian precept and example on hand for his defense, and soon won his fellow dramatists, including Shakespeare, to join him upon the well-known path. Song, satire, elegy, story, epic, epithalamium, epigram, epitaph, and pastoral each had its well-defined laws no less faithfully observed because the poets breathed with remarkable freedom within their own self-imposed conventions. Certain of these conventions, altering and hardening, produced in time the rules of the Augustans.

Eighteenth-century criticism became largely the embodiment of this conservatism. The Elizabethans had won a temporary freedom for style if not for genre; the Augustans, like the Chaucerians, became once more conventional in both. Their assiduous servitude created a certain sterility. When the romanticists in freeing the political and the spiritual man freed also the man of letters, one of the most drastic revolutions in the history of literature was effected. The old genres weakened even before the old rhetoric, the weakening of their hold upon the nineteenth century leading at length to the present degree of license. The ardent radical sees art freed at last from the imitation of art and so become the better mirror and servant of life. Our criticism at times carelessly accepts this romantic point of view. But far more than we are generally conscious today, genres accumulated through the centuries are still observed. In most cases the modern author is tacitly aware of his conservatism. In others it becomes the place of the historian to show that, where older analogues are indisputably known to the author, an influence, even if unconscious, must exist. Even so naturalistic a poet as Merrill Moore is often conventional in his methods and ideas. The literate poet today conforming to the ancient patterns will do so the more readily and effectively because of his knowledge. The more intelligent the poet, the more closely he realizes this indebtedness. And while pedantry is occasionally a fault even among the moderns, the worst pedantry is always in style, not in the larger contours of form.

Where the greater part of English poetry, both of today and of the past, is concerned, any presentation of the case must be highly condensed. The mention of a few prominent poems, new and old, in connection with each of the types readily suffices to sketch the lines of continuity and indicates how little the subject matter and general plan of poetry have changed during ten centuries. Such cards have long rested in the hands of literary historians to play, but it is remarkable how seldom in recent years they have been sorted for the game and placed upon the table.

The epic is a heroic narrative expressing a national culture, which as far as it celebrates the outer life of the race becomes historical and as far as it celebrates the inner life becomes mythological. It tends to commemorate the military struggles of a people for existence. In its most complete form, as in the *Iliad*, the *Aeneid* and *Beowulf*, it proves both historical and mythological. Its inclination toward the historical appears best in Lucan and in the *Chanson de Roland*, its inclination toward myth in Du Bartas and in Milton. On the whole the secular element is generally the more important in the poetry of highly civilized peoples. Certainly the political epic, Milton notwithstanding, has the stronger tradition in English. Save *Paradise Lost*, the great religious poems have been of a comparatively limited—hardly a national—appeal. *Piers Plowman* is a satirical protest representing national strife rather than national unity; and *Pilgrim's Progress* still further voices the dissidence of dissent. Poets are closer to the epic in medieval verse before the romantic Malory, in heroic poems composed in the alliterative meter, such as the *Morte d' Arthur* or *The Destruction of Troy*, or even in the heroically and patriotically inspired *Chronicle* of Robert of Gloucester. Michael Drayton's *Poly-Olbion* is similar poetry. If Kipling had possessed a more powerful imagination or a better cause, he might conceivably have written the epic of imperialism.

There is undoubtedly an epic intention in patriotic poems such as Stephen Vincent Benét's brilliant if erratic *John Brown's Body* and Mark Van Doren's *Jonathan Gentry*, both poems celebrating the life of a nation on a new continent. Epic aspirations fired John Neihardt in a series of loosely related poems on the winning of the American West. But these authors have been happier in their less ambitious productions, and they have drawn only casually on the inspiration of epic form. For such inspiration Hardy, as author of *The Dynasts*, turned to the Napoleonic Wars. Unhappily most modern poets who have come closest to the epic spirit have gone behind the present or recent past to treat broadly and at times symbolically the life of more primitive peoples. The best literary epic of our times is probably MacLeish's *Conquistador*, a narrative poem depicting the conquest of Mexico by Cortes. As a narrative told in the first person, as a work of only moderate length, and above all as an essentially scholarly and antiquarian production, it departs from the true epic. But in its heroic style and spirit, militant scene, narrative method, and lofty idealism it unquestionably reflects its author's appreciation of the epic tradition in general and of *Beowulf* in particular The epic, with qualifications, is still a living form.

As epic poetry loses its objectivity and its popular appeal, becoming philosophical instead of naïve, cosmic instead of nationalistic, and allegorical instead of mythological, it gradually passes from the true epic to the major philosophical poem. All of the dignity and much of the imagery of the more primitive form are retained with new increment from an aging civilization. The poet paints an affirmative picture of human destiny. Long poems, such as Pope's *Essay on Man*, Young's *Night Thoughts*, or Wordsworth's *Excursion*, dealing with man's place in the universe without the aid of semimythological fable, do not fall into the present category; nor do strictly metaphysical poems, such as the allegorical Psyches and Psychomachias of mystical tradition. But an intermediary category lies between epic narrative and romantic fantasy, between racial myth and fine-spun introspection. Lucretius and Seneca, Dante, Langland and Spenser suggest such a classification of earlier material. All poets attempting to pluck out the mystery of life with the aid of a heroic fable must, so far as they are aware of each other at all, feel a community of spirit. A philosophical poem thus inspired becomes a spiritual epic, the primitive transfigured by a more advanced culture. Ezra Pound in his learned *Cantos* obviously feels an affinity with predecessors in this lofty and difficult domain. So did W. B. D. Henderson, author of the too-little-known *New Argonautica*, based on an allegorical interpretation of the astronomical and geographical explorations of the Renaissance.

On the right of the epic stands the major poetry of the imaginative philosophers, on the left the romances of the novelists in verse. Here is a long tradition hardly less conscious and powerful than that of the true epic. Every century since the Chaucerian period has left contributions. Chaucer's *Troilus and Criseyde*, the first and best of amorous novels in English, is followed by countless tales. Interestingly enough the two finest to approach it during the next two centuries are in poetic prose, namely, Malory's *Morte d' Arthur* and Sidney's *Arcadia*. William Chamberlayne's *Pharonnida*, a platonic romance, gained much favor in the Cavalier period and has been occasionally remembered ever since. George Crabbe's *Tales of the Hall* contains so strong a central stem as to be comparable despite the tales branching from it to a novel in the Augustan style with many digressions. Byron's *Don Juan* notwithstanding its satirical flavor is a novel of the picaresque school; while the uncommon form assumed by the narrative in Browning's *Ring and the Book* slenderly conceals novelistic tendencies. Such poems are uncommonly long, with complex major and minor actions; they differ from the shorter and simpler tales in verse.

Usually material for a number of tales is contained within the scope of the verse novel itself.

Although literary historians have been reluctant to find the roots of the modern novel in early romances, the settings of romantic verse novels themselves strongly suggest such origins. Crabbe trod on comparatively fresh ground when he approached the novel and at the same time chose a contemporary scene. Other poets preferred the past. Wordsworth in his *White Doe* writes of Elizabethan England; Coleridge with philosophical catholicity is content merely with a strong medieval atmosphere; Keats's fancy dwells on medieval Italy; Southey prefers Islam and Spain; Scott clings to his Scottish border; Swinburne, Arnold, and Tennyson retell tales of the age of Chaucer; Browning advances to the Renaissance; but Morris in his voluminous paraphrases includes early German and Icelandic legends. It is of interest that E. A. Robinson, most indefatigable of romancers, chose for his longest tale the many-times-told story of Tristram, after having already recorded the tragedies of Merlin and Lancelot. And from a powerful medieval ballad, *Edward*, Robinson Jeffers has taken the title and plot of a recent novel in verse, *Such Counsels You Gave to Me*. The Middle Ages may not again yield even the setting for such a novel as Robinson's *Tristram*, but this setting itself points to inherited characteristics from what is still easily recognizable as a parent stock. Romantic novels in verse are today not uncommon: Christopher La Farge's *Each to the Other* is an example; Jesse Stuart's *Man with a Bull-Tongue Plow*, another. They express a point of view and employ a narrative technique essentially the same as that of Chaucer's *Troilus and Criseyde*.

Jeffers and Robinson have been among the most effective narrative poets in recent years. Only about half their longer poems, however, rise in complexity of situation from the class of the short story in verse to that of the novel. In the latter category by Robinson are *Tristram, Lancelot, Merlin, Talifer*,

King Jasper, and *Matthias at the Door.* Although the action of
Roman Bartholow is relatively simple, the story progresses with
Shandean leisureliness and, being one of the longest of all
Robinson's poems, certainly equals a novel in its scope. He
writes the modern psychological novel in a singularly dry,
analytical style. His chief debts are to the prose writers of his
own times or a little earlier, as Henry James and George
Meredith. But as an intelligent reader he must certainly have
realized his affinity not only with Browning and Tennyson but
with Malory and Chaucer. His characters of Tilbury Town are
the most direct and legitimate descendants of the Canterbury
Pilgrims that English verse affords. It would indeed be difficult
to believe that the realistic portraiture in the *Canterbury Tales*
and the consummate art in *Troilus and Criseyde* failed to make
some impression on the American romancer. Jeffers acknowledges and presumably feels fewer debts to English poetry than
any contemporary writer of equal magnitude. Striding somewhat morosely over his Californian headlands with a Greek
tragedy in one hand and an American dime novel in the other,
he admits comparatively few literary companions. But his silence
as to the conventionality of his themes and narrative methods
conceals neither his unavowed literacy nor his obligations even
if at second hand to the romance tradition. Such a story as *The
Women at Point Sur* resembles in its extravagance a "Gothic"
effusion such as Thomas Chatterton's *Tragedy of Ella.*

The shorter tale, confined to little more than a single un-
complicated action which might constitute an episode in a
longer novel or romance, has, of course, as long a tradition and
is actually the basis of all narrative verse. *The Miller's Tale* or
The Pardoner's Tale in Chaucer exemplify it as a type. Marlowe
and Chapman's *Hero and Leander* is perhaps the finest short
romance in English. Almost as vital are the translated stories by
Dryden, the romantic tales by Keats, and the realistic tales by
Crabbe. Practically all the romantic poets attempted this briefer

form of narrative. Despite the efforts of Masefield the verse story has appeared neither abundantly nor brilliantly in twentieth-century England; it has fared somewhat better in America. Again Robinson and Jeffers stand out most prominently, although others, as Frost in his *Witch of Coös*, occasionally tell a good tale in verse. In narrative technique and delicate handling of suspense Robinson has few equals or none. His *Avon's Harvest* is by modern standards almost a perfect short story, while *Cavender's House* and *The Glory of the Nightingales*, though less expert as narratives, are clearly to be taken more seriously as poetry. In this phase of his art Robinson was doubtless aided by his wide reading of detective stories. But he himself points emphatically to at least one source of poetic inspiration. There are obvious likenesses between his stories and those in the best collection in verse since Chaucer, namely Crabbe's *Tales*, and in an often-quoted sonnet Robinson acknowledges Crabbe's greatness. Enjoying Crabbe's power and dryness and writing as he did, Robinson can hardly have escaped some literary inspiration from the older poet. And Jeffers's tales of horror, however much they may differ from the chief romantic poets in style, still bear certain resemblances in spirit and imagery. Such a story as *Roan Stallion* is Coleridgean in effect, even though the exceptionally crude manners which it depicts would probably have offended the English poet. In one of Jeffers's few acknowledgments of literary indebtedness, he mentions his *Tamar* as reminiscent of Shelley's *Cenci*, a romantic tale cast in a not-too-dramatic form.

The ballad is very commonly a highly compressed narrative poem. Not as a type of versification but as a type of narrative poetry we may, then, consider this shortest variety of the verse tale. During the earlier part of the romantic period the ballad form was revived as a part of the indiscriminate vogue of things medieval. It accorded, too, with the democratic tendencies of the nineteenth century. Native American ballads and

English sea chanteys were collected in large numbers. In the hands of Meredith and Hardy, however, the ballad took on a new aspect. The nineteenth-century novelists discover in this form a means for satisfying both their love for storytelling and the growing demand of the finer artistic conscience of the age for compression. Hardy's ballads and other poems closely related to the ballad may be regarded either as sketches for novels or as the shortest possible examples of the short story. Here is narrative fully embodied and stripped of all superfluous ornament. In some of his earlier volumes Hardy meticulously imitates the ballad form with its refrain and verbal archaisms, quite as Morris and Swinburne had done before him. Among his more traditional ballads are A Sunday Morning Tragedy and A Tramp-woman's Tragedy. In his later poems he more frequently follows the spirit of the popular ballads without verbal echoes, retaining only the compressed narrative, the lyrical stanzas, and the tragic irony. Poems of this character which he wrote after the War of 1914–18 may fairly be called modern in temper as well as in time. Although at present on the decline, the form has shown a remarkable tenacity and adaptability. The earliest ballads have an extraordinary power to inspire the newest verse. The relation of the old ballad Edward to the story and spirit of Jeffers's Such Counsels You Gave to Me has already been mentioned. Robinson at least experimented with the form. Its popularity in England has been even greater than in America. Kipling's adaptations of naval and military songs are especially admired by the younger and more radical British poets, in revolt from the aestheticism of an era epitomized by Moore and Proust. Yeats wrote several fine ballads, a good specimen being his Father Gilligan. In short, the form still lives in the literary as well as in the plebeian world.

Many ballads are largely or wholly in dialogue form. This, in addition to the violent action which they depict, gives them their dramatic quality. Much of the most vigorous and objective verse is always written in direct speech, either between three or more characters, between two characters, or even as the uninterrupted utterance of one person to his neighbor or to himself. Nondramatic poetry in these semidramatic forms is, of course, of great antiquity, in the idyls of Theocritus reaching a technical skill seldom thereafter to be equaled. Medieval lyrics are also singularly rich in dialogue and debate, the scene often including several speakers. Such themes as the Magi and the adoration of the three Shepherds at the manger were commonly treated in direct speech and lyrical verse. Again, Spenser, in imitation of both Theocritus and Virgil, introduces three or even more speakers into the eclogues of his *Shepherd's Calendar*. The form is followed again in verse by Landor in some of his poetical *Conversations* (for he was not always content with prose as the medium for this type of writing). A few of Browning's most successful poems, as *In a Balcony*, are incipient dramas with three or more speakers. A useful tradition of vigorous dialogue between several persons in poems dramatic figuratively and not literally was thus passed on to modern hands. And these hands have accepted it. Robert Frost, whose fondness for the spoken word has already been noted, employs three or more speakers in such poems as *The Self-Seeker* and in his brilliant eclogue, *Snow*. Yeats uses the same practice in *The Seven Sages*. Elinor Wylie's fine poem, *This Corruptible*, is a traditional debate in the seventeenth-century manner between Heart, Mind, and Spirit.

But far more common is the dialogue of two. Medieval poetry contains hundreds of such poems. There are dialogues of the soul and the body, the owl and the nightingale, the flower and the leaf, the Virgin and the Lord, the Lord and the Cross, Christ and the soul, the clerk and the maiden, the shepherd and the shepherdess, and, perhaps best known of all, the knight and the nut-brown maid. The possibilities of the inevitable form were merely augmented by the New Learning that admired debates in the classics not only in Theocritus, Virgil, and Horace, but in Plato, Lucian, and Boethius. Hence the Elizabethan lyric proved a new garden for this species. Poems written to be sung as duets became dramatic duets by virtue of such technique. De Vere's charming dialogue between Melibeus and Faustus beginning, "Shepherd, what's love, I pray thee tell?" is typical. In each stanza Melibeus asks substantially the same question and each time Faustus gives a different reply. Shakespeare, Spenser, Sidney, Drayton, Daniel, Raleigh, and virtually all the chief poets of the age wrote similar pieces. The Cavaliers followed suit with undiminished vigor. Some of the most charming of Herrick's trifles are duets, as the too-little-known song of Charon and Philomel. Herbert carried on the Elizabethan phase of the tradition. A few of the most widely admired of Marvell's poems take this shape, as his *Dialogue between the Soul and the Body*. A mild type of the dialogue is revived from Horace by Pope and Churchill in their satires and by Young in graver mood. Burns writes naturally not only dialogues between men and women but between two bridges or two dogs.

The more purely romantic poets turn less frequently to conversation partly because of their greater subjectivity and partly because of their love for description. It does not appear that Wordsworth tested the conversational sprightliness of Lucy Gray, the Solitary Reaper, the Happy Warrior, or Simon Lee; and the Leechgatherer had hardly begun to speak before, as the poet unblushingly admits, his richly stored mind wandered at its own sweet will. Even so, a few of Wordsworth's poems are conversation pieces, and this holds as well for Southey. The extreme of the anticolloquial is achieved in Whitman, whose poems, recording scarcely an oral word, deal almost exclusively in action or description. Whitman even describes the musical quality of a voice without giving the word spoken. Browning stands at the opposite extreme, although the monologue rather than the dialogue is his forte.

The long tradition of the dialogue emerges in contepmorary verse with new sprightliness. Half of Frost's best-known work, especially his many rural eclogues, are largely if not wholly a talk between two persons. The title poem of his volume *West-running Brook* affords an instance—a conversation between husband and wife. *Nicodemus* and *Ponce de Leon* stand among Robinson's ripest work in simple dialogue. English poets from Hardy to MacNeice have freely cultivated the form. Hardy's fondness for dialogue appears not only in many earnest talks between two persons but in conversations between inanimate objects, as between an old house and a new. This device Hardy may have taken from Swift or Burns, who wrote several such fantasies. Hardy's skill in dialogue is reflected in a score of novels and still more eloquently in *The Dynasts* and a few minor verse dramas. Another poet who wrote plays both for the library and the stage turns frequently in some of his happiest short poems to an interchange of words between two speakers. A dozen of Yeats's most memorable poems follow this pattern. An instance is his unforgettable lyric, *The Rose Tree*, a terse colloquy between Pearse and Connolly as to what affords the best moisture for the parching tree of Irish freedom. T. S. Eliot's *Conversation Galante* is a graceful instance of dialogue in lyric form.

But a lyric may have dramatic speech without dramatic dialogue. Many poets write at their best in poetic monologue with a dramatic flavor. Someone speaks or writes to another person. The active figure may be a historical or an imaginary character or the poet himself. In fact the dramatic spirit is seldom purer than in certain lonely debates, when the poet or one of his creations soliloquizes with his own soul. The essential thing is that someone conceives himself as speaking to another or to himself. Some poems are in this sense wholly undramatic. And there is a sliding scale from these to the most intensely dramatic work or that depicting the closest relations between two speakers face to face. To clarify this statement we may consider an exceptionally undramatic poem, as Keats's sonnet, *The Human Seasons*:

> Four seasons fill the measure of the year;
>   There are four seasons in the mind of man:
> He has his lusty Spring, when fancy clear
> Takes in all beauty with an easy span:
> He has his Summer, when luxuriously
>   Spring's honied cud of youthful thought he loves
> To ruminate, and by such dreaming nigh
>   His nearest unto heaven: quiet coves
> His soul has in its Autumn, when his wings
> He furleth close; contented so to look
> On mists in idleness—to let fair things
>   Pass by unheeded as a threshold brook.
> He has his Winter too of pale misfeature,
> Or else he would forego his mortal nature.

To indicate, on the contrary, what a dramatic poem is, one need only quote the first line of one of Shakespeare's *Sonnets*: "Then hate me when thou wilt; if ever, now . . ."

The truly dramatic monologue has a history as old as English poetry itself. The Anglo-Saxon *Dream of the Rood* in which the Cross passionately addresses the dreamer is substantially such a work. The finest dramatic monologue in English is very possibly the long prologue to Chaucer's *Wife of Bath's Tale*. Any poem which addresses itself to this or that, such as Chaucer's *Complaint to His Purse*, necessarily has a dramatic setting. No dramatist, not even Shakespeare, has been more dramatic than Donne in many of his lyrics. Donne is forever addressing someone passionately, whether it be his God, his friend, his mistress, or his reader. "I'll tell thee now (dear Love) what thou shalt do," begins one of his lyrics. One of his elegies commences, "Here, take my picture." His famous apostrophe to his mistress commences with a fatal conjuration,

"By our first strange and fatal interview." The reader of at least one of his lyrics is startled by the very first line, which sets him the astonishing task: "Go, and catch a falling star." "Batter my heart, three person'd God," begins a sonnet. And not to be less importunate to the angels than to God he begins another:

> At the round earth's imagined corners, blow
> Your trumpets, Angels, and arise, arise
> From death, you numberless infinities
> Of souls, and to your scattered bodies go.

Or he passionately soliloquizes, as at the opening of a third sonnet when he exclaims: "Oh, to vex me, contraries meet in one." When contraries meet in one, we await the dramatic spark. But only in his satires does Donne allow a third person to speak with the personal freedom which the poet uses in his other writings. In short, we may distinguish between the subjective and the objective monologue. Such egoists as Donne and Milton are masters of the former, such happier spirits as Chaucer and Browning are masters of the latter. The first type of poem is epitomized in the great medieval lyric, *Quia amore langueo*, Mary's lyrical appeal to man to ponder his redemption through the Crucifixion. The second type is represented in Chaucer's *Wife of Bath's Prologue*, already mentioned, and in Browning's *Bishop Orders His Tomb*.

With the objective monologue must logically be associated the address to another in writing, or, in short, the epistle. Just as in prose, so in verse the eighteenth century is par excellence the age of letters; but wherever men are literate they will write letters, as English poetry of all periods evinces. Thus the modern epistolary poet can never want for models. Anglo-Saxon poetry preserves a charming letter of a husband to his wife. Some of Chaucer's best short poems, as the address to Scogan, are in this form. Lydgate and Occleve employ it, notably in the dedicatory epistle. Some of Skelton's poems are news letters from abroad. But a greater vogue and art of letter writing follows the rediscovery of the Latin poets. Wyatt writes as pleasing verse letters as any poet in our tongue. And almost all the Elizabethans resemble Don Adriano de Armado in an affected passion for poetical epistles. One of the longest pieces put at least superficially into epistolary form is Spenser's *Colin Clout's Come Home Again*. Some of the briefest and best are to be found in Ben Jonson's Minor Poems. Daniel and Drayton appear to great advantage in their epistles; Donne writes over a score; and few types of serious verse prove more popular among the Cavaliers. Obvious subdivisions of the form appear, as the congratulatory epistle and the invitation to dinner (of which Jonson has good examples) or to the country (of which his friend Randolph wrote an admired specimen). Several times when Jonson was visiting at a country house he offered a poem as an elegant thank-you note. A number—possibly all—of Shakespeare's *Sonnets* must be read in an epistolary light. Milton's best epistolary verse is in Latin, but later poets have written less learnedly. Among subsequent masters of epistolary art are Dryden, Pope, Prior, Gay, Swift, Goldsmith, Churchill, Burns, Praed, and Byron. One of the most personal and charming, though least characteristic, of Shelley's works is his *Letter to Maria Gisborne*. Something in Victorian society and the Victorian view of bardic dignity forbade the fullest development of the epistle. The poet who was straining to report a revelation from heaven seldom consented to pen a friendly note to his neighbor. But the old tradition is at times rejuvenated by the most active spirits of our own days. Auden and MacNeice include specimens in their colloborated volume, *Letters from Iceland*, while MacLeish has an *American Letter* and the Louisianian, Robert Penn Warren, has several times used the form with distinction.

Models for the objective monologue at its simplest, where actual speech is represented, were among the most popular of English poems when many of the poets now living were in an impressionistic youth. No pieces received warmer appreciation at the beginning of the present century than the dramatic monologues of Browning, such representative work as Tennyson's *Ulysses*, or Kipling's spirited *M'Andrew's Hymn*. Thus E. A. Robinson came naturally to express himself in this form in such pieces as *Ben Jonson Entertains a Man from Stratford*, *Rembrandt to Rembrandt*, and his masterly *Toussaint L'Ouverture*. Even several of Robinson's sonnets, as his excellent *How Annandale Went Out*, are lively dramatic monologues. This treatment of the sonnet is also typical of Thomas Hardy and Merrill Moore.

The still commoner monologue wherein the poet speaks in his own person to a specific listener creates a type best exemplified in many of the poems of Donne and sonnets of Shakespeare. In the traditional manner, therefore, Elinor Wylie opens one of her sonnets thus:

> I hereby swear that to uphold your house
> I would lay my bones in quick destroying lime . . .

The opening of an amorous trifle by Ezra Pound is amusingly imitative. Writes this scholar-poet: "No, no! Go from me. I have left her lately." Whether or not Pound had recently left the lady, he had certainly been no long time away from John Donne.

The spirit if not the letter of dramatic style is preserved in the interior monologue or lonely debate. Shakespeare's clash of fearful opposites appears as dramatically in the debates of Hamlet's divided personality as in the music of Hamlet's sword against the sword of Laertes. This most subjective form of the address in poetry has its clear and ancient history, hardly necessary to trace here in detail. Medieval poets, writing in the manner best cultivated by Villon, tormented themselves over the ironies of old age and death. The Elizabethans dramatize the form in their dramatic soliloquies. That these soliloquies are in fact often lyrical is indicated by anthologies drawing upon the Elizabethan drama, from Charles Lamb's *Specimens* to Charles Williams's *New Book of English Verse*. Actually no body of verse has more enriched the English poetical tradition than the Elizabethan soliloquy. Much of Blake is interior monologue. Wordsworth obviously spent a great part of his life muttering heaven-inspired music to himself. The interior monologue is found in almost any collection of sensitive subjective writing. Elinor Wylie's magnificent poem, *O Virtuous Light*, is a typical debate between the halves of her tense personality. The larger part of Conrad Aiken's verse consists in these broodings. Two of his recent volumes, *Preludes for Memnon* and *Time in the Rock*, are wholly comprised of soliloquies undoubtedly under the influence of Elizabethan dramatic tradition. Aiken broods with a distraught and pitiful tension upon the cruelties of time, life, and death. In earlier volumes imaginary characters did the brooding for him; but since in their solitude there was no one to call them by name, the reader rightly and naturally assumes that King Borborigmi, Forslin, Senlin, Festus, and the unnamed victim-hero of *The House of Dust* are all the poet himself. The life of the metaphysical poet tends to become a tragically protracted soliloquy, a song of myself whose music ends only in death.

The word death brings us to one of the most fertile of all poetical conventions, the elegy or, as the Cavalier school less ambiguously termed it, the poetical obsequy. The two chief themes of poetry are love and death; and since there are more ways of courtship than of dying, the dirge is more conventional than the love song. The circumstances behind the dirge beget in themselves a formal pattern, so that in the mind death acquires a more comely body than life itself. Life is manifold, death one. The elegy almost inevitably states who has died, for what he is remembered, how the survivors feel on the occasion, and what, if anything, is to be viewed as the future of the soul of the deceased, in earth, in heaven, or in hell. Not every poem dealing with death is elegiac, but most of them are; and so familiar is the pattern on which the poet usually finds himself at work that he almost inevitably feels some pressure from the scores of poems known to him. For death, as the Cavaliers observed ruefully, is the great leveler. Almost every poet has written an elegy. The passion and the mystery of death and love—which become at times, of course, the same—confront us with the inadequacy of common speech and demand a ritual of precisely chosen words.

The English elegy does not, as conventional criticism sometimes carelessly states, begin with Spenser and Milton. It commences, of course, with English poetry; many of the best remembered Anglo-Saxon verses, as the elegiac passages in *Beowulf*, are in this key. One of the earliest English lyrics is the quatrain with a hundred variants which begins, "erthe to erthe." Chaucer, Dunbar, Skelton, Sir Thomas More, and most of the medieval poets have left us elegies. Their most popular theme, however, is not the lament of one mortal for another but of Mary for Jesus. The finest lyrical verse of the Middle Ages is contained among the thousands of variants of the *planctus*. So conventional had the human elegy become under the influence of Dante, Petrarch, and Boccaccio that Spenser's chief elegies, closely imitated from Chaucer and Marot, are cool consolation. Milton's *Lycidas* is certainly better poetry, but as an elegy its form is digressive. More moving as a lament is the memorial by Bishop King to his wife, a tender poem which exercised its spell upon Poe. There are affectionate and distinctly classical elegies by Dryden and Cowley, sentential and almost impersonal monodies by Collins and Gray, and exquisite memorial verses by Wordsworth and Byron and the too-little-known George Darley. Whitman's chant for Lincoln is actually a most conventional requiem, although a refreshing dew of totally new imagery easily leads the reader to overlook how traditional the great master of free verse really is. His briefer tributes to dead soldiers in *Drum Taps* are equally notable. Arnold's *Thyrsis* is so far overlaid with the descriptive and didactic material which it shares with *The Scholar Gypsy* that personal grief becomes obscured. His slighter *Requiescat* is the more purely elegiac. The most celebrated Victorian elegy, *In Memoriam*, resembles the didactic poem on the rambling Scholar Gypsy. Thus no elegy in the language keeps so close to the human norm or to the classical and ancient tradition as Shelley's *Adonais*. Others may or may not be better poetry. Shelley's dirge, however, best represents all the folds and adornments with which mankind has found it helpful to cloak the dead body and magnify the living soul.

The elegy can hardly die for the simple reason that man is forever dying. Consequently many dirges well worth attention for their traditional beauty of form and spirit have been composed by poets whose idiom otherwise justifies their inclusion in the modern school. These poems rarely conclude, as earlier elegies often do, on the theme of personal or Christian immortality. Thy are also less narrowly classical than the Renaissance elegies, less ascetic than the medieval. But the continuity of the type remains unmistakable. Hopkins's longest and in some ways strongest poem, *The Wreck of the Deutschland*, commemorates the death of five nuns lost at sea. A number of his shorter poems sound the elegiac note, as his fine sonnet, *Felix Randel*. Mortuary tones characterize a large number of the dirgelike poems by Hardy. His graveyard meditation, *Friends Beyond*, equally human and austere, gives the traditional stoical interpretation of death in singularly delicate images. His elegies often contemplate animal as well as human death and even the decay of inanimate things. Yeats's poetry sheers up a strong bulwark against death, as in his six lines, *Oil and Blood*, on the revolting spectacle of the battle field, and in his magnificent tribute to the political martyrs of the Dublin Rebellion, *Easter,*

1916. In fact, the Irish excel in the elegiac vein. The sonorous and much-quoted lines by T. W. Rolleston on the heroes long dead at Clonmacnoise is typical of Irish romantic threnody, and so, too, is James Stephens's *Deirdre.* The Sitwells, revolutionary as their poetic style often is, at least observe the full decencies and proprieties of the elegy. Osbert is the simplest, with his bucolic elegies on Miss Mew and Mr. Goodbeyer. *Mademoiselle Richarde,* by Edith, shows the sister also combining the elegy with the sentimental character sketch. After 1914 endless elegiac flowers appeared (as now) on the graves of soldiers, but when most of the poems were written the graves were perhaps too raw to yield fragrant blossoms. Some of the best known of these elegies are by Rupert Brooke and Laurence Binyon. One of the most exquisite poems, Owen's *Anthem for Doomed Youth,* has already been quoted in relation to the sonnet form. Another rare growth of this crimson harvest is *Commemoration,* a poem by Henry Newbolt inspired by the chapel of his school from which so many youths departed on the unreturning road.

The formal elegy as produced by the Old World has been perfectly transplanted to the New. Allen Tate's *Ode to the Confederate Dead,* written for a war cemetery, is one of the stateliest of American obsequies. MacLeish's *Lines for an Interment* remembers the American dead of the War of 1914–18 fifteen years after their ordeal. His *Memorial Rain* is even fresher and more powerful, with a keener irony and satire; while his striking *Burying Ground by the Ties* returns from the ravages of war to the almost equally inhuman ravages of industry. Even Wallace Stevens, best known for his wit, composes artful and tender threnodies, such as *Two at Norfolk* and *Cortège for Rosenbloom,* the latter modeled on the old eighteenth-century rhyme, *Who Killed Cock Robin?* Ransom's many elegies are the more sincere for the presence of wit and irony, introduced always with modesty and good taste. Almost all of Lindsay's true poetry is romantically elegiac. He is forever remembering a buried past, as the political campaign of 1896, the ancestors of a Chinese laundryman, the ghosts of the buffaloes, Andrew Jackson, Johnny Appleseed, Pocahontas, General Booth, John Brown, St. Francis, or a forgotten Congo. He was on his home ground when writing his delightful *Dirge for a Righteous Kitten.* Lindsay's elegiac note is sincere, exquisite, and pervasive. A *Soldier,* Robert Frost's poem on a calamity of America's last war, completes the evidence that the genre of the elegy has remained basically unchanged since the inscriptions by Simonides. For the epitaphs of Simonides are perhaps the most perfectly preserved poems of antiquity, much as the funeral oration by Pericles and the figure of the mourning Pallas remain respectively the most easily intelligible of ancient works in prose and marble. Time rather than the Athenian dead lies buried in these urnlike elegies. And the same may be said of so intensely human and yet finely polished a poem as Frost's sonnet:

> *He is that fallen lance that lies as hurled,*
> *That lies unlifted now, come dew, come rust,*
> *But still lies pointed as it plowed the dust.*
> *If we who sight along it round the world,*
> *See nothing worthy to have been its mark,*
> *It is because like men we look too near,*
> *Forgetting that as fitted to the sphere,*
> *Our missiles always make too short an arc.*
> *They fall, they rip the grass, they intersect*
> *The curve of earth, and striking, break their own;*
> *They make us cringe for metal-point on stone.*
> *But this we know, the obstacle that checked*
> *And tripped the body, shot the spirit on*
> *Further than target ever showed or shone.*

The epitaph is frequently the elegy in little. This form, of great antiquity, played small or no part in medieval English, but gained much prominence in the Renaissance, due to the discovery of classical poems and to the new individualism encouraging elaborate inscriptions upon tombs. Poets composed many verses actually used for monumental purposes. Such epitaphs and many others appear in their printed works. So compelling was the vogue in the mid-seventeenth century that Herrick apparently published an epitaph for his cook before her death, doubtless confident that in any case the good woman could not read.

In this little Urne is laid
  Prewdence Baldwin (once my maid)
From whose happy spark here let
  Spring the purple Violet.

The fondness for epitaphs is several times reflected in Shakespeare, as in *Timon of Athens* and *Much Ado about Nothing*. Scholars usually express the hope (it can be nothing more) that the great dramatist did not write his own epitaph. The art was polished by the classical Jonson and skillfully continued by William Browne, Robert Herrick, Bishop King, Mark Akenside, and Pope. Modern poetry conclusively shows that its authors have pondered the older inscriptions. Among the best examples are Bridges's *On a Dead Child*, Abercrombie's *Epitaph* and Gogarty's *Per Iter Tenebricosum*. De la Mare, who has written epitaphs of his own, has compiled an anthology from tombstones. Being romantically inclined, he calls his book *Ding Dong Bell*; had he been more classically minded he might have called it "Asphodel." Among other traditional epitaphs composed in our own times are Stevens's *Death of a Soldier*, Elinor Wylie's *Epitaph*, and Swift's *Epitaph* as rendered by Yeats. It is almost impossible for a poet, even if it should be his desire, to write an epitaph without treading in the narrow path worn by countless predecessors.

The epitaph, which became the briefest form of the elegy, is also the most serious form of the epigram. How close together

the sad saying and the witty saying may come appears in many
of the quaint poems cited by De la Mare. Whether the following poem on a deceased baker of Bristol is more epitaph than
epigram would not be easily determined:

> Like to a baker's oven is the grave,
> Wherein the bodies of the faithful have
> A setting in, and where they do remain
> In hopes to rise, and to be drawn again:
> Blessed are they who in the Lord are dead;
> Though set like dough, they shall be drawn like bread.

The rarer form of the satirical epitaph stands still closer to the
epigram.

The humorous epigram has at all times been as popular in
English verse as it was to the first readers of the Greek Anthology. Such pieces were in the Middle Ages generally pro-
verbial; so that when John Heywood, the epigrammatist of the
early sixteenth century, anticipating Carl Sandburg in the twentieth, came to collect and parody them, he found an enormous
mass of familiar material at hand. Jonson, Donne, Herrick, and
their contemporaries in large numbers remade the form under
classical influence, handing it on to Pope, who composed the
perfect epigram in honor of his Highness's dog at Kew. That a
modern poet may be well aware of the tradition is shown by
Hilaire Belloc, some of whose Popian epigrams are quoted in an
earlier chapter. The aim of the epigrammatist has always been
to put as much wit as possible into a surprisingly small space and
to come to a pungent conclusion. Where compression is the
ideal, Wallace Stevens must always be eminent. He wastes not
a syllable, as appears in the rhyming syllable of the first line of
an epigram, *Boston with a Note-Book:*

> Lean encyclopaedists, inscribe an Iliad.
> There's a weltanschauung of the penny pad.

Here is a world in a nutshell. In Chaucer's language, "there is nomore to seyen."

The satirical epigram leads on to the ampler poetical form, the satire. Here modern poetry shows the continuity of the poetic tradition with unusual clarity. The group of contemporary poets which has gone farthest back for poetical inspiration has returned above all to the satirists. Auden and Lewis look backward to Langland and Skelton, to the satirical element in the *Canterbury Tales*, and to political satire in general. The enthusiasm of Yeats for Swift and of almost every modern writer for the satirical Donne represents the affinity which the modern author finds with his predecessors. The revived popularity of *The Beggar's Opera* and of Gay's satire generally and the recent attempts to restore Churchill to his rightful place and to rescue Dryden and Pope from damaging errors of romantic criticism are significant. It is significant, too, that nearly a quarter of Auden's anthology of light verse, which presumably represents his own taste, is political. This book begins with a political song concerning Henry III in the thirteenth century and ends with a comment on public opinion concerning Edward VIII. One notes that it includes such political satires as Skelton's taunt of the Scotch, the anonymous pro-Catholic poem, *Little John Nobody*, excerpts from *Hudibras*, an admirably chosen satire on George III by "Peter Pindar," examples of Burns's lampooning, Confederate poetry against the Northerners, and specimens of Belloc's antiparliamentarianism. An age like our own, in which public issues press upon the public mind, turns especially to satire on social and political institutions. And despite the obscurity of allusions to forgotten issues and men, a surprising amount of vitality survives in the political propaganda of the past. The men, the issues, and above all the literary style and form of political satire remain basically unaltered. Yeats in his parliamentary career in Ireland pictured himself as another Swift. All three of the younger Sitwells are lovers of the Augustan age, but it is of Swift in particular that Osbert's numerous political lampoons are reminiscent. Roy Campbell follows suit with his elaborate neo-Augustan satire, The Georgiad. And in America MacLeish, Cummings, and such entertaining poets as Ogden Nash, Dorothy Parker, and Peggy Bacon write at their best in a virulent style for which English poetry affords ample precedent. A recent anthology, compiled by several distinguished critics under the general guidance of Charles Williams and particularly addressed to persons interested in the problems of the poet, gives useful evidence of trends in modern taste. In his preface Williams writes at length of the Earl of Rochester, from whose satires thirteen pages are included in the collection, while Byron is represented by thirty-one pages chosen exclusively from satirical poems. The latter part of Don Juan and all Rochester's work, both generally slighted a generation ago, have once more become life-giving material for the poet. The same volume also includes a selection from Doctor Johnson's satire inspired by Juvenal, The Vanity of Human Wishes. Strange as it may seem at first, satire on politics and manners, if it is well enough done, does not grow old. Horace and Aristophanes are quite as death-less as Virgil and Lucretius. Indeed Horace has probably been the most insistently imitated of all. And the English satirists will undoubtedly enjoy as long and vigorous an influence as the heroical or sentimental poets.

The satire is closely related to the verse essay, a more expan-sive and less caustic form of didactic poetry. Not always easily distinguished from varieties of the Horatian epistle, the most influential essay has proved to be Virgil's Georgics. Didactic and utilitarian poems of an expository nature have been written in almost every century of English history. The school of Gower, Occleve, Lydgate, and Hawes found verse an attractive medium for giving advice on all manner of topics. Had Chaucer been Gower, he would have written his essay on the astrolabe in rhyme. There are no pleasanter essays than Daniel's Musophilus, a sober study of Elizabethan education, or Dryden's *Hind and the Panther*, a fanciful sketch of religious sects under James II. But the great age of the essay, of course, whether in verse or prose, was the century of Addison and Doctor Johnson. It is unnecessary to recall at length the innumerable didactic poems of the times, most of them, rightly or wrongly, held today in only moderate esteem. They include, however, such readable works as Pope's *Essay on Criticism*, Thomson's *Seasons*, Gay's *Trivia*, Churchill's *Rosciad*, and Cowper's *Task*, in turn an account of literary criticism, English country life throughout the year, the streets of London, the art of acting, and British society as seen by a sentimental and highly religious country gentleman. The more conservative of the poets at the beginning of the nineteenth century continued the tradition, as Crabbe in his *Borough* and Byron and Rogers with poems on travel, literature, and morality. The genre, so far as English poetry is concerned, achieved its last triumph in *Childe Harold*. Didactic as the Victorian poets were, they lacked the simplicity and the literal-mindedness to set down their thoughts in a manner so close to prose. More and more our prose has come to absorb material long treated in this type of verse. So we generally overlook the charming and genuine aesthetic sense with which poets such as Thomson, Young, and Cowper lead us in their long and chatty poems through seeming digressions without abruptness or irrelevancy, displaying a tact analogous to that of the artful conversationalist. On inspecting their work, we find arrangement almost as much an art as creation. This genre has, then, of late occasionally been read, but seldom imitated and rarely given its merited praise. Yet even the verse essay is consciously or unconsciously revived. Frost's *New Hampshire* closely corresponds to the didactic and elaborately digressive poems from the eighteenth century. This type of verse may be minimized by a romantic philosophy, but its chief masterpieces cannot be eclipsed nor imitation of them extinguished.

One type of descriptive poetry, however, has retained considerable popularity, namely the verse portrait. Such character sketches are, of course, from time to time included in longer poems. Chaucer, Pope, and Crabbe incorporate sketches in their major works; Goldsmith's *Retaliation* is built upon the same principle. But in Masters's *Spoon River Anthology* and in Osbert Sitwell's *England Reclaimed* the sketches may certainly be regarded as constituting separate poems. Moreover, many of Robinson's most widely admired pieces are character sketches in one form or another. English verse since Chaucer has witnessed few more fascinating pageants than the procession at Tilbury Town: the exile Flammonde, Bewick Finzer, Richard Cory, Aaron Stark, Cliff Klingenhagen, Fleming Helphenstine, Reuben Bright, Aunt Imogen, Uncle Ananias, Miniver Cheevy, and the "Poor Relation." To these might be added Robinson's sonnets to Crabbe, Zola, and Erasmus. The poem as portrait seems an inevitable consequence of our individualistic culture pattern. By no means confined to conservatives such as Robinson, it may be found also in T. S. Eliot and Edith Sitwell. And the examples of the earliest writers just mentioned stand too close to the practice of the latest to admit a doubt as to the vital continuity of the tradition.

More in harmony with modern theories of aesthetics is the poetry of the myth. The myth is for aesthetic purposes defined as a legend generally accepted by a people and combining narration with a spontaneously grasped symbolism. The image and the meaning, in other words, are discovered simultaneously and held inseparably, with the aid of the magic of either the witchman or the poet. An example is the legend of Johnny Appleseed in Lindsay's poem of that name. Any artist who arrives at an idea through an image is, to be sure, his own mythmaker. When such an imaginative achievement becomes a part of the race consciousness, it becomes a true myth. Poetry and mythmaking are thus intimately associated. Allegory, on the other hand, is defined as a sophisticated symbolism where image follows idea and is merely decorative, not organic. Thus in his respect for myth and distaste for allegory Blake expressed a point of view over a century in advance of modern speculation. According to this view a genuine myth is both a primitive poetry and an ideal theme for a modern poem. The poet is advised merely to translate the myth into the idiom of his own day. So Eugene O'Neill translates the legend of Electra, T. S. Eliot that of Agamemnon, Robinson Jeffers that of Medea, H. P. Putnam that of Daphne, and Genevieve Taggard a sun myth from the Pacific Islands. Modern philosophy seemed about to deprive both poet and public of the Christian myth, when modern psychology abruptly restored it to our hands.

In search of genuine myths and eager to shun a supposedly superficial allegory, the modern poet and his critical guides have turned from the allegedly artificial creations of the Renaissance master, Spenser, to the esoteric mysticism of the inspired Blake. Although they have seldom revived Blake's dark and original symbols, they have imitated his method. He has been discovered to be the summation of mystical literature and esoteric myths, much as Dante summarizes patristic and scholastic learning. George Russell (Æ) and Yeats, once an editor of Blake, have been prominent in this movement. The quest for myths generally leads the poets beyond the fields of accepted English and American literature. But folklore is still theirs. Edith Sitwell composes an allegory on the Sleeping Beauty and other legends of the nursery. Lindsay writes of Johnny Appleseed. Eliot's *Waste Land* uses a mythological interpretation of Arthurian legend. Roy Campbell turns to the biblical legend of the flood. D. H. Lawrence resorts to Indian lore, while Hart Crane at least follows Lawrence in following the Indians. More interestingly, Conrad Aiken finds what he considers a genuine myth in the story of Punch, the subject of his striking poem, *Punch, the Immortal Liar.* His *John Deth* makes use of much mythological material, but most of it alien to earlier English poetry. As long as the aesthetic theories lauding the primitive myth and decrying the intellectual allegory find favor, it must be expected that poets will turn frequently to mythological themes and that, with a growing psychological subtlety, more in English poetry than we have ever supposed will be found mythical. Thus Delmore Schwartz treats the Coriolanus story virtually as myth in his stimulating volume, *In Dreams Begin Responsibilities*.

Whatever critical subtleties may be drawn, allegory has been and still is a prevalent form of poetry. An allegory may be simply described as an artificial work of considerable length organized symbolically. No one is likely to dispute the statement that most of the major poetry of Langland, Spenser, and Dryden is allegorical. Although the word often chills the modern ear, we find the thing created in our midst quite on the pattern of older work. Robinson's allegories, *Amaranth* and *King Jasper*, are Swiftian in their fancy. C. S. Lewis's *Pilgrim's Regress* is indebted to Bunyan and to Langland. An age numbering Joyce and Yeats, Lawrence and Melville, among its literary guides and sitting at the feet of Frazer and Freud is not likely to witness a diminution in allegorical poetry or lack of attention to earlier English masters of the symbolical technique.

An allegory is simply a protracted network of metaphors. The Elizabethans, in fact, often speak of metaphors or similes as "allegories." Although we use different terms, it is apparent that in the family of literary genres the short poem based on a single figure is closely related to the major allegory. This variety of short poem has been recognized by writers on seventeenth-century lyrics as a definite literary type. Flourishing especially in the Cavalier period, it is nevertheless a type older than Chaucer and younger than ourselves. Yet its aesthetic importance has been emphasized for modern poets by the strong revival of interest in Donne and his school, begun a quarter of a century ago under the leadership of Professor Grierson. The

Elizabethan and metaphysical lyric still remains an inspiration in this particular technique.

Presumably every good poem—even a nonsense rhyme—has some unifying elements in thought, image, and versification. It is obvious that throughout many short poems a simple image is kept in view. In other cases a leading image may appear in the first lines, to reëmerge in the last. But the typical lyric by Donne is intellectually most rigorous. The image is announced like a musical theme at the beginning and its general significance is clear, although the poet has surprises in store. The poem then progresses with logical variations upon the single figure or "conceit." In his book *The World's Body*, John Crowe Ransom regards this as the ideal type of the lyric. The judgment may be questioned: simply because the fugue is the most rigorous form of musical composition, it does not follow that it is the best. No pattern ever determines the ultimate excellence of a poem. But the mathematical perfection of Donne's imagery has undoubtedly been a guide for contemporary poets. An attractive instance of the merciless logic of the neometaphysical writers may be seen in Ransom's own poem *Captain Carpenter*. Here life is pictured as an eccentric warrior fighting quixotic battles in which he loses in turn his nose, ears, legs, arms, eyes, and finally his heart, each torn away from him by his foes like limbs lopped off a tree. Another instance of exceptionally logical development is MacLeish's well-known poem *You, Andrew Marvell*, where the title acknowledges indebtedness. The universality of the mind is figured by an imagination conceiving the continuous sweep of day and night across the earth. For stanza following stanza the poet depicts the evening shadows creeping over Asia, the Mediterranean, and the Atlantic. A poem deserting the metaphysical image for a more complex structure illustrates the point by contrast. MacLeish's *Prologue* is written to an antiphonal formula which he several times effectively employs. The stanzas alternate between a succession of ideas crowding on the poet's mind and a meditation on the mental attitude of Columbus and his crew. Again the geographical image suggests seventeenth-century poetry. But Donne or Marvell would have been content to focus the imagery on the ship of Columbus, as Donne unified his remarkable poem which transforms the thought of his voyage to Germany into a voyage through realms of pure spirit. Elinor Wylie, an even more devoted student of metaphysical poetry than MacLeish, composed lyrics in Donne's strict imagistic pattern. *This Hand* resembles in its ingenious consistency such a poem as Donne's meditation on his name scratched on a windowpane.

While Donne affords the best examples of a rigid pattern, a consistent and successful poem with adequate unity may be written less fastidiously. This Elinor Wylie seems herself to have observed when in two poems in her finest manner, *Minotaur* and *True Vine*, she argues against preciosity and over-refinement in both art and life. Although Ransom regrets Shakespeare's freer movement, most readers continue to prefer the license of the great dramatist. A less stringent unity in the lyric may at the same time afford adequate unity and give a more variegated play of light. Frost, who has avoided the metaphysical cult and observed the more catholic tradition of form in his shorter poems, has composed many pieces each with a dominant image freely developed. His celebrated *Birches* is one; *Two Look at Two*, depicting the meeting in a wood of two lovers with two deer, *A Star in a Stone-Boat*, and *Tree at My Window* afford equally good instances.

These poems keep the best lyrical tradition partly because image and idea are felt as inseparable. Although the "meaning" may be stated only in the last lines, the poet avoids the shallow romantic practice of tagging a descriptive poem with an imperfectly expressed generality. Hence Frost stands happily midway between Donne's pedantic consistency and Wordsworth's sentimental irrelevance. In any case the human mind is so far com-

mitted to the interplay of spiritual and material that most of
even the briefest poems are fundamentally allegorical. In simpler
words, the images have a meaning. The hardest thing is in fact
to succeed without allegory. Mere image produces fatuous description, mere abstraction becomes unlovely and prosaic.

Modern taste as a rule finds the lightly concealed metaphor
more pleasing than the image made explicit. Some of Frost's
most admired poems are highly suggestive, in the Cavalier manner, rather than obvious, in the Victorian. One cannot well
regard such poems as *The Cow in Apple-Time, The Runaway,*
and *Stopping by Woods on a Snowy Evening* as mere description. In art's half-tones they hint half-conscious meanings. The
cow drunk with apples is very humanly exuberant; the runaway,
a young colt out on a stormy night, is anyone who disregards
prudence; while the deeper meaning of the last of the three
pieces lies in the line: "The woods are lovely, dark and deep."
Even so. Some arresting darkness always lies in depth and
beauty. Frost simply follows a tradition as old as poetry itself.
A successful poem which presents a dominating action openly
and unreflectingly is more than ever exceptional. Yet exceptions
can be found where direct statement avoids both banality and
sentimentality. Michael Drayton's ballad on the battle of Agin-
court is a classical example; such a simple and direct poem as
Frost's lines on the boy in a sawmill who loses first his hand and
then his life affords a modern instance.

Contrary to current theories of verse, much good poetry has
been and is written without any conspicuous image or action
whatsoever. Apparently Longfellow's didactic and generalizing
poetry, so often cited during the present century as an instance
of outmoded style, is outmoded not by its didacticism or its
abstraction but for less obvious causes. The didactic and reflective lyric has a long history; its masterpieces are still admired,
their influence is still felt, and the genre remains thoroughly
extant. The dignified and measured didactic lyrics by Chaucer,

Jonson, Daniel, Dryden, Pope, Cowper, Blake, Wordsworth, and Arnold continue to have their large band of admirers. It is this tradition of the didactic lyric which Emily Dickinson follows in her lines beginning, "The Brain is wider than the sky," and "I reckon, when I count at all." Even the contemporary poets who love imagery and action best, as Robinson Jeffers, frequently compose equally naked and austere verses. Such a piece as Jeffers's *Age in Prospect* gives a favorable example. Poets as different as Robinson, Elinor Wylie, Auden, and Yeats are alike in writing from time to time powerful poems of this description. Their method is thus far at least singularly orthodox. The "naked, thinking heart" changes little.

If the present century has added any new type of poem to Time's anthology, it must be the ultra-impressionistic lyric. Subtlety has assuredly been known to English poets always, but seldom have they consented to offer as a finished poem a glimpse, a few ungrammatical phrases and nothing more. Emily Dickinson ground her poems like cut diamonds. The fragments of Walt Whitman were better guides to the creation of the new impressionism. A favorable example of this wispy form may be taken from the postimpressionist lyrics of E. E. Cummings:

> the
>   sky
>   was
> can dy lu
> minous
>   edible
> spry
>   pinks shy
> lemons
> greens coo 1 choc
> olate
> s.

                un der,
                a lo
        co
        mo
                tive   s pout
                            ing
                                vi
                                o
                                lets

Even the typographical design of this poem expresses the wispi-
ness of light clouds and evanescent puffs of smoke.

Nevertheless, some minor eccentricities aside, such art has
a few roots in the past. The Elizabethan madrigal poets occasionally wrote lyrics almost as brief, delicate, and suggestive.
The song *Sweet Suffolk Owl*, with its overtones of mystery and
magic, bears remembering in this connection:

> *Sweet Suffolk owl, so trimly dight*
> *With feathers, like a lady bright,*
> *Thou sing'st alone, sitting by night,*
> > *Te whit, te whoo! Te whit, te whoo!*
>
> *Thy note that forth so freely rolls*
> *With shrill command the mouse controls,*
> *And sings a dirge for dying souls,*
> > *Te whit, te whoo! Te whit, te whoo!*

And still further back, the Middle English poets also dealt
occasionally in mothlike lyrics. This is an example:

> *Nou goth sonne under wod,—*
> *me reweth, marie, thi faire Rode.*
> *Nou goth sonne under tre,—*
> *me reweth, marie, thi sone and the.*

Last of all the genres for consideration—last because it merges
with another art—is the true song. Writing for the singer is

obviously one thing, for the reader another; and while many poems never composed for music have been successfully sung or been the inspiration for instrumental music, definite traditions in writing words especially appropriate for music have developed. Broadly speaking, there are two traditions: that of the stanzaic poem with corresponding musical repetitions, which originated in the earliest times and has never grown obsolete, and that of the chant or song in freer verse forms, which reached its highest development in the age of Lawes, Purcell, and Handel. This freer tradition, once almost obsolete, has of late been consciously revived.

The popular song is usually the simpler product. It tends to conservatism in thought, feeling, and imagery, to brevity, lucid construction, and emotional coloring. To the stanzaic form, with musical repetition, is often added a musical and poetical refrain. (Herbert Spencer, irritated by Victorian ballads, defined the refrain as "an inane repetition of an idea.") A strongly marked and often a trisyllabic rhythm is preferred. Whether due to artistic professionalism, the distractions of other arts and amusements, or a decline in popular taste, there are today few rivals of the lovely and popular songs of a century ago. The song is undoubtedly immortal but suffers at the moment from unfavorable conditions. None of the major types of poetry has fallen so far out of the control of the better writers. The close collaboration of musician and poet so remarkable in the sixteenth and seventeenth centuries is wanting. Nevertheless where a good song is written today, it generally bears, as we shall see, the clear marks which have characterized the genre from the earliest period to our own.

A large number of short poems undoubtedly sung survives from the Middle Ages, conforming in every respect to the standards in such verse from earliest times to latest. Clearly no lyrics can be more exquisitely adapted to music than many of the carols and love songs of the thirteenth, fourteenth, and fifteenth centuries. The subsequent lyrics by Wyatt, Sidney, Campion, Carew, Herrick, Jonson, and Milton reflect new subtleties in the development of English music. Images and ideas in the poems are carefully designed to lend themselves to musical coloring. A group of speakers in the poem often becomes a group of singers in the part song. The stanzaic form decreases in favor. This was incomparably the greatest age for the development of the true lyric, the Shakespearean half of the period on the whole more inspired than the Miltonic.

But succeeding periods are also changeful and brilliant. Most of the chief poets of the Restoration composed musical odes for Saint Cecilia's Day, with much freedom in verse structure and what the Elizabethans would have found too literal a relationship between music and words. When words thundered, drums thundered; when words cooed, strings cooed. Shakespeare and Milton arranged such things far more delicately than Dryden or Pope. The simpler instrumental accompaniments of the Elizabethan song—usually a lute would suffice—were more favorable to the role of the poet than Handel's orchestra—Briareus with his hundred hands, as Pope termed it. In the odes and more formal productions the new music thus drowned out the words. But the purer song, still true to its popular simplicities, flourished with melodic sweetness. Many poets, at least remembering the peculiar requirements of this type of writing, restrained themselves from empty display on the one hand and inept intellectual subtleties on the other. Hence a classical purity of diction is reached in songs by Dryden, Sedley, D'Urfey, Prior, and Gay. In the mid-eighteenth century new lyrical fervor appears as an attendant to the revival of emotional religion, producing the hymns of Wesley and Cowper. Meanwhile medieval, Augustan, and romantic tendencies combine to make Burns perhaps the greatest song writer since the Cavalier period. The beauty and importance of the true song in the early romantic period and at least the potential permanence of its contribution are too readily overlooked. Many poets who in other fields seem to us to have been quite incapable of producing great verse excelled in this. It was an age of melodies, such as the *Hebrew Melodies* of Byron and the *Irish Melodies* of Moore. Scott, long devoted to northern song and ballad, became himself a superb song writer. And lesser spirits often contrived to write the most admirable songs, such as Chatterton, Campbell, Beddoes, Kirke White, Allan Cunningham, John Clare, and George Darley. The songs of Tennyson and Christina Rossetti may well outlast their more ambitious works.

The modern poet, accordingly, finds a vast quantity of good song writing available for him, falling chiefly into two schools and reflecting the musical setting: on the one hand the repetitive stanzas and on the other the freer verse. He has availed himself of both. The more conservative form is represented in such songs as Hardy's much-quoted *Weathers*, Belloc's drinking songs, and lyrics by Davies, De la Mare, and Housman. The strong ballad meter beloved by the last-mentioned poet helps to make his poems peculiarly adaptable to musical setting. Frost's earliest volume, *A Boy's Will*, is felicitously lyrical, containing as it does such pieces as *Flower-gathering* and the haunting final poem, *Reluctance*: these are exceptionally expert lyrics quite in the nineteenth-century manner.

Highly ingenious, significant, and effective is much song writing in the more complex manner which discards the stanzaic form. This style lends itself equally to poetic and to musical modernities. Eliot's complicated patterns in his hymnlike religious poetry are of a brilliantly musical inspiration, as seen in many of the verse choruses in his plays. The same or even a finer musical quality appears in the "echo songs" by Hopkins. This poet obviously had a musical feeling for words akin to that of the Cavaliers, just as he possessed a taste for music which led him to write an ecstatic sonnet in praise of Purcell. Hopkins would have agreed with Dryden, who observed that beyond a doubt God let down the scale of music from the sky as a ladder on which Purcell's soul might climb to heaven. The worst that can be said of Hopkins's unique and extraordinary language is that it is too far from English and too close to music. His echo songs and his rhythmical patterns generally are on the side of the more complex writing. He was little given to the simpler stanzaic song.

The Sitwells are devoted to baroque music, poetry of the school of Dryden, and a poetic style of their own consciously adapted to musical setting. Much of their writing with musical values seems a compromise between Hopkins's poetry and that of Whitman. A remarkable amount of Whitman's verse has, incidentally, been finely set by twentieth-century composers. The Sitwells have been almost as fortunate. Sacheverell's *Rio Grande* has received a striking musical arrangement. The degree to which the three authors are possessed with the theory of the marriage of poetry and music of all sorts they themselves thoroughly realize; it appears even in the titles of their poems, some of which read: *Trumpets, Barrel Organs, Valse Estudiantina, Ten Serenades, The Italian Air, New Water Music, Gypsy Song, Solo, Song with Bagpipe, Village Band, Fugal Siege, Grande Adagio, The Drum, The Serenade at Morning, Lullaby for Jumbo, Trio for Two Cats and a Trombone, Dark Song, Hornpipe, Aubade, Fox Trot, Cacophony for Clarinet, Two Kitchen Songs, Spinning Song, Songs for Sunday, Three Nocturnes, Prelude,* and *Grande Finale.*

The lyrical beauty of the Elizabethan madrigal, with verbal form perfectly married to music, has recently been imitated with some fidelity and success. A revival of interest in madrigal verse has been especially notable in England, where the old music has recently enjoyed a remarkable resurrection. The artist-poet T. Sturge Moore, for example, has among many other pieces of musical quality a song distinctly an echo of the most

famous of Elizabethan madrigals. Moore retains the drooping
cadences of the old *Silver Swan* in his own *Dying Swan:*

> O *silver-throated Swan,*
> *Struck, struck!* A *golden dart*
> *Clean through thy breast has gone*
> *Home to thy heart.*
> *Thrill, thrill, O silver throat!*
> O *silver trumpet, pour*
> *Love for defiance back*
> *On him who smote!*
>
> *And him, brim o'er*
> *With love; and ruby-dye thy track*
> *Down thy last living reach*
> *Of river, sail the golden light—*
> *Enter the sun's heart—even teach,*
> O *wonderous-gifted Pain, teach thou*
> *The God of love, let him learn how!*

Ballad and lyrical traditions from a preindustrial world still
flourish lustily in parts of the American South and West. These
traditions have exercised a profound effect on outstanding poets,
such as Vachel Lindsay, Stephen Vincent Benét, William Rose
Benét, Roy Helton, and Carl Sandburg. The last mentioned
stands today as perhaps the most remarkable exponent of verse
potentially or actually to be chanted or sung. His selections
from American folk poetry in *The American Songbag* point to
some of the chief sources of his own inspiration. Many of his
best poems, as his charming *Potato Blossom Songs and Jigs*, are
molded on banjo improvisations. His title *Jazz Fantasia* suggests much of his happiest work. A large number of his brief,
tender, and almost sentimental trifles in free verse have even
more the quality of musical impromptus than of impressionistic

sketches: their inspiration is even more subjective and musical than objective and imagistic. In his fine metaphysical tone poem, *Slabs of the Sunburnt West*, depicting the Grand Canyon, the rythmical recurrence of certain themes comes closer to musical than to pictorial form and spirit. Sandburg, in short, is the most successful of the American troubadours. Although, as Rebecca West observes in her preface to his *Selected Poems*, he is one of the most representative of American poets writing today, his feeling for the relation of words and music represents a cultural development extending far back not only into the American but into the English and the European past. Sandburg's prairie reverses Chaucer's famous metaphor; in the American we see the oldest corn springing in the newest fields.

IV: THE HERITAGE OF SPIRIT

WHEN THE CRITIC OF POETRY PASSES FROM THE technique and forms to the indefinable spirit, he merely shifts his place of emphasis. In our studies of style, versification, and genres we found it impossible to overlook the broader aspects of the poet's meaning. Conversely, as we now begin a more liberal and direct, a less technical and detailed inquiry into the hereditary spirit of twentieth-century poetry, we shall not neglect its verbal or formal aspects but merely add new material to previous inquiries and go deeper beneath the troubled surface of modern verse. A view of the spirit of poetry is logically built on accumulated studies of its technique and form.

If, as I believe to be the case, the most fruitful interpretation of a poem is usually the sociological, it follows that the best method of examining the spirit of a work is generally to view it in the light of the times and the culture which have produced it. So far as this book is concerned the spirit of our own times is largely taken as known or at least elucidated without formal comment as the argument of the book unfolds. The significance of the poets' inheritances of culture is chiefly explained by the character of the ages from which these debts are acquired. While modern poets have drawn much from the specific technique of their medieval predecessors, what they have assimilated from the distant and mysterious culture of medieval times is less tangible.

In considering in this final chapter the spirit of poetry which has survived or been resurrected from earlier times, it is convenient to recognize three periods: the dynamic age of Shakespeare, brief and amazingly varied; the age of Augustan formalism which persisted for over a century and a half; and the romantic age, of slightly less duration than the preceding. We shall note survivals of the Elizabethan ideal of tragedy in Robinson Jeffers, of the sentimental Shakespearean lyric in Cummings, Davies, and De la Mare, of the intellectual and emotional Jacobean lyric as practiced by Donne in such moderns as Elinor Wylie and Yeats, and of the old tradition of learned poetry in Eliot. The taste of the later Renaissance or the Augustans for measured artificiality in poetry, as well as in life, leaves its mark most clearly upon the writing of the three Sitwells, Edith, Osbert, and Sacheverell, and on the American poet Wallace Stevens. Finally, we shall observe survivals and developments of the metaphysical temper of the romanticists in Aiken, of the romantic idealism and glorification of the poet's mission in Lindsay, and of the nineteenth-century passion for character analysis in Robinson.

FROM THE ELIZABETHANS

Although Robinson Jeffers has viewed all but a few of his contemporaries—such as E. A. Robinson—somewhat cavalierly, it would be manifestly an error to infer that his powerful work is inspired merely by Californian wine and Californian mountaintops. And though he deliberately shuns the learned style cultivated by Joyce, Eliot, and Pound, it must not be assumed that he is poorly read in verse. He is clearly studious in prose, for he is devoted to the romantic schools of Schopenhauer and Nietzsche in philosophy, Freud and Jung in psychology, and Frazer and Sumner in anthropology. His reading in belles-lettres, though less obviously marked in his own writing, can hardly be less extensive. One of his longer poems is based on the Volsung Saga, another on a story out of Pausanius, a third on several Greek tragedies concerning the House of Atreus, and in other cases he has acknowledged his indebtedness to Shelley, to Scott, and to the medieval ballads. He has been an ardent student of law, medicine, the natural sciences, and languages, new and old.

Since most of Jeffers's narrative poems depict uneducated people seen against the barren mountains and virgin forests of California, their more literary background is obscured. In one or two cases, as *Give Your Heart to the Hawks*, the plot might serve for a short story in a sensational magazine. In most cases the tragic spirit is too intense, the view of sex too frank, philosophy too obtrusive, and abnormality too common to admit such a suggestion. If he actually has literary antecedents or companions, it is not at once clear who they may be.

Of his major poems, nine have settings on the contemporary Pacific coast and four, less representative and not so well received, deal, on the contrary, with ancient themes. *At the Birth of an Age* is based on the Volsung Saga, *The Tower beyond Tragedy* on Greek tragedy, *At the Fall of an Age* on the Trojan legend, and *Dear Judas* on the Bible. *Tamar* also shows his continuous interest in biblical literature while *Solstice* is the *Medea* of Euripides transposed to a Californian setting. The mere fact that Jeffers bases by no means a negligible part of his work directly on literary material should give pause to the judgment assuming the majority of his poems to be innocent of poetical sources, however much they use prose sources from philosophy, psychology, and anthropology. Jeffers is a great and original artist; he excels in depicting the California desert, but he is in no sense the voice of an unlettered man crying in the wilderness.

The one word written conspicuously over all his major work is tragedy. It is often on his own lips. His works approach tragedy in both spirit and form. He finds it pleasurable and profitable to contemplate images of misfortune. He grounds his vision of the Clytemnestra story on a theory concerning tragedy, calling his poem *The Tower beyond Tragedy*. Many digressions in his stories, even in so brief and relatively early a piece as

Roan Stallion, explicitly discuss the tragic idea. He is fascinated not only by the idea embodied in tragic experience, but by the tragic genre in drama. This his own practice clearly intimates. He has, to be sure, written only one brief work wholly in dramatic form: *At the Fall of an Age.* None of his works has won on the stage the recognition which all have received as poetry. Nevertheless, three of his long poems, *The Tower beyond Tragedy, At the Birth of an Age,* and *Dear Judas,* are substantially poetic dramas, with the unconventional feature of having their stage directions in verse. And all of his longer poems have some dramatic feeling, since they are all of a length usual on the stage, present only a few characters in violent and concentrated action, and in certain respects obviously comply with the spirit of theatrical tragedy. Even their philosophical passages are made partially dramatic by a reminiscence of the Greek Chorus. The superb apostrophe on the death of the eagle in *Cawdor* is such a choral lyric as Aeschylus might have written. Much the same may be said of the bold choral and lyrical ejaculations in *The Women at Point Sur, Roan Stallion,* and other of the poems. Jeffers literally employs a chorus in his plays on Greek themes, while his extraordinary version of the Volsung Saga is graced not only with a chorus but with Christ as the ideal *deus ex machina.* Jeffers, like Robinson, is a poet with an eminently dramatic mind who through accidental circumstances fails to turn this dramatic instinct to theatrical account. Both men are incomparably more dramatic than many romantic poets whose collected verse includes extensive dramatic work. The romantic closet drama is today increasingly superseded by the dramatic poem.

If, then, Jeffers is haunted by the idea of tragedy and highly conscious of dramatic form, it is only natural to assume that his creative mind also responds to the theatrical heritage. His paraphrase of Greek poets in *The Tower beyond Tragedy* supports this view. Even more striking is his free and effective

adaptation of Greek dramatic methods in *At the Fall of an Age*
and of Greek dramatic material in *Solstice* His first long poem,
Tamar, defining much of the course for his subsequent work,
owes more than a casual or unconscious debt to Ibsen. Atmosphere and method alike are Ibsenesque. We have the usual
morbid spirit, insistent symbolism, haunting images of the sea,
and psychiatric probing into character. The depth of antecedent
action so conspicuous in Ibsen is here much furthered by the
theories of Freud. The young Jeffers is the old Ibsen migrated
to the Pacific coast. Nor should we overlook the relationship of
America's chief narrative poet to her leading dramatist. Jeffers
and O'Neill, both of Irish stock, have so much in common in
their love for psychologically inspired tragedy that it is difficult
to suppose either was unconscious of the other.

Shakespeare, however, has clearly meant more to Jeffers than
any other of the older English poets or dramatists, and among the
plays *Macbeth* has left the deepest mark. The facts must first be
demonstrated before probing further into his view of tragedy.
As his critics have occasionally noted, his strong poem, *Give
Your Heart to the Hawks*, is a free and imaginative but none-
the-less unmistakable and searching adaptation of *Macbeth* to
a new setting. One is reminded of Turgenev's story, *A Lear of
the Steppes*. Jeffers changes the scene from a bleak Scotland to
a titanic California and from Scottish castles to small Western
ranches. More tender and less august than the original drama,
Jeffers's poem depicts a murder of one brother by another.
Where in Shakespeare Duncan's guards are drunk, in Jeffers
the murderer himself is drunk and thus stirred to ill-founded
jealousy. The essential likeness lies in the remorse of the
murderer, in his insane dread of detection, his ghost-haunted
imagination, the valor of his wife in vainly offering her support,
and the final defeat, the murderer betrayed by evil spirits which
he has himself conjured up. Lance, Jeffers's creation, stands
halfway between Macbeth, the villain, and Hamlet, the hero.

He has, too, something of the blend of nobility and stupidity characteristic of the Wagnerian heroes, Siegfried and Parsifal. He is the hero-clown.

The Shakespearean background becomes noticeable only after the crime has been committed. But shortly Lance observes: "I don't make a good murderer." In its context the Shakespearean echo is strong. "No more of that," says Fayne, Lance's wife, on an occasion similar to that which evokes exactly the same words from Lady Macbeth: "No more o' that; you mar all with this starting." "Oh, we'll live well," exclaims Fayne hopefully, reminding the reader of the encouragement given by Lady Macbeth to her timorous husband. Lance, like Macbeth, is assailed by horrible visions of hell. There is sleep-walking in both poems, but perhaps to avoid artless repetition it is in Jeffers the murderer and not the wife who walks. A few lines in quotation give an impression of the Shakespearean atmosphere at this point:

"The angels wi' the hooky beaks . . . What in hell," he said
Sharply, "who's there?" "I, Lance. Oh come to bed, dear.
You wandered out in your sleep." "No: that spying devil,"
He said, "Hm?" "Your father, your father, Lance.
He was here when you came." "Oh . . . . Did I talk?"
Hardly a word. Nothing, dear." "I sleep better
Alone," he said, "now."

Here are the guilty sleeplessness and the harrowing sleepwalking, as in the drama. The simple words "come to bed" are a Shakespearean reminiscence. And "who's there?" following the references to hell, suggests Macbeth's gatekeeper.

As Jeffers's story advances, Lance, and he only, sees the ghost of the murdered man, suffers the same maniacal madness that bedeviled Macbeth, harkens to omens especially of birds, watches a war in the sky above his house, and fears blood springing from the ground. Again the very words of Shake-

speare are used with unaltered meaning and obvious indebtedness. Fayne, like Lady Macbeth, to encourage her husband to
believe that he has worsted the evil spirits, says, "We'll not
fail," and Lance, observing his bloody hands, whispers, "I'll go
wash." Where specific phrases and the general spirit and plot
of the story both point to indebtedness, the conclusion is beyond question.

Give Your Heart to the Hawks is not the only poem by Jeffers
written with recollections of Macbeth. Macbeth's simile for
life as a tale told by an idiot is remembered in Tamar, where
Jeffers writes

. . . life is always an old story, repeating itself always like the
    leaves of a tree
Or the lips of an idiot.

When in The Tower beyond Tragedy Clytemnestra says of her
husband who has murdered their daughter:

Not the deep sea's green day, no cleft of a rock in the bed of the
    deep sea, no ocean of darkness
Outside the stars, will hide nor wash you.

Jeffers recalls two distinct passages from Macbeth, the green sea
crimsoned by murderous blood and the hand which no seas can
cleanse. When in another poem a character exclaims that "all
the opium of India" cannot procure forgetfulness, the poet is
varying an old theme by Shakespeare, "all the perfumes of
Arabia cannot sweeten this little hand." Again in The Tower
beyond Tragedy when Electra, more manful than her brother,
declares she has been the arm to his sword, Lady Macbeth
inciting her husband is recalled. The Shakespearean phrase "no
more o' that," already noted in Give Your Heart to the Hawks,
also occurs with a similar connotation in Cawdor. And magical
charms in At the Birth of an Age recall Macbeth by allusion to
"a birth-strangled man-child" in a witches' brew and further
suggest Shakespearean witchcraft by reference to the fiend

Grimalkin. The intensely masculine women in *Solstice* and *Such Counsels You Gave to Me* presumably owe a part of their magnificent vigor to Shakespeare's portrait of Lady Macbeth. In both *Tamar* and *Cawdor*, as in *Macbeth*, crimes are accompanied by equally monstrous disturbances in the elements. Indeed, in this field Jeffers proves as resourceful and effective as his predecessor.

Jeffers occasionally adapts the language and spirit of other Shakespearean plays to his purpose, and always with quiet skill. *Hamlet*, for example, is recalled when, in reference to a grave, the question arises, "how long will these planks last?" Hamlet's bitterness to Ophelia is echoed by Lance in *Give Your Heart to the Hawks:*

> God made them male and female but men have made
> So and so.

Fera, one of the chief characters in *Cawdor*, soliloquizes in a manner almost too reminiscent of Hamlet, arguing at length to be or not to be and asking, "how can anyone be sure that death is a sleep?" Jeffers, like Hamlet, is fond of seeing life as dreamlike, sleep as lifelike. Mark, the mad visionary in *Thurso's Landing*, converses in Hamlet-fashion with his father's ghost:

> "Make we sure of it. For if the blind tugging here
> And self contempt continue, and death's no peace,
> It would be better to live forever . . . but best, best,
> Never've been born."

Hamlet and other Elizabethan plays presumably contribute to the two or three "candid and loving" women in Jeffers's gallery, as "the loving shepherdess" in the poem of that name and Mary Abbey in *Give Your Heart to the Hawks*. These women not only suggest Ophelia and her tenderhearted sisters; it is probable that they were drawn in part on the Shakespearean models.

The darkest and most horrible of Shakespeare's plays afford

Jeffers the most aid. One notes, for example, paraphrases from *Lear*. Remembering Edgar's "ripeness is all" spoken to his blind father, Jeffers writes, "blindness is all." Recalling Lear's mad words regarding flies in the shambles and his advice to lustful men to "go to't," the mad Mark, who has somehow read Shakespeare, speaks of deer who "go to it like dogs in the bushes." Cawdor, in a more compassionate mood, echoes the same speech when he recalls a promise "not to kill fly nor stinking beetle." One of Jeffers's boldest and most successful adaptations of Shakespeare is a powerful satire in *Cawdor* on life itself —"ah, there's the question"—closely resembling the Duke's superb speech in *Measure for Measure* beginning, "Be absolute for death." Mark's pessimism in *Thurso's Landing* comes closer in its intense bitterness to the misanthropy in *Timon of Athens*. There are passages in Jeffers that might have been written by Timon's "vile dog" Apemantus. Some of Lance's dreams of the world of ghosts suggest bloody brows seen in a horrible dream by Clarence in *Richard the Third*. Especially the Senecan horrors of such a play as *Titus Andronicus* have their counterparts in Jeffers's poems. There are only a few reminiscences of purer but less sensational poetry from other of Shakespeare's plays. In *Cawdor*, as in *Othello*, a woman talks of life and death while pinning her dress; Antony's gorgeous image of imminent death as a sunset seems reflected also in *Cawdor*. In *The Tower beyond Tragedy* the words "Ah, soldiers!" spoken by a dying woman in defiance of a crowd were suggested by the "Ah, soldier!" spoken in the scene of the dying Cleopatra; while the last words of Shakespeare's Queen of Egypt, nursing an asp at her breast, inspire what are almost the last words spoken by Helen in *Thurso's Landing*:

. . . "Oh that's all? Old fool.
Those little white things, meant to fight the seed of our lovers,
Are seed themselves, I'm pregnant and swell fast,
Baby death, darling darling."

Jeffers's affection for Shakespeare is openly attested not only in his silent borrowings but in an excellent short poem suggested by the rhyme on the Shakespeare monument at Stratford Church. His borrowings from Shakespeare do not extend to the comedies, nor is there any evidence that he has read any comedies whatsoever.

He has profited, however, from a knowledge of other Elizabethans than Shakespeare. Several of his poems contain paraphrases of speeches in Marlowe's *Faustus*, notably from Faustus's lines to Satan, his apostrophe to Helen, and his final soliloquy. This last speech has left a deep impression on Jeffers's work. In *Give Your Heart to the Hawks* he uses the line, "see where Christ's blood streams through the firmament," and in *Such Counsels You Gave to Me* the Ovidian line quoted by Marlowe, *currite noctis equi*. Jeffers, like the Elizabethans, enjoys tragedies of revenge. Like Ford and Massinger, he delights in the theme of incest; like Webster and Tourneur, he uses macabre imagery; like Marston and Jonson, he writes satirical tragedies rich in disillusionment. He follows all the Elizabethans when he says: "It is beautiful to see men die by violence." His stories use soliloquies much as do the old plays. They abound in ancestral ghosts, like that of *The Spanish Tragedy*, and in masculine-minded women like the famous heroine of the realistic tragedy, *Arden of Feversham*. George Chapman would certainly have applauded the lines:

> Pure action would make a good life, let it be sharp-
> Set between the throat and the knife.
> A man who knows death by heart
> Is the man for that life.

Jeffers, in short, is both Shakespearean and Elizabethan. For like all the Elizabethans he loves tales of blood and agony, concentrated as drama demands and rising to a full realization of the tragic ideal. An authentic experience of an emotional storm leads to an awful and consummate peace.

Nevertheless the common ground of tragic understanding shared by Shakespeare and Jeffers is defined most clearly as we recognize large areas in Shakespeare strikingly opposed to similar areas in Jeffers. So different in important respects are the two men that even their strong similarities easily escape notice. To avoid misconceptions it is also worth while to sketch the negative side.

All Jeffers's major poems are grim, but not all are in the highest sense tragic. The early *Roan Stallion*, one of his most brilliant works, is perhaps a little too brief to rise fully to the accumulative climax of pure tragedy. In his *Women at Point Sur*, and less notably elsewhere, the allegorical, intellectual, and didactic elements crowd tragedy to the wall. Doubtless this is a good aphorism: "No one ever tastes triumph until the mouth is rinsed with despair." But the tragic sense freezes in contemplation of what Jeffers terms "abstract existence, consciousness abstracted from feeling; the wires of pain-pleasure burned out; the way of consciousness cleared perfectly." A chill falls on the scene which, in the poet's words, depicts "no benevolence, but only knowledge." The heroine of *Cawdor* upon a bed of pain reflects on her tragedy: "She lay and contemplated it with little emotion." His more orthodox work, like *Othello*, resembles a mountain rising from green valleys to the austere gleam of an icecap. But such a poem as *Cawdor* is an arctic mountain, ice to the very base. In its concentration upon only the fiercer emotions Jeffers's poetry is less heroic and sublime then gigantic and inhuman. He himself indicates his position in his highly provocative title, *Tower beyond Tragedy*. This poem concludes not with an action but with a denial of action. The ending, neither Greek nor tragic, betrays the quietism and mysticism prominent in Jeffers's thought. These doctrines and moods may produce admirable poetry, but they do not produce pure tragedy and contribute less than the more active attitudes toward the fruition of art and verse. Intellectual poets have always confronted the problem of reconciling the action demanded by art with the more austere demands of contemplation. Goethe faced the difficulty in his *Faust* without fully resolving it. A chorus is likely to run away with any play; the didactic element damages the purity of the tragic experience which demands to a certain extent a naïve acceptance of life and death. The difficulty appears in *At the Birth of an Age*, where a stirring action is followed by an exceptionally long philosophical chorus. It appears also in *Dear Judas*, which even begins as a struggle between conflicting ideas rather than persons or wills and becomes decreasingly dramatic as it advances. This austere atmosphere is not the realm of pure tragedy. *At the Fall of an Age* depicts a Helen so far supernatural as to be virtually allegorical. The symbolism injures the force of a still powerful tragic scene. *Tamar*, the first of Jeffers's long poems, is one of the least skillfull in ordering the wealth of its material, in harmonizing the poet's reading in psychiatry with his feeling for life. Tragedy, as occasionally in Ibsen, is left groping in a portentous fog. But Jeffers's grasp of tragedy—together with his appreciation of Shakespeare—has been growing with the years. All his palpable limitations in the field notwithstanding, there have been no finer tragic poems written in America than *Cawdor*, *The Loving Shepherdess*, *Thurso's Landing*, *Give Your Heart to the Hawks*, *Solstice*, and *Such Counsels You Gave to Me*. With his knowledge of the Elizabethans and his own obvious grasp of tragedy, it is unthinkable that his imagination should have failed to draw important stimulus from the chief fountainhead of tragedy in English literature.

Often where he departs from the Elizabethan tradition he does so only to approach, as he is well aware, the still older tradition of the medieval drama from which Elizabethan tragedy itself in part arose. The serious medieval plays, it will be recalled, appeared in three easily distinguishable varieties: relatively short plays on the lives and miracles of the saints; the great mystery cycles based on the mystical interpretation of the Scriptures; and morality plays gradually evolving from theological and allegorical pageants to secular representations of the vanity of human wishes or, to use the language of the period itself, of the fall of princes. The last type of play in its latest manifestations merged with the academic or Senecan drama to produce Shakespearean tragedy.

Of the countless saints' plays in English only two or three survive, one of the earliest a fragment so obscure as to be virtually unknown to all but a few scholars and yet curiously like a number of Jeffers's works. *Duk Moraud* tells the story of a father who corrupts his daughter and thereafter contrives to set himself right with God and the universe. This is likewise a leading theme in *Tamar* and *The Women at Point Sur*. At least half of Jeffers's long poems may be described as metaphysical disquisitions upon incest. The similarity between these works and *Duk Moraud* may appear accidental, but it points to a really fundamental likeness between the American poet and the medieval stage.

Jeffers's relation to the mystery plays is both more intimate and more important. Ever haunted with the sense of tragedy, he has from the earliest of his long poems shown extreme interest in the idea of self-torment: suffering self-sought and cherished within. This he acknowledges in the concluding sentences of his recent introduction to his *Selected Poetry*. Through studies in anthropology and psychology he has become especially fascinated by myths of the tortured and the self-tormented God. Thus *Roan Stallion* ends with the shooting of a horse that has assumed divine significance in the mind of the leading character. *At the Birth of an Age* concludes with the intervention of "the hanged God" as *deus ex machina*. And *Dear Judas* develops the same theme with a full-length portrait of the passion of Jesus. The attainment of serenity through passion is the theme of most of Jeffers's poems, barely distinguishable from salvation through passion, an important subject of the medieval mystery play. That type of drama was based almost wholly on the Scriptures. Jeffers's *Dear Judas* enjoys an identical foundation. Although the modern poet substitutes a rationalized and detached interpretation of Jesus for a mystical and sacramental one, in every detail he follows the course of the old plays. In psychological import, also, the new poem and the old mystery play are extremely close. Jeffers deliberately leans upon the Christian dramatic tradition, which he regards as a part of the myth-loving mind of humanity. The Christian story is for him simply the last and best-known version of "the hanged God."

This relationship proves of much significance for the peculiar quality of the tragic idea in Jeffers's poems. The mystery play was not in itself in any strict sense of the word a tragedy, for it depicted the ultimate triumph of Christ. Not the mystery play, but the morality play contributed to the rise of Shakespearean tragedy. The mystery play is essentially a metaphysical poem, highly serious and dramatic but not fundamentally tragic. It deals at bottom with an inner rather than an outer action. For the mystery play developed as a part of the celebration of the Blessed Sacrament as established by the festival of Corpus Christi. Exactly so Jeffers's poetry tends to an intellectual and inner action: in his own admirably critical words, to a "tower beyond tragedy." The mystery play, containing in its original setting a tower of salvation on which God was enthroned, is also this tower beyond tragedy, and in each case, that of the old drama and the modern poem, the tower's foundation is cemented by sacrificial blood. While Jeffers's affinity with Shakespearean tragedy explains his tragic strength, his affinity with the sacramental drama of the Middle Ages explains why his art at times deserts the purer ideals of tragedy for a more daring and to some persons, no doubt, a less profitable flight. Jeffers himself protests that despite the lukewarm reception of his *Dear Judas* by the public this poem stands upon the same basis as his other major works. And this statement seems correct, since all his chief poems show an uncommon absorption in man's evil lot, with the view that for men to find life pleasant is shallow, to find it miserable, profound. But while the suffering God and the psychological theory which it implies are highly conspicuous in the relatively untragic *Dear Judas*, these elements become comparatively subordinate in the other poems. In short, Jeffers's doctrine of the purgation of all emotions threatens but does not destroy his tragic art.

The similarity between Jeffers's poems and the early morality plays is no doubt largely fortuitous, but none the less notable. Too few persons have read the first secular play in English, a morality play known as *The Pride of Life*, written in a chaste and admirable poetic style strongly suggesting the poetry of A. E. Housman. As a study of the vanity of life this drama has much the same spiritual meaning as any one of Jeffers's austere poems. And since both the new poem and the old depict human beings in a violent action and a chastening misfortune, each is essentially tragic. From the point of view taken by true tragic poetry, both have also the same defect, namely, a tendency toward didacticism and abstraction. So Jeffers in one of his own poems, *Night without Sleep*, shuns "the ignoble and cruel incidents," to contemplate "the vast abstract order." Even when retracing, consciously or not, the path of the old tragic moralities, or moral tragedies, he makes frequent excursions to his tower beyond all tragedy.

The evolution of the scholastic medieval drama into the humanistic Shakespearean drama thus helps to interpret the intermediate position occupied by Jeffers's poems. On one hand they are as doctrinaire as the medieval plays, on the other as spontaneous as the Elizabethan. Here they seem pedantically humorless and professionally melodramatic, there profoundly human and genuinely tragic. Even the Elizabethans in fashioning their plays occasionally used their own psychological studies pedantically, Ford's *Lover's Melancholy*, for example, is founded on Burton much as Jeffers's *Tamar* is based on Freud. And yet few poets between Shakespeare and Jeffers have dealt with abnormality and madness so successfully as Ford. The Jeffers poems become at times as poetic as Greek tragedy itself and at times as intellectualized as the coldest and most unfeeling dissertation on the mere theory of tragedy. The question is one of sympathy. How far is Jeffers the psychiatric analyst and how far the tragic poet of literary tradition?

One of his stories less generously admired than might be wished, *The Loving Shepherdess*, at the same time reflects his relation to the Shakespearean playwrights and indicates in a surprising way his own position. This is the only poem in which his leading figure is not an egoist and a rebel against the moral law. It is his only poem dealing fundamentally with tenderness and one of his few pieces wholly free as a work of art from disturbing traces of a doctrinaire psychology. The title itself suggests that Jeffers is writing a Californian pastoral, or tragic idyl: it resembles Fletcher's *Faithful Shepherdess* and many similar dramatic and nondramatic poems of the Renaissance. Moreover, the affectionate picture of Clare, the shepherdess, who "loveth well both man and beast," breathes a gentleness and pathos scarcely equaled in English poetry since Shakespeare's Perdita in *The Winter's Tale* or Beaumont and Fletcher's portraits of Aspatia and Spaconia in *The Maid's Tragedy* and *A King and No King*. Jeffers states that he received his idea for his poem while reading to his young son a few pages in one of Scott's novels—he tells us that he has forgotten which one. Scott, himself a master of pathos, undoubtedly learned his own more tender notes chiefly from the Renaissance plays which he loved so well. In short, Jeffers's poem is related to the Elizabethans as a cousin once removed. We are much more willing to admit reality in the portrait of the gentle Clare than in such a portrait of monstrously exaggerated crime and passion as Barclay in *The Women at Point Sur*. Tragedy, as the Elizabethans discovered, demands a certain sympathy of the reader or spectator with the imaginary figures. It requires that the figures shall seem not monsters or diseases or mere symbols of ideas, but men and women. The figures in Jeffers's finest poems are human, although a tendency toward the doctrinaire intrudes, especially in his early poems and those ambitious pieces in which he leaves his beloved Californian background for settings in ancient or medieval Europe.

Such, then, are the serious obstacles which Jeffers's rich imagination raises against his own achievements in the tragic field, his remarkable attainments notwithstanding. He owes much to the Elizabethans and has a ponderable though less direct indebtedness to the medieval stage. This, of course, does not exhaust the story of his relationship to English poetical tradition. In his most mystical moments he follows Whitman, in his cloudy symbolism and dream imagery he uses Blake. Despite all his originality, he remains a typical romanticist in his philosophy of primitivism and the individual and in his impartiality between unreasoning faith in violent action and profound repose. His extravagant pictures of the passions curiously suggest Macpherson's *Ossian*. In his elegiac poems on Irish tradition Jeffers acknowledges his own descent in spirit as well as in blood from the Celt. But this is a peculiarly intangible relationship. It is certain that his art has a more generic relation to the great age of the poetical drama in England, from the medieval mystery plays to the last works of the Jacobean school, than to any other chapter in English literary history. More than any other non-dramatic poet, he shows the power of Elizabethan drama to mold contemporary poetry.

The Shakespearean drama remains a definite although perhaps not a great or a salutary force in the poetical drama of our own times, in the work of Maxwell Anderson in America and T. S. Eliot in England. Not even among writers for the stage itself is there a contemporary author who writes with so searching a study of the tragic tradition as Jeffers in his narrative poems. E. A. Robinson, to be sure, composed many sad and moving verse tales suggesting the dramatic style. But he is much less concerned with violent action than Jeffers, much more leisurely in his analysis, and closer to the modern novel or the old romance. Unlike Jeffers, Robinson was never deeply interested in the theory of tragedy. His narrative poetry stands nearer to Chaucer's *Troilus and Criseyde* than to Shakespeare's *Macbeth*. Accordingly we may be content to begin and end our view of the survival of Elizabethan theory and practice of tragedy with the contemporary writer best exhibiting this heritage.

The lyrical and shorter poems of the early Renaissance fall into two distinct groups, each of which is still an influence on the poetry of today. These groups are the emotional or sentimental lyric as perfected by Shakespeare and Spenser and the intellectual or critical lyric as practiced by Jonson and Donne. One type of verse is based on the theory that the poem should possess above everything else a simplicity and purity of feeling; the other, that it should harmonize emotion and idea. One type complies with our notion of all that is naïve, romantic, and ethereal in the Elizabethans. It is manifested in the clear voices, whether in the days of Elizabeth or Charles, as heard in the simple songs of Peele, Greene, Dekker, Lodge, Campion, Fletcher, and Herrick. The other group, laboring under the name of "metaphysical," comprises in addition to Donne a large number of poets of the Cavalier school from Raleigh to George Herbert. A distinguished poet of the age will almost inevitably show both tendencies; but Englishmen for well over a generation leaned fairly definitely in one or the other

direction. By the middle of the seventeenth century the Elizabethan enchantment had all but vanished and Donne's tre-
mendous energy seemed increasingly removed from his admirers.
Although, as argued in the first chapter, Milton is primarily a
neoclassicist and an Augustan, his genius lifts him into a sphere
virtually his own. The Augustan decorum and artificiality as
ushered in on the smooth and beguiling verses of Waller and
Denham announced a new taste if not a new culture. All three
traditions still have some power to stimulate contemporary
writers, although the school of Donne is perhaps today more
fruitful than that of the Shakespeareans or the Augustans.
Though roughly following in chronological sequence, they are
not strictly governed by time; it is best, therefore, to consider
the tendencies rather for what they are than with too scrupulous
a thought of their times of manifestation. They all lie now in
one field from which the new corn indiscriminately springs.
And since Donne is by far the greatest master of the intellectual
type of poem, and since most of his verse was written during
the lifetime of Shakespeare—possibly even within the reign of
Elizabeth—it is legitimate to associate metaphysical poetry with
the age of Shakespeare rather than with the times of Milton or
Cowley. Critics more conscious of literary types than of poetic
values overlook the fact that Donne has more in common with
such dramatic poets, Elizabethan and early Jacobean in origin,
as Marston, Webster, and Tourneur than with lyrical poets of
nearly two generations later, such as Carew, Vaughan, and
Marvell. The golden age died with Shakespeare; the Augustan
age is now seen to have commenced considerably earlier than
was once assumed. Donne stood in every way closer to the generation of the great Elizabethans, to which he belonged by birth,
than to that of the Cavaliers: while most of the Cavaliers stand
nearer to the Augustans of the Restoration period than to the
Elizabethans. Indeed, the Augustan spirit harmonized with
the temper of some of the belated followers of Spenser, as the

charming and highly artificial poet William Browne and such sober versemen as Samuel Daniel and Sir John Beaumont. Although its roots were medieval, the sentimental lyric grew under the inspiration of a new school of music. The intellectual lyric, on the contrary, reflected the influence of the new critical spirit in humanistic poetry, or in other words the development under Jonson's guidance of neoclassical satire, epigram, epistle, and elegy.

The sentimental lyric itself is based on a simple action, mood, feeling, or conjunction of images. Dispensing with logical subtlety, it is also without an immanent idea. What the Elizabethans achieved by intuition and spontaneous imitation, the moderns struggle to attain with the additional aid of theory. The psychological doctrine of the intuitions contributes to a theory of the pure lyric as an art uncontaminated by intellectualism. So the preface to E. E. Cummings's *Collected Poems* is an apology for a type of poetry wherein the experience itself is spontaneous and unreflecting, no matter how delicate is the technique. "Life, for eternal us," writes this truculent author, "is now. . . . Everywhere tints childrening, innocent spontaneous, true. . . . Nothing believed or doubted; brain over heart, surface: nowhere hating or to fear; shadow, mind without soul. Only how measureless cool flames of making; only each other building always distinct selves of mutual entirely opening; only alive. Never the murdered finalities of wherewhen and yesno, impotent nongames of wrongright and rightwrong; never to gain or pause, never the soft adventure of undoom, greedy anguishes and cringing ecstasies of inexistence; never to rest and never to have: only to grow."

Precisely because Cummings's technique, temperament, and ideas so frequently clash with work of the Elizabethans, his agreement in lyrical inspiration proves all the more striking. And not only is this agreement as such worth examining, but it will be seen that Cummings himself owes a conscious debt to

the masters of the Renaissance lyric of sentiment. The final
poem in his collection is a sonnet expressing in verse what the
just-quoted preface voices in prose.

> you shall above all things be glad and young.
> For if you're young, whatever life you wear
>
> it will become you; and if you are glad
> whatever's living will yourself become.
> Girlboys may nothing more than boygirls need:
> i can entirely her only love
>
> whose any mystery makes every man's
> flesh put space on; and his mind take off time
>
> that you should ever think, may god forbid
> and (in his mercy) your true lover spare:
> for that way knowledge lies, the foetal grave
> called progress, and negation's dead undoom.
>
> I'd rather learn from one bird how to sing
> than teach ten thousand stars how not to dance

Such is the doctrine of the spontaneous lyric expressed in a far-
from-spontaneous poem. A large number of Cummings's pieces,
however, fully realize this ideal.

There are at least two indications in the foregoing lines of
the reverence of the usually outrageous Cummings for the older
school of poetry. That he writes many of his seemingly revolutionary poems in the sonnet form is an amusing evidence of his
reliance on tradition. And the words "for that way knowledge
lies" are a deliberate imitation of Lear's "for that way madness
lies."

Cummings's interest in the English Renaissance appears most
notably in his first book of poems, *Tulips and Chimneys*. The
first lyric, for example, has the spirit of an ode by William
Drummond or some latter-day Petrarchist. The imagery is

pastoral, with its silver streams, willows, flowers, meadows, pastures, shepherds, sunsets in May, and trees drenched in the full moon. The verse form is a regularly rhymed nine-line stanza of ten-syllable lines wholly in the Elizabethan spirit. That the poem and its language also bear many marks of modernity in no way prevents it from leaning heavily on the Renaissance. It is essentially a poem of mood, and of an elegiac and melancholy mood familiar in verse from Petrarch to Spenser.

The second poem in the same volume has the pastoral, amorous, and elegiac atmosphere of one of Herrick's lyrics without Herrick's style. The fourth lyric is a paraphrase of that great Jacobean poem, the King James version of *The Song of Songs*. The fifth piece, a sonnet with Shakespearean rhyme scheme, like many other of Cummings's sonnets proves especially Shakespearean in its first line: "it is at moments after i have dreamed." The following lyric begins with another thoroughly Elizabethan line: "All in green went my love riding." Its ending contains one of the most common of all Elizabethan puns, that on heart meaning both deer and beloved. The next few pieces bear distinct traces of exuberant Marlovian rhetoric and hyperbole. The ninth (his poems are numbered without titles) curiously combines Renaissance images with a suggestion of the modern symbolist painters whom Cummings knows well. His tenth recalls the neoclassical lyric by reference to faun and syrinx. The eleventh, deriving from the nonliterary tradition of nursery rhymes and nonsense verse, plays games with arithmetic and reminds one of such quaint and ancient songs as *The Three Huntsmen*, *The Twelve Days of Christmas*, and *I'll Sing You Twelve O*. The twelfth poem in *Tulips and Chimneys* is a sonnet directly of the Italian Renaissance, since it consists in a remarkably imaginative description of the painting of Fra Angelico. The stanza scheme of the fifteenth song is freely adapted from Marvell's ode on Cromwell's return from Ireland. As often occurs in the seventeenth-century poet, the stanza

closes with a trimeter couplet. Marvell's diction and his special
fondness for meadows are recaptured in such lines as these:

> whose bodies strong with love
> through meadows hugely move.

Cummings recalls Marvell's platonism, "a green thought in a
green shade":

> while in an earthless hour my fond
> soul seriously yearns beyond
> this fern of sunset frond on frond
> opening in a rare
> Slowness of gloried air . . .

The following piece shows even more conventional pastoral
imagery, while the eighteenth is composed with a recollection
of such a well-known lyric as Nash's "Spring, sweet Spring, is
the world's pleasant king." Cummings's forty-third poem, a
magnificent sonnet on the possible future infidelity of the beloved, is not only written in direct emulation of Shakespeare
but conceivably surpasses a few of the great dramatist's own
sonnets on this theme. The extent of Cummings's archaism is
shown by little things as well as by great, by his habit, for instance, of using the word "utter" in its Elizabethan sense of put
forth. He may have remembered the flower in Spenser's *Shepherd's Calendar* which "uttered his tender head." His play on
words, as "Rolls Royce" and "Professor Royce rolls," is truly
Elizabethan.

Although his later volumes indicate his persistent memory of
his reading in the Renaissance lyric, his first book of verse shows
this debt most clearly. As his art grew he dispensed with a
pedantic following of the letter and cherished the spirit of his
predecessors. The Elizabethans had more than one attraction
for him. Impatiently despising our contemporary culture, he
returned to them as to a more robust and less prudish age than

our own. He combined the tenderness and idealism of Spenser with the bitterness and brutality of Marston. He could find these rival views expressed by the author of A Midsummer-Night's Dream and Timon of Athens. Even a lesser spirit, such as Robert Herrick, excels equally in extremes of refinement and coarseness. His eccentric mannerisms notwithstanding, Cummings is therefore a thoroughly Renaissance figure. He stands closer to the Elizabethans than poets who have protested their admiration more loudly, as Swinburne and Rossetti.

The essence of Cummings's obvious affinity to the Elizabethans is aesthetic rather than moral. Aspiring to a pure lyricism, the American poet recognizes in the singers of Shakespeare's age the purest embodiment of his own lyrical ideal. That Cummings remains fundamentally a lyric poet is demonstrated in both his doctrine and his practice. His views of art, expressed in the already quoted preface and concluding sonnet, clearly lend themselves best to the lyric, for in the lyric moment the poet realizes his goal of unreflecting experience more fully than in longer or more meditative forms. His collected poems consist of over three hundred lyrics and no pieces of any other description. If some of the cryptic poems in his latest volumes defy the patience, if not the intelligence, of most readers, every indication is that he has remained undeviating in his devotion to the lyrical ideal. In his own words, he celebrates "a thing most new," "complete, fragile, intense," a "breathless" moment. He aims always "to face suddenly" his experience. In one of his latest sonnets he writes:

> let must or if be damned with whomever's afraid
> down with ought with because with every brain
> which thinks it thinks, nor dares to feel (but up
> with joy; and up with laughing and drunkenness)

In another lyric he defends his aesthete against the enmity of a critical world:

. . . let all
unfools of unbeing

set traps for his heart,
lay snares for his feet
(who wanders through only white darkness
who moves in black light

dancing isn'ts on why, digging bridges with mirrors
from whispers to stars;
climbing silence for ifs
diving under because)

Each of Cummings's lyrics expresses a simple feeling, sometimes dramatically aroused by a violent action, sometimes
quietly determined by inner or outer climatical conditions. His
poems have fluid motion to a definite goal, each brief and thoroughly self-contained. The pieces on the physical nature of sex,
whether elaborately metaphorical or bluntly literal, are the least
imaginative and most easily spared of his works, original, perhaps, as verse, but hardly unusual as obscenities. But the satirical poems are almost as lyrical as the idealistic ones. He makes
the modern sonnet, so often a vehicle of meditation or didacticism, as truly lyrical as it appears in Sidney, Constable,
Spenser, or Shakespeare. In a flash he gives us a poetic interpretation of the boulevards of Paris, an evening in a Greek restau-
rant in downtown Boston, a night by the sea, a cheap dance
hall, a character, a Christmas tree, a locomotive, a street scene,
a hand organ, or a sudden death. The lyric spirit is embodied in
a lyric form. Sometimes his free verse is actually stanzaic, as in
the captivating poem beginning, "Jimmie's got a goil." Sometimes what is virtually a stanzaic form lies hidden beneath the
free verse, as in poem number 124, which begins, "nobody
loses all the time." More often still, a thoroughly modernistic
style, dispensing with stanza, line, rhyme, and even rhythm and

syntax as these are commonly practiced, attains lyrical movement and unity through an intensely imagined organic structure. *Memorabilia*, his poem on American tourists in Venice, achieves this consummation. Cummings, who is equally a lover of modern music and modern painting, of Stravinsky and of Picasso, shows in this case the strong influence of the radical composers. Even his notorious obscenity, "She being Brand-new" (number 134), is at least pure in its lyricism. The following *jeu d'esprit* seems printed deliberately to conceal its affinity to English nursery rhymes at least as old as Shakespeare:

> IKEY(GOLDBERG)'S WORTH I'M
> TOLD $ SEVERAL MILLION
> FINKLESTEIN(FRITZ)LIVES
> AT THE RITZ WEAR
> earl & wilson COLLARS

That Cummings should reach the objectives of the Elizabethans, whom he knows and emulates, by means so thoroughly modern makes the original relationship all the more fascinating.

While Cummings hides his literary obligations by a glaring cloak of modernity, affecting the humors of a literary cult which includes James Joyce and Gertrude Stein, W. H. Davies with hardly less success hides his literary obligations by advertising his life as spent among day laborers and the unemployed, in town and country. In 1906 he published his prose *Autobiography of a Super-Tramp*, picturing himself as a bohemian nearer to the true gypsy pattern. The book was prefaced by Bernard Shaw, who declared that on reading the poems he felt "there was indeed no sign of his ever having read anything otherwise than as a child reads. . . . Here, I saw, was a genuine innocent, writing odds and ends of verse about odds and ends of things; living quite out of the world in which such things are usually done." The fact, however, seems to be that just as in the case of so many other "innocent" poets Davies by living outside the circle of literary clubrooms enjoyed leisure to be a patient reader of the older poetry and a studious craftsman in his own. Where Burns derived even more from oral than from literary tradition, Davies derives most from books. Although he has written a few short verse essays and some verse epigrams, nine tenths of his work is clearly lyrical, and how brief his poems are may be judged from the fact that his 1935 volume of collected poems contains many more poems than pages. Davies naturally leans the most heavily on the authors of the same type of short poem as his own. He is a twentieth-century Welsh Herrick. Although he has written little about his reading, his poems sufficiently betray his habits. He several times mentions his library as being his most valued possession and, like Herrick, speaks of the labor of polishing and refining his verses. Intelligent in his reading and scrupulous in his craftsmanship, he is as legitimately literary a poet as any of our times. While the likeness is chiefly to Herrick, few modern writers suggest so many of their predecessors. Verbal similarities are too close to permit the possibility that in any but a few cases the likeness is accidental. Although he knows English lyrical verse only too well from Chaucer to Landor, it is in the greatest period of the English lyric, between Shakespeare and Milton, that he feels most at home. In almost all cases it is to the simple song or poetic trifle rather than to the intellectual poetry of Donne and his school that his work finds its affinity. His critics have invariably described his style as "Elizabethan" rather than "metaphysical" or "Cavalier." This, no doubt, is substantially correct, although it must be added that he shows a fondness for many of the simpler poems by writers of the Cavalier period.

In a number of cases Davies paraphrases the Latin lyrists, either remembering them in the original, in translation, or through the mediation of the intensely neoclassical poets of the age of Campion, Herrick, and Milton. His poem *Truly Great*, for example, paraphrases classical odes on the quiet life as these have been variously rendered in English poetry by Wyatt, Campion, Pope, and countless others. Horatian echoes are by no means rare. One of the poems, for instance, begins, "Happy the man . . ." Although he prefers light verse, he occasionally writes a brief, passionate lyric closer to Catullus than to Horace. When in *The East in Gold* he writes

> *Since first I heard the cock-a-doodle-do,*
> *Timekeeper on green farms,—at break of day—*

he follows Chaucer, who wrote of "the cok that horologe is of thorpes lite"—Chaucer in his turn borrowing from the French.

Davies is apparently not a medievalist, but close parallels in his work may be educed to any number of Elizabethans. He attacks his theme in an Elizabethan manner, as in his lyric which begins, "When primroses are out in Spring." In several poems Davies uses Lodge's favorite image likening Cupid on the bosom to a bee in a flower. Such an allegorical trifle as the song *The Best Friend* might stand as easily in Campion's *Book of Airs* as in Davies *Poems. The Starved,* his poem depicting the lament of a mother for her fatherless babe, recalls Greene's sentimental poems on the same theme. *The Moth* might be a new song sung by Shakespeare's Ariel, while other of Davies's poems contain reminiscences of the singing of Puck, as well as of the clowns in *Love's Labour's Lost.* One of Spenser's sonnets may have suggested the image of the spider and the bee in Davies's "That day she seized me like a bee." He has an interesting allusion to Spenser's heroine, Una. The homely drinking songs in Dekker's *Shoemaker's Holiday* may have helped him to write *A Drinking Song;* the line, "We'll laugh, ha! ha! to see them weep," seems reminiscent of a song in Dekker's *Old Fortunatus,* while Dekker's lyrical tenderness is approached in *Robin Redbreast.* Davies's poem beginning, "Oh, sweet Content," must have been written with a recollection of Dekker's song in *Patient Grissill* having a refrain that commences with the same words. All of Davies's poems on the joys of poverty share something with Dyer's well-known song, *My Mind to Me a King-dom Is. Knitting*, which contains the phrase, "let her still uncertain be," derives from such Ovidian conceits as that which Jonson's Lovewit sings in *Epicoene*. The lusty verse movement of *The Life Divine* has the true Fletcherian swing. No Elizabethan scholar would be surprised to read the song *Death* in a play by Beaumont and Fletcher.

> Beauty'll be no fairer than
> Agèd dame so shrunk and wan,
> Whom she looks on proudly. Now,
> Did Death strike them sudden low,
> Strike them down, a little while
> Vanished Beauty's velvet smile,
> Ugly grinner she, and few
> Mark the difference 'tween these two.
> Nothing here shall arbitrate,
> Chivalry intimidate,
> Hour of doom, or change Death's laws;
> Kings hire no ambassadors.
> Death makes monarchs grinning clowns,
> Fits their skulls for bells, not crowns.

Such a song as *Nature's Friend* might easily have been inspired by a sympathetic reading of the part of the Good Satyr in Fletcher's *Faithful Shepherdess*.

But Davies's most profitable reading is Robert Herrick. He sees himself with the same eyes that Herrick used for self-analysis. In *The Doll* Davies depicts himself as an old lover of a young girl. Elsewhere, like Herrick, he acknowledges that his lyrical loves are imaginary. In *I Am the Poet Davies, William*, he paints his face as physically ugly, a course that Herrick had set before him. He follows the older poet in imagining that he is dead and mourned by his sweetheart. Like his predecessor, he recounts his amorous dreams. He unblushingly records the lady's physical charms, as when, in *Around That Waist*, he de-

scribes an amorous girdle or, in *Her Body's a Fine House*,
declares that her body has three stories divided by garter, belt,
and necklace. Her head, by way of afterthought, turns out
a roof garden. Boldly imitating his master, he composes a little
poem on earrings: *When Diamonds, Nibbling in My Ears*. Entirely in Herrick's vein he writes:

> To think the world for me
> Contains but her alone,
> And that her eyes prefer
> Some ribbon, scarf or stone.

His lines *Waiting* palpably imitate Herrick's famous *Corinna's
Going a-Maying*. His *Farewell to Poesy* follows the earlier poet's
Farewell to Sack. Entirely in the mythological vein of his pred-
ecessor he sings:

> Her golden hair gave me more joy
> Than Jason's heart could hold,
> When all his men cried out—Ah, look!
> He has the Fleece of Gold!

With the Devon poet he sings of Charon's ferry, of the Court
of Queen Mab, and of the festivities at Christmas. With Herrick, too, he has a mad maid's song, here called *Mad Poll*. Like
him he praises the freedom and ease of the country life. That
he has learned much from the metrical and stanzaic technique
of his forerunner needs no emphasis, but may at once be seen
by comparing the songs in *Hesperides* with such pieces as
School's Out, with its lusty dimeter, *The Example*, and *To
Sparrows Fighting*. *The Posts* is extremely close to the movement of many of Herrick's trifles. Davies's poem begins:

> A year's a post, on which
> It saith
> The distance—growing less—
> To Death.

Davies clearly follows the *Hesperides*, though at a greater distance, in epigrams and brief, satirical verse portraits. The true significance of all these relationships, however, lies not in any similarities, accidental or deliberate, in subject matter or technique, but in the attitude of the two men toward their art. Each is essentially the light and tender lyric poet, delicate in craftsmanship, Epicurean in philosophy. It is in their occasional graver notes that they differ most, for the War of 1914–18 touched Davies more deeply than the Civil War touched Herrick; and the modern humanitarianism which caused Davies to write so feelingly of the London poor was a sentiment unknown to the Cavalier poet. Davies even expressed surprise himself at these occasional digressions into an unwontedly serious vein. In his few poems against liquor he seems as unlike Herrick as unlike his true self. Here Herrick, despite enforced absences, proved the more faithful lover. But for delicately carved, refreshing, and sentimental trifles wholly free, nevertheless, from all vulgar sentiment, Davies and Herrick still have few rivals in English verse.

Davies has profited not only from Herrick but from much of the lighter poetry of the mid-seventeenth century that carries on the tradition of Shakespeare and Campion rather than that of Donne and Chapman. Milton he recalls chiefly as author of *L'Allegro*. In *Fancy's Home*, for example, he gives fantastic mythological genealogies resembling those of Milton's poem. In his lines *Music* he reflects the words and meaning of the most devoted musician among the English poets.

Of the lesser poets of the age, Marvell means most to him. "O what a life is this I lead," begins his piece *A Happy Life*, echoing "What wond'rous life is this I lead!" from Marvell's *Garden*. Such lines as the following can have but one literary source:

> *I make a fallen tree my chair,*
> *And soon forget no cushion's there;*

> *I lie upon the grass or straw,*
> *And no soft down do I sigh for.* . . .
> *The dappled cows in fields I pass,*
> *Up to their bosoms in deep grass.*

One infers that Davies has read not only *The Garden* but *Appleton House.* His *Sheep,* unlike Marvell's *Bermudas* as it may be in subject matter, rivals it in clarity and directness.

The style of *Shopping,* with the line, "Take not advantage of that hand," strongly suggests Carew. Davies has several drinking songs close to the carefree manner of Randolph. He remembered Suckling's well-known ballad when he wrote, "Her cruel hands go in and out," and perhaps again in the not-too-ambitious couplet,

> *To hear her moving petticoat,*
> *For me is music's highest note.*

Some of his excellent epigrams suggest Quarles's *Emblems.* He recaptures the quiet humor of Isaac Walton when he says:

> *For, free, he lives his simple life,*
> *And has not risked it with a wife;*
> *Prefers tobacco's quiet blisses*
> *To Love's breath-mixture sealed by kisses.*

From Vaughan's *Retreat* he borrows almost shamelessly in his *Time of Dreams:*

> *What sweet, what happy days had I,*
> *When dreams made Time Eternity!*
> *Before I knew this body's breath*
> *Could not take life in without death.*
> *As fresh as any field of grass*
> *This breath of life was, then: it was* . . .

His quiet and mystical joy in such a piece as *A Great Time* may well have been aided by the poetical instruction of the didactic Thomas Traherne. Some of his most guileless and naïve verses, on the other hand, approximate George Wither. And, finally, there are parallels to Herbert, but only to Herbert's simplest and least intellectual poetry.

Although the purest vein of the Shakespearean lyric is the chief literary inspiration for this felicitous singer, his art from time to time reflects a reading of later poetry. Some of his less ethereal songs lending themselves most readily to musical settings, as *My Youth* or *Jove Warns Us*, might be read without surprise in the group of poems written for music by Matthew Prior. Again in his less fanciful and chaster manner, as in *Days That Have Been*, he approximates Cowper's craftsmanship. Some of his more formal epigrams, as *Here Am I*, seem the work of a less powerful Landor. His country songs, as *Early Morn*, have the charm and freshness of John Clare. That Davies borrows from Blake has been observed by several of his critics. Such a phrase as, "they're laughing at once with sweet, round mouths," can have only the author of *Songs of Innocence* for its verbal inspiration. The passionate directness of such simple lyrics as *The Weeping Child, In the Country,* and *Facts* lifts them out of Davies's customary province of light verse into a more romantic and more deeply felt lyricism. As a conservative nature poet Davies can hardly forget Wordsworth, although he happily makes it his rule to seek models more often in the seventeenth than in the nineteenth century. One of his poems alludes to Wordsworth's *Solitary*, the pacific hero of *The Excursion*. And as Davies returns occasionally to the medieval ballad and to the sterner elements of life, he may well have conversed on the way with Housman's *Shropshire Lad*.

Davies is a closer and happier follower of the Shakespearean lyric than a contemporary even more often mentioned in this regard, Walter de la Mare. For De la Mare is three parts romantic to one part Elizabethan. More a poet of delicate moods than of ideas or strong feelings, he repeats again and again the atmosphere of the romantic ballad of wonder. *The Listeners* is his masterpiece in this kind. Nor can we see in his well-known *Old Angler* a brother of Walton's Angler, but rather a decadent descendant, last of a fast-fading line. De la Mare has studied his Shakespeare, but he more often recalls Coleridge and Poe. A representative collection of his work, *Selected Poems*, published in 1927, contains distinctly more poetical meditations than genuine lyrics. His many pleasant children's poems are for the most part either ballads or lyrics in the Victorian vein of Stevenson's *Child's Garden of Verses*. Yet occasionally the rare combination of the scholar and the true poet makes itself felt. With an ear attuned with almost Elizabethan delicacy to the music of words, he has written several lyrics that might pass for excellent Elizabethan madrigals, such as *The Linnet, Forgiveness, Who?* and *The Moth. The Blind Boy* is an Anacreontic trifle on Cupid only a little less spirited than those by Drayton and Cowley. *An Epitaph* represents the fruits of long study by the poet in the verse inscriptions on seventeenth-century tombs. *The Little Salamander to Margot* is a song in Ariel's vein, while *The Familiar* may be imagined as a dialogue between Ariel and Prospero. *The Mermaids* is an exquisitely lyrical, musical piece such as might have adorned any masque by the best of the old poets who practiced in that field: Jonson, Daniel, Campion, Chapman, Beaumont, Shirley, or Milton.

To many of the poet's critics it has seemed that by his verses for children he is destined to live longest. As already observed, many of these are narrative or sentimental in the Victorian manner, without showing the scholar behind the poet. Yet a few lyrics catch the spirit of the nursery rhyme, nonsense poetry, and folklore carrying the reader back at least to the Elizabethan age. *The Huntsmen* is such a homely and delightful trifle. *A-Tishoo* is at least as light as Herrick; *The Fairies Dancing* contains a recollection of Spenser; *The Hare* has something of Dekker's fancy and pathos; while Shakespeare or any poet of the later Renaissance cultivating pastoral fields might have been pleased to have composed De la Mare's *Flower*. Nevertheless it is difficult to see the lyric of sentiment in this fragile poet as more than a lonely mistletoe in a nocturnal forest of phosphorescent decay. Whether or not Cummings and Davies are better poets, their blither spirits stand much closer to Shakespeare's lyric of the heart.

The perplexed modern world has on the whole remembered better the intellectual lyric written by Donne, finding the darker vein more answerable to present needs. Poets who have acknowledged their indebtedness to the seventeenth-century "School of Night" have been as numerous as the critics who have recently acclaimed it. Among the poets a typical example is Genevieve Taggard, editor of an anthology of metaphysical poetry from Donne to E. E. Cummings and of a lyric significantly entitled *Vaughan in New England*. It must suffice here to consider, first, the original significance of Donne's contribution to the lyric and, secondly, the work of two powerful poets, recently dead, who came under his spell: Elinor Wylie and William Butler Yeats.

Donne himself, his contemporaries, and his recent interpreters have agreed in regarding his work as a revolt against the leading tendencies in English verse at the close of the sixteenth century. Then Spenser was the dominating figure, with Sidney still revered and Marlowe's luscious *Hero and Leander* among the most popular of poems. Affected sonnets, sentimental pastorals, patriotic verse chronicles, and decorative madrigals comprised a large part of the nondramatic poetry. Petrarch was still the leading model in lyrical verse, Ariosto in the verse narrative. Light verse tended to pretty artifice, English serious poetry to literal-mindedness and woodenness. Under the guidance of Shakespeare and Jonson a revolution was being effected in dramatic poetry in terms of a freer and fuller expression of personality. Donne attained similar leadership in the lyrical field, aided by a group of young radicals embracing Raleigh, Chapman, and Marston. But Donne towered so far above his associates and achieved so individual and memorable a manner that it is actually misleading to speak of the school of Donne. For present purposes it is better to consider his own work than his relation to his first admirers, all of whom felt his influence, none of whom fully captured his idiom.

Executing an about face from the decadent Petrarchan style, Donne became above all else intellectual. With his Jesuit training he commanded a logical subtlety and breadth of learning that became the envy of his age. Almost every poem he wrote proved a challenge. He subtly debated and questioned the poetic religion of love as well as the Anglican religion of the State; he reveled in the doubts germinated by the new science. The sentimental lyric was of popular origin and appeal; his own poetry sprang from his special training and addressed primarily the intellectuals in court circles. It was intended not for the popular stage but for the scholar's library. Always more or less difficult to read, it bristled with learned allusions and strange and rapid turns of thought. His favorite technique was to torture a single image as a dog worries a bone. He deals freely with disillusionment. Most of his poems are arguments, often paradoxical and with a dramatic conclusion that quite reverses the first stated proposition. In short, these poems are always for the specially trained or specially informed reader. For the simple harmonies of the popular song they exchange the dire intricacies of "the thinking heart." If a few of his pieces seem mere intellectual gymnastics, written, as he said, "to outdo Sir Edward Herbert in obscureness," the great majority remarkably combine agility of thought with intensity of feeling.

Such emotional tension and mental pyrotechnics as Donne loved had small charms for the Augustan period, which worshipped above everything else serenity and ease. The tenacity with which Donne clings to his conceits and his studious ingenuity in developing them also attracted scant attention in poets from Wordsworth to Swinburne. That our own age of stress, strain, and ingenious self-torment has turned back to

Donne, revolting from Victorian sentiment as he revolted from Petrarchistic sentiment, is well recognized as an important episode in literary history.

Elinor Wylie is the most gifted of American poets to fall powerfully under his influence. This relationship she acknowledged, as when, in one of her poems, she speaks of enjoying "with Donne a metaphysical frolic." Her allusions to alembics, mandrakes, and the cutting properties of the diamond show her acquaintance with such verse. Science supplies a number of her images. The word "centrifugal," for example, appears in one of her lyrics. Theological subtleties, which play so large a part in Donne, directly or indirectly appear in a large number of her poems.

That she had much of Donne's temperament aided her in successfully following the paths of his art. Their common forms sprang from a common need as shown both in lesser things and greater. More than once, like Donne, she dwells morbidly upon physical decomposition after death. The body she calls a "fresh embroidered shroud." Her poetry, too, combines intellectual subtlety and emotional directness. Inner tension becomes the leading feature of her poetical character. Thus she writes a *Malediction* upon *Myself* close to the style of numerous maledictions in Donne. Her *Self-Portrait* might with the omission of a single redundant syllable serve even better as a picture of him than of her:

> *A lens of crystal whose transparence calms*
> *Queer stars to clarity, and disentangles*
> *Fox-fires to form austere refracted angles:*
> *A texture polished on the horny palms*
> *Of vast equivocal creatures, beast or human:*
> *A flint, a substance finer-grained than snow,*
> *Graved with the Graces in intaglio*
> *To set sarcastic sigil on the woman,*

Repeatedly inner strife appears her formula for lyric art. Her famous *Birthday Sonnet* represents her fierce struggle to retain her integrity. In another sonnet she gives the formula itself:

> . . . *all your beauty is the work of wars*
> *Between the upper and the nether stars.*

Three of her best-known poems continue this theme. In one she records the struggle between "a private madness" and "this virtuous light." Another is a debate between three aspects of her nature—heart, mind, and soul—regarding a fourth, her querulous body. A third, entitled in the words of Hamlet *Absent Thee from Felicity Awhile*, is the age-old problem of the man who meditates suicide: to be or not to be. More than once she considers the relative claims of a fastidious beauty and "the savage lovely," renouncing her earlier allegiance to the former. Again and again she traces her inner struggles: sometimes the battle seems over, sometimes it looms in the future. So in *This Hand* she reflects on her old love for a man whom she now views coolly. In *"Desolation Is a Delicate Thing"* she wonders at her rapid changes from grief to ease. In *Valentine* she foresees a coming struggle to keep her mind, despite the world, fresh and sweet till death. In *A Proud Lady* she depicts a woman after her own heart, scorning the world without losing temper.

Her intellectual tendencies are self-confessed. As a true admirer of Donne she writes of thinking, "by some mental twist," of "a line knotted about the brain," of a combination of "spice and salt," and of the "clean envolved precision of my mind." It is the moral of one of her striking lyrics that wisdom is greater than love or pity. Many of her poems are built about paradoxes and contradictions. Thus with a subtlety reminiscent of Dante she finds only love in the lion who slays the tiger to save the lamb; and she wonders if wind can be the same "element" when at one hour it exudes heavy fragrance and at another rushes in swift and terrible sterility against the mountain-top.

Certain border-line poems which may or may not be considered lyrical show as clearly as her purest lyrics her indebtedness to Donne. Under the heading *Elegies and Epistles* she includes three pieces which Donne would undoubtedly have called elegies: The *Broken Man, The Lie,* and *The Loving Cup.* These personal poems are chiefly distinguished from the majority of her lyrics only by their rhyme scheme, a distinction equally valid for the elegies of Donne which they clearly emulate. The first is an ingenious effusion to a china statuette, the second a subtle argument regarding degrees of mendacity, and the third, a farfetched development of the loving-cup image, wholly in the manner of the metaphysical conceit as practiced by Donne. The Elizabethan himself wrote satires as well as elegies, but Elinor Wylie's genius was the more lyrical. Her nearest approaches to Donne's satires are two or three withering verse portraits of ladies who fell into her disfavor, as *Portrait in Black Paint* and *To a Lady's Countenance.* They have at least something of Donne's bitter wit.

It must be acknowledged that a few of her poems are better classified with the sentimental than with the intellectual lyric. Such charming trifles as *The Bird* or "*As I Went Down by Havre de Grace . . .*" have a lyrical intention close to the poetry of Herrick or her contemporary, W. H. Davies. This type of verse is one to which she relaxed in spare moments. Some of her most graceful light verse remains to this day only in the newspapers and periodicals to which she contributed; it was gathered neither into the four volumes of poetry published during her lifetime nor into the beautiful posthumous *Collected Poems.*

Nevertheless her genius was chiefly for the serious and difficult poem. Most of her memorable pieces are in one way or another obscure. Thus in some of her best ballads and brief narratives she tells a story in the most abrupt and puzzling

manner possible. This is true of her apocryphal tale of the
Three Wise Men entitled *Twelfth Night*. Another poem consists of twenty lines about pearls, but the word is never used.
A few of her pieces, as *Benvenuto's Valentine*, carry some weight
of learning. Especially in her more personal lyrics her imagination leads her to hint rather than to explain. A profusion of
farfetched images, as in the highly "metaphysical" *Doomsday*,
makes slow reading. But the chief obscurity of her finest poems
arises from her mysticism. As religious as Donne, but even less
orthodox in her thinking, she is probably at times more difficult
than many of her readers imagine. In this stanza, for example,
she comprehends Donne and goes beyond him upon the metaphysical way:

> *There I walked, and there I raged;*
> *The spiritual savage caged*
> *Within my skeleton, raged afresh*
> *To feel, behind a carved mesh,*
> *The clean bones crying in the flesh.*

The first group of poems, headed *Breastplate*, in her volume
Black Armour contains some of the most interesting verse of a
distinctly mystical character written since Emily Dickinson.

In the eminent Irish poet William Butler Yeats we find an
even more prominent modern who came under Donne's spell.
The influence of Donne is interesting in such a case as being
spiritual and elusive rather than technical or formal. Unlike
Elinor Wylie, Yeats never imitates details of Donne's technique,
but with a manner thoroughly his own he assimilates much of
the Elizabethan's intellectual ruggedness and spiritual realism.
Yeats's understanding of lyrical art was deepened and directed
by the Donne tradition.

The commanding position in the field of English poetry
which Yeats enjoyed throughout the postwar period was largely
due to his extraordinary breadth and catholicity. He reminds us

that literary Dublin is at once more conscious of its nationalism and more deeply international than cumbersome London or forward-looking New York. And Ireland, apologetic as to its present, fosters a phenomenally vivid sense of the past. In no respect has Yeats been more faithful to Irish literary tradition than by his cosmopolitanism and depth of literary perspective. He warmly appreciated many classics, and especially the English poets of all centuries. Homer and Sophocles—the latter he translated brilliantly—had special attractions to him; and more successfully than any modern poet in the language he reproduces at least in part the passionate Greek love lyric and the graceful Anthology. His studies in philosophy and mysticism led him to Plato and Plotinus. These, together with his Celtic temperament, led him also to the Middle Ages, to Dante and to the long tradition of Christian poetry. In Ireland no forced medieval revival is possible: the Christian and even the pagan Middle Ages linger on as the national inheritance of a country still wholly Catholic and partly primitive. Yeats not only delighted to retell old stories in old settings, but to give his verses an atmosphere suggesting the frank-speaking and passionate age of Langland, Chaucer, and Malory. Both his romance and his satire have more than a faint medieval flavor.

The Elizabethans were less often on his tongue, but seem to have lain still nearer his heart. He wrote of their age as the greatest in our literature. His literary tastes and social philosophy led him increasingly toward the Renaissance, an inclination fostered by his early friends Lionel Johnson and Walter Pater. But all this enthusiasm seemed more natural and less forced in the Irishman than in the Englishmen. His view of the past was intensified not only by his race but by his ideas of racial and family tradition and spiritualism. Might he not even commune with the great Dean of St. Patrick's ghost? In his poem *The Seven Sages* he pictures as the last wise men of his country Goldsmith, Burke, Swift, and Bishop Berkeley. These men conversed with his own ancestors; he in turn converses as intimately with them. Yeats, then, by no means repudiates the eighteenth century. And he remains equally friendly to the romantics, remembering the romantic verses of his own youth. In speaking of the Irish Revival, with which his own thought and life were so closely connected, he writes:

> We were the last romantics—chose for theme
> Traditional sanctity and loveliness;
> Whatever's written in what poets name
> The book of the people; whatever most can bless
> The mind of man or elevate a rhyme.

His poetical and philosophical powers and his romantic nature were early nursed in his studies as editor and lover of Blake. The fascination which metaphysics and aesthetics held for him brought him, apparently despite his own wishes, close to Wordsworth and Coleridge; his taste naturally attracted him to Shelley and Keats. With a grand gesture of eclecticism he built his own modernistic poetry on the foundation of the romantic verse which he wrote as early as the eighteen-nineties, often wholly in keeping with the spirit of the times. Age drew him away from Swinburne and back to Arnold. As public affairs grew increasingly critical, his own social conscience became aroused, with the result that some of his later poetry—his fine *Meditations in Time of Civil War*, for example—resembles the grave dignity of the Victorian poet who most successfully expressed the issues of a strident age in the deep musical harmonies of verse. Yeats's passionate love poetry, too, realizes some of the most typical ideals of the romantic school.

Enjoying this wide literary background he pondered more seriously than most poets over the general problem of literary heritage. Sometimes he sees the claim of the individual as foremost, sometimes that of tradition. In his *Sailing to Byzantium* he says:

> Nor is there singing school but studying
> Monuments of its own magnificence.

In *Ego Dominus Tuus* he debates both sides of the case. The traditionalist argues thus:

> A style is found by sedentary toil
> And by the imitation of great masters.

To which the romanticist in him rejoins:

> Because I seek an image not a book.
> Those men that in their writings are most wise
> Own nothing but their blind, stupefied hearts.

Yeats knew both sides of the case feelingly, possessing far too strong an imagination to lean unduly upon predecessors and far too shrewd a wisdom to neglect their aid. In such an artist indebtedness is likely to be deep rather than obvious. In view of his profound sympathy with all major schools of tradition, and his obvious preference for the Renaissance in particular, it would appear likely that beneath the surface of his own work would lie a considerable obligation to English poetry of the age of Shakespeare.

We need not be detained by the question of precisely how much the leader of the twentieth-century revival in the Dublin theatre owed to the great leader of the sixteenth-century revival of the London stage. For criticism in recent years has increasingly emphasized the importance of Yeats in lyrical rather than in dramatic poetry. By the dramatic lyric rather than by the lyrical drama he promises chiefly to be remembered. At times he follows the pastoral poets of the Renaissance. His surprisingly beautiful *Shepherd and Goatherd* is perhaps the finest close imitation of the elegiac pastoral eclogue since *Lycidas*. The platonic melancholy of *Il Penseroso* seems to have attracted him. He is author of a few sentimental songs, written chiefly in his younger years, which suggest sympathy with the naïve phase of the Elizabethan lyric. As an enthusiastically romantic love poet he readily falls into Petrarchan hyperboles and conceits— such extravagances as would delight the author of *The Arcadia*. Even the gently archaic titles in his most romantic volume, *The Wind among the Reeds* (1899), point to a fondness for the verse of Wyatt and Surrey. An example would be *The Lover Mourns for the Loss of Love*. But it is not here that his finest work nor his most important contribution to modern poetry lies. Yeats is primarily the author of some fifty or hundred highly memorable lyrics expressing at the same time a passionate heart and an ironical intellect. The result is a frankness, an honesty, and a realism not commonly found in romantic poetry but much sought for today. He pictures the inflammable human heart with the detached sagacity of an Oriental seer and with the satire and wit of a Swift or a Goldsmith. This combination of emotion, sensitivity, and critical acumen has won the admiration of a public devoted to rereading John Donne and his associates. Nor is it really plausible that Yeats himself arrived at his own position without some aid from these seventeenth-century masters.

His poetry, to be sure, shows only a few verbal borrowings and contains few allusions to the movement. Once he expresses his contempt for the crowd in the words of one of the most indefatigable aristocrats in verse, Ben Jonson. Yeats will stand "beyond the fling of the dull ass's hoof." He hastens to add, "Ben Jonson's phrase." One is reminded of Jonson in other of Yeats's poems, such as *The Leaders of the Crowd*, where the bold, almost prosaic diction resembles the great Elizabethan, although Yeats's plea for the philosophical recluse contrasts with Jonson's defense of the sulking lion sharpening his claws in retirement. Yeats's most distinctive verse comes the closest, however, to Donne and to the pithiest work of his immediate followers. A phrase presumably derived from Donne is "household spies," words found with a similar context in one of Donne's finest elegies. While Yeats never elaborates conceits as Donne does in his longer poems, he does resemble the Donne of the shortest lyrics and the most dramatic of the lyrical sonnets.

Responsibilities, published in 1914, represents with its trenchant realism a new note in English poetry. In literary history it ranks with the *Lyrical Ballads* of over a hundred years before. It is significant that this volume concludes with the quotation from Ben Jonson. Significant also is its appearance shortly after the first revival of popular enthusiasm for John Donne as promoted by the scholarship of Professor Grierson. In this volume occur the oft-quoted lines:

> And I may dine at journey's end
> With Landor and with Donne.

Yeats has something in common with the grave and eloquent romantic, Landor, but clearly it is with the poet whose name closes the lyric (*To a Young Beauty*) that Yeats owes most. The first poem in *Responsibilities* praises his early friends who had chiefly studied the Jacobean masters of the intellectual lyric:

> You kept the Muses' sterner laws,
> And unrepenting faced your ends,
> And therefore earned the right—and yet
> Dowson and Johnson most I praise—
> To troop with those the world's forgot,
> And copy their proud steady gaze.

In *A Coat*, the last poem in *Responsibilities*, Yeats declares that he will throw off his cloak embroidered from old mythologies:

> For there's more enterprise
> In walking naked.

Whether or not he remembered Donne's superb phrase, "a naked thinking heart," there can be small doubt that he owed his predecessor a considerable debt in the formation of his bitter, new style.

This style signifies a departure from both the sentimental and the coolly rationalistic verse of his predecessors, and in its stead comes a complete fusion of intense thought and feeling. In his earliest volume, published twenty-five years before *Responsibilities*, some few poems very close to this style appear, but they stand in a marked minority. During the nineteen-twenties his increasing devotion to mysticism often threatened to put an end to the most vigorous vein in his own verse. But Yeats entered all the chambers of human thought, including mysticism, without incarcerating himself in any. Not even the charms of mysticism proved sufficiently strong to control his entire powers. In *Michael Robartes and the Dancer* (1921) appeared some political poems rivaling in intellectual and emotional energy the best of Donne's satires. His powers in the short, highly critical lyric seem steadily to increase, through the series entitled *A Man Young and Old* to his highly effective *Words for Music Perhaps*. The latter series contains poems on the symbolical Crazy Jane and may be considered to include also the group *A Woman Young and Old*. Not one of these pieces, to be sure, is modeled closely on a sixteenth- or seventeenth-century poem or shows extensive verbal indebtedness to Donne and his school. Many of them express a mystical or metaphysical doctrine foreign to Donne's. They are so original as to indicate a new way of writing. And yet as poetry they show how valuable to a truly imaginative mind an earlier tradition may become. Yeats is an heir to Donne in spirit.

In his literary character Yeats has some more specific likenesses to Donne which probably represent not only accidental similarities but a sympathetic reading of the Elizabethan. In

Her Anxiety, for example, Yeats's insistence on love as inevitably wearing itself out suggests one of Donne's favorite biological theories. Something of Donne's macabre imagery and sense of the terror of death appears in such pieces as *Crazy Jane Grown Old Looks at the Dancers* and *The Mother of God*. When Yeats ends a poem with a reference to the biblical text concerning the lion and the honeycomb, he quotes a verse especially beloved by Donne. His poem *Towards Break of Day* in its imagery and frankness suggests Donne's remarkable erotic lyric, *The Dream*. Such a bold metaphor as "ram them with the sun" has a distinctly reminiscent flavor. *The Second Coming* has weird imagery better known in Donne's religious poems and sermons. Finally, such lines as Yeats's prologue to *Responsibilities* and *An Irish Airman Foresees His Death* have a manly directness and persuasive force which Yeats could have found in no book so readily as in Donne's poems.

However much Yeats really owed to the intellectual lyric of the age of Donne—and there can never be a precise estimate of such a debt—the character of his obligation contrasts with that of several of his contemporaries who have followed more pedantically in the footsteps of Donne, Drayton, Spenser, Milton, and other of the learned poets of the Renaissance. To the distinctly literary poets of the age of Dante, Chaucer, Lydgate, and Skelton, learned poetry in one form or another was a rule rather than an exception. Spenser and Milton were deemed successful by their first readers largely because of their ability to display a wide learning. Abraham Cowley fairly smothered his verses in erudite commentary. The age of Dryden and Pope held bookishness in similar esteem. Learned poetry glossed by explanatory prose remained a commonplace from the *Odes* and the *Poly-Olbion* of Michael Drayton to the lyrics of William Collins. Classical or romantic paraphrase or allusion was deemed necessary in the high style, delightful in the low. Learned poetry passed out of fashion, though never really out of use, only with the ascendency of romantic sentimentalism and the rise of the democratic Muse.

Those poets of our own day, as Yeats, who not only possess wide learning but have made something of a boast of it, have shown a particular affection for the verse of the latter Middle Ages and the early Renaissance. This is the field most congenial to Ezra Pound and T. S. Eliot. That Eliot's poetry has often become a composite of paraphrase and allusion is too obvious a point to bear emphasis. That his treatment of learning contains little new and much in keeping with Elizabethan humanism seems to have attracted less general attention. References to Shakespeare and his fellow dramatists, to Donne, Spenser, and Milton crowd the pages of his poetry from his earliest volume through his *Waste Land*. The last-mentioned poem represents the climax of his work in this academic and esoteric vein. Thereafter he has been at times equally obscure, but never quite so allusory.

Not only have most periods witnessed learned poetry; they have witnessed some debates as to its propriety and use. They have attempted to answer the question of when it is pedantic, esoteric, and socially futile, when really original, fresh, and invigorating. In the last few years, judging from the works produced, it appears that some of the most ardent practitioners of learned poetry have had serious qualms as to their more extreme and fantastic practice of the art. Learning they have seen to resemble sugar, useful, but easily cast on too thickly. There can be no simplified rules or theories as to the application of the more intellectual spice: criticism may offer general advice, but not recipes in the manner of a cookbook. No account of the Elizabethan poetic heritage, however, seems complete without a backward glance at this general attitude toward poetic tradition itself. Eliot is a neo-Elizabethan not only through his critical essays and his own detail, but because of his occasionally excessive reliance upon poetic tradition and the general resources of a library. Spenser—though hardly Shakespeare—may be fancied as a child curled up among ancient tomes, as Eliot in his *Animula* pictures himself curled "in the window seat behind the Encyclopædia Britannica." Yeats resembles Shakespeare, the wiser man and more felicitous poet, since his reading was put to more substantial human use and at no time made the display of empty vanity.

FROM THE AUGUSTANS

A distinguished group of writers best represented in England by the three Sitwells—Sacheverell, Edith, and Osbert—and in America by Wallace Stevens represents at once a brilliant experimentalism and an unmistakable indebtedness to the late Renaissance. While the number of these writers is not great, their debt is equally broad and profound. As students they are quite as much aware of art and society as of mere literature and more conscious of Europe as a whole than of provincial England. Either the aesthete or the sociologist is better qualified to view their inheritance than the historian or the philosopher, for they are more concerned with taste and manners than with accurate statements or serious ideas. They show no fondness for a single period limited so narrowly as the reign of Elizabeth or the lifetime of Shakespeare; knowing precisely what they wish, they are willing to go far afield to procure it. Cosmopolitan urbanity and aristocratic elegance mean more to them than fondness for a single land or generation. Their enthusiasm is for the courtly or upper-class culture of Europe and Great Britain during the entire baroque period from Mantegna to Mozart. To their fastidious taste the greater Elizabethans show an uncongenial exuberance of the intellectual, emotional, and imaginative life. They have more in common with the romances of Peele and Greene than with the plays of Shakespeare or Jonson. Youthful spirits and extreme vitality disturb their serenity. In English poetry Dryden and Pope, Marvell and Gay, best represent their ideals. The neoclassical period of the French eighteenth century as represented by Chardin, Houdon, and Haydn pleases them most. They like definite patterns in women's dress, cherish the memory of the minuet, prefer a perfumed atmosphere to a natural one and silk breeches to woolen trousers. They are suspected also of preferring a certain past to a confused present. To hostile critics they appear decadent, affected, and obscure. Even to themselves they sometimes seem futile, esoteric, and obsolete. But to their admirers and to themselves in their own happier moments they are the cream of our age— the rest, skimmed milk. Such is the general outline of the present Sitwellian school as seen in relation to the past.

The most fascinating paradox of their position is the modernity of their technique in contrast with the antiquity of their ideals. Emphatically they put old wine in new bottles. While much of their thought and feeling remains a faithful imitation of Augustan precedent, their form is as radically new as form well can be. Their versification, for example, proves as a rule most original. Alexander Pope would certainly stare with amazement at such licentious verses as the syncopated lines of Edith's *Sir Beelzebub*. The Augustan couplet and the Augustan rhetoric are undiscoverable in the Sitwells and hardly discernible in Stevens. In short, they boldly attempt to continue much of the cultural tradition of the eighteenth century without literal imitation of older methods.

Moreover, the moderns have what might fairly be called a romantic view of the Augustans themselves. For the Augustans were at the same time less frivolous and less despairing than the Sitwellian school supposes. They were deeply concerned with materialistic achievements and sober thinking. No sound historian imagines them living in a dreamworld of pastoral dances, incessant wit, delicate serenades, and elegant play. Above all, in England eighteenth-century thought and life, deeply affected by the accession of the House of Orange and the Hanoverians, assumed a bourgeois complexion. English poetry of the period by Whig and Tory alike, Dryden and Pope, Swift and Thomson, reflects a society stirred by materialistic and imperial ambitions, based upon rising mercantilism and industry, and infused with a largely Protestant temper. As the age advanced the Gallic spirit burned consistently lower. A period ultimately accepting Doctor Johnson as its idol was no age of polite and idle trifling. Thus the Sitwells have not only skimmed the cream off the eighteenth century; they have whipped it into a baroque *meringue glacée.* Whatever value we may place upon the Sitwells' dilettante writing in biography, art, travel, and criticism, we must concede them justified in giving to poetry at least the things which they deem proper to poetry. Their task as poets is to use the Augustan heritage in their own creative art, not to attempt a judicially balanced picture of an age forever past.

If it be true, as Edith observes, that the Sitwell family derives from "the dead Angevin kings," it is not to be supposed that its members will remember only a part of their long and legendary past or that each will recall the same matter as the others. Sacheverell, for example, is clearly the most interested in the more remote times, since he has written at somewhat injudicious length on Gothic tapestries and early baroque architecture. Edith is more occupied with the Augustan tradition in its riper forms, while Osbert has special fondness for Palladian simplicities, for Hogarthian realism, and for the great age of the English novel. Sacheverell, most voluminous and discursive of the three poets, seems most at home in the times of Charles I, Edith (to use her own quaint language) in those of "the great Queen Anne," and Osbert among the early Hanoverians. However much the three agree in their literary tastes, the individuality of each determines the reading which he utilizes. Sacheverell, with a peculiarly abstract and masculine mind, derives most from the pastoral or strictly neoclassical poets and painters; Edith remembers best the most bitter and wittiest writers;

Osbert divides his attention about equally between the savage political satirists and the genial and sentimental authors of verse "characters." Although the verse of all three reflects an aristocracy of leisure, Sacheverell's strong tendency to abstraction dissuades him from the poetry of actual manners or, in other words, from the representation of a social class. The best work of Edith and Osbert, on the contrary, depicts the life of the English county family under conditions largely typical of the Augustan age. Sacheverell is the most prolific as a poet and the most literary and academic; he leaves little doubt as to the chief writers and painters on whom he leans most heavily. In this respect in particular he best represents the cultural traditions of the family and supplies the clearest picture of their common background. The poetry of the other two flows in narrower but swifter channels, duplicating something of Sacheverell's own art and adding their more markedly individual notes. Sacheverell's poetry tastes flat; it obviously lacks seasoning. To it Edith adds salt and vinegar and Osbert adds a certain amount of sugar. Anyone reading the three with their cultural background in mind accordingly does well to begin with Sacheverell.

While their diversified studies in the most brilliant spirit of dilettantism have carried them into many fields, it is clear that they owe most to the aristocratic traditions of the seventeenth and eighteenth centuries. Again not all three have pursued precisely the same course. Just as Sacheverell has delved further into medievalism than his companions, Edith has traveled more widely in the nineteenth century. While the romantic period has hardly influenced her as much as the Augustan, she has felt its spell strongly. Thus she has anthologized not only the Augustan school of English verse, but the romantic and the Victorian. Her numerous studies in the Victorian period have even been crowned by a biography of the Queen. Nevertheless the prose publications of all three show the superior attractions of the earlier age. Edith is author of a volume of criticism on Pope and a "biography" of the city of Bath; Osbert has written on Rowlandson; while Sacheverell has written at considerable length on the music, art, and architecture of the age. Here is their home of love, to which, however far they wander, they always return. For the old regime represented the last age of genteel culture uncontaminated by the obnoxious evils of modern society to which all these authors prove acutely sensitive. Without falling into the banal error of bluntly idealizing the past, they would find life unthinkable without their inheritance from their ancestral fields. Educated amid a wealth of material possessions owned by their family and their friends, they live more effectively in a dreamworld of the past than any other writers of their own country and incomparably more fully than any Americans. All are peculiarly poets of the land, but not of the land as seen by Walt Whitman or that lyrical tramp, W. H. Davies. The land for them is the typical estate of the British landowning aristocrat. As their poems eloquently remind us— Sacheverell's *Hortus Conclusus*, Edith's *Troy Park*, and Osbert's *England Reclaimed*—this British aristocracy is rapidly being interred by its own gardeners on their beautifully landscaped estates, perhaps the finest heritage ever bequeathed by a social class to posterity. For the England of the future to neglect the necessary care of these estates would be a crime against civilization similar to the neglect of the richly hereditary poetry of the Sitwells, which preserves not only an image of the landscape but an idealized reflection of the taste and manners of the old county places.

"I am no mystery, for what have I to hide?" writes Sacheverell in one of his poems clearly referring to himself. He remains, on the whole, a singularly open poet. Although he has experimented in a number of typical modern types of verse, he invariably returns to the type which he loves best. This is a poetry cool, austere, abstracted, and, as he himself understands it, classical. He many times states his ideal explicitly. He seeks "plumed gardens of the mind," an art where "Cupid and Psyche go forever kissing"; each poem becomes an "oaten tragedy," a "Claudian hour" (with reference, of course, to Claude Lorrain, not to the wicked Roman); each piece results from "toying with another figured shape." If he toys with ideas, it is only to drop them impatiently. Especially for a brief period in his career an intellectual poetry fashionable at the time intrigued him. Hence he wrote *Two Clowns' Psychology*, a debate on the rival merits of neglecting or challenging the Philistines, *Actor Rehearsing*, containing a few debts to modern psychology, and *The Thirteenth Caesar*, a thoughtful, effective, and forward-looking study in the tragic ills of military dictatorship. His *Doctor Donne and Gargantua*, a poem in six cantos, well exhibits, however, his habitual fondness for slipping away from troublesome intellectual or moral problems. This poem begins as a bizarre allegory of the rival claims of hedonism, science, and religion; it ends in a pastoral ballet. Doctor Donne and Gargantua not only make their peace but, judging from their abrupt departure from the action, fall asleep, while supernatural religion yields to an exclusive preoccupation with fauns, satyrs, and shepherds playing in pastoral and amorous beauty. The only reflection which the last two cantos leave in the reader's mind is stated more briefly in lyrics by Herrick and Ben Jonson: that beauty is more pleasing when naked than when adorned. Donne wholly forgets to pursue his star, Gargantua to seek his mandrake, and the poet to follow his lost theme. Whether Sacheverell regards his poem as literally finished is here beside the point. The last two cantos show his unwillingness to cling even humorously to an intellectual theme and his proneness to fall back upon a pleasant imagism.

The key to Sacheverell's inspired art is, then, his love for the school of garden poetry best represented by Andrew Marvell. Sacheverell, too, is a quietest, a lover of green thoughts in a green shade, always preferring an imaginative metaphor to a tragic passion. He writes:

> What dreams of other life than this
> Lived in another emphasis,
> Where boughs of lively coral turn
> To meadows by the river's urn?

Like Marvell, he writes coolly of the parliament of flowers. With him, also, he sings of flowers as "lamps in deepest dark" and of oranges burning in the trees. His typical poem on a sundial suggests not only Marvell's dial of flowers but many seventeenth-century metaphysical lyrics, as well as a famous image in Butler's *Hudibras*. Something of his love for "pure form" he acquired no doubt from current schools of art criticism, notably from Clive Bell. But being a highly sensitive poet, he turned primarily to the achievement itself as he discovered it in English verse from Peele to Marvell and to Pope. One sees him as a studious lover of Milton's pastorals. His *Hortus Conclusus* contains poems which he avows to be imitations of Marlowe, Peele, Milton, Pope, Lyly, Herrick, and Browne. It would be more revealing, however, to say that his lyrics were inspired by the manner of these poets than that they are in strict imitation of their style. The Sitwells at their best follow the spirit, not the letter, of the past. Their object is not to echo or reproduce, but to assimilate the older works into their own individual or modern idiom.

Of Robert Greene's verse Sacheverell writes: "His poetry, or that of Nashe or Marlowe, has always appealed more to me than the work of Keats or Shelley, because it is less occupied with spiritual recipes for remaining unhappy and misunderstood. The bold premises of these former men were uttered without the hope of contradiction, and with a surer eye and ear for beauty. Listen to this madrigal by Roberto Greene . . .

The swans, whose pens as white as ivory,
eclipsing fair Endymion's silver love,
floating like snow down by the banks of Po,
ne'er tuned their notes, like Leda once forlorn,
with more despairing sorts of madrigals,
than I, whom wanton Love hath with his god
pricked to the Court of deep and restless thoughts.

This carries you, in the space of a tiny instant, to the absolute fountain of poetry, and it is not necessary towards that objective to quote the madrigal in its entirety. . . . They are not positively the last words, but almost the first few syllables in the paradisaical language of poetry; but whatever may be their degree of merit, they are unmistakably in the right dialect."

To inquire into the exact meaning of all terms in Sacheverell's criticism is hardly wise. The important thing is that he seeks an "absolute" and "paradisaical" poetry and finds it in Greene's poem. The passage in question, differently spaced, he works into the second canto of *Doctor Donne and Gargantua*, where it serves both as motto and beginning. His poetry serenely moves through the forest of the dying swan, the burning phoenix, the captured unicorn. No lover of strenuous action, unlike Shakespeare he depicts Antony solely in the relaxing company of the Queen of Egypt; while to celebrate Alexander the Great he is forced to picture him after death in a sort of Mohammedan paradise of luxury and idleness.

Both his ideal of poetry and its origin in the neoclassical and baroque tradition which he knows so well appear strikingly in his ambitious work, *Canons of Giant Art: Twenty Torsos in Heroic Landscapes*. Although a minority of these admirable torsos depict pastoral characters, the spirit is as aloof, abstract, and idealized as his own garden or "paradisaical" verse. The first and the last of the torsos indicate the two opposite and extreme limits of the poet's mood, beyond which he never deviates. Here the clearest inspiration comes from painting rather than from earlier poetry. The two painters selected indicate the historical period with which Sacheverell throughout his poetry shows closest sympathy. Mantegna died at the beginning of the sixteenth century, Claude Lorrain at the end of the seventeenth. Mantegna is here celebrated for his austere detachment from the violent actions which he often depicts and for a high serenity and superciliousness often called by the Renaissance itself magnanimity. Whether or not these observations are historically just, they are deeply imaginative and aesthetically convincing. Mantegna affords Sacheverell a true poetic vision and one highly significant for the explanation of his own art. This austerity dominates all the graver pieces in the poems which follow, such as *Agamemnon's Tomb, The Laocoon of El Greco,* and *Upon an Image from Dante.*

The concluding piece, *Grande Adagio: the Enchanted Palace,* is developed from a picture by Claude. The mood is a harmony of Parnassian grandeur, elegant langour, and luxurious melancholy—in short, the mood equally exploited in Claude's pictures and Sacheverell's poems and dominant in a vast amount of the poetry and painting of the later Renaissance. It is, however, the mood not of the second birth of classical culture, but of its second decline and fall. To the sunset hues of a great tradition Sacheverell's poetry appears as the final seal. That shadows similar to those of Poe fall upon Claude's castle is for Sacheverell the merest accident; it is to the Renaissance rather than to romantic or classical springs that he goes to fill his own melancholy urn. "The Claudian hour" is studiously composed of seventeenth- and eighteenth-century elements. Here are allusions to favorite subjects of Augustan art: Harlequin stands beside Virgil's tomb, Psyche weeps by moonlight to the accompaniment of an adagio serenade in rooms decorated with Italian frescoes.

O seek not the reason, let it have its way,
We will lie in the moonlight and look upon the windows.
The palace is the soul of man,
Deserted, now,
But haunted in the moonlight,
In the Claudian hour,
The hour of ilex and of nightingale;
No more a shore of mourning,
Every window burns,
The waves are bright with lanterns for the serenade;
For the palace stands in water,
With long colonnades to cool the sea born wind,
High doors of stateliness, and painted ceilings
In Italian histories of street and tavern
Transmuted by magic to this palace air.
They show on balconies above stone doors,
And their lingering music in the curtain folds
Fills the volutes and the fluttering ends,
While trumpet and mandoline, like trophies formed,
Are the fine heraldry of this rare existence.

Although this scene, being the last of the *Canons of Giant Art*, is fittingly more crepuscular than most, its mood is not essentially unlike that of other of the poems, such as the lovely elegy for Cephalus and Procris, the disillusioned poem entitled *Bohemund, Prince of Antioch*, and the glowing *Landscape with the Giant Orion*, the last suggested by a picture by Poussin. Still other "torsos" are developed from paintings of the neoclassical school.

The best of the Sitwellian poems are serenades sung in the twilight of a vanishing culture deeply convinced of its own futility. In this respect *Bohemund, Prince of Antioch*, proves a typical figure. Bohemund, a surprising intruder into the subject matter of English poetry, was, Sacheverell asserts, a medieval prince with small ability or integrity but with a certain capacity for the enjoyment of life. He is now capriciously honored by Sicilian peasants in their traditional puppet shows. Puppet and Harlequin, Punch and Pierrot, Jack in the Box and Scaramouch, prove among the familiar figures in the Sitwellian world which conceives life itself as a trivial mechanism. From such a poem we see clearly how this art is an echo's echo: an imitation of an art itself an imitation of another art; in other words, a re-Renaissance and as little as possible a fresh image of contemporary life.

Sacheverell's poems are incense burned in reverence of Augustanism. The first page of his *Collected Poems* dismisses the contemporary public as a savage herd. When a very young man Sacheverell joined the other two poets of his family in social satire, but he soon weaned himself from his bitterness, preferring a genteel moan to a shrill cry. His pages almost immediately transport us into the old Hampton Court world which earlier produced *The Rape of the Lock*. So phenomenally sensitive are all the Sitwells to the poets, artists, and musicians of the Augustan age. Sacheverell's second poem introduces an old, sentimental dowager, his third reads like a reminiscence of the eighteenth-century *Bath Guide*. We are shortly acquainted with Pierrot, the ballet and the trapeze, a belated mythology, a multitude of statues, fountains, gardens, parasols, nursemaids, and gay importations from the Far East, not the five-and-ten-cent trinkets from modern Japan but the elegant Oriental importations from eighteenth-century China. In *Church and Stage* Sacheverell displays the love of serenity and hatred of enthusiasm, especially in matters religious, characterizing the best of Augustan thought. In his charming *Hochzeit of Hercules* he depicts that primitive hero as an elegant dandy, the perspiration wiped forever from his limbs. Nothing in his world possesses a utilitarian value; all has a fine, cool glitter. His poem *At Breakfast* reminds one of Pope's couplet on country life:

Or o'er cold coffee trifle with the spoon,
Count the slow clock, and dine exact at noon.

Like the Augustans themselves, Sacheverell turns to whatever is
artful and confined: to the fantasies of the circus tent, to the
glamour of playing cards, to life reflected in a looking glass.

His actual references to the poets and artists of the age become numerous. One receives an impression that the entire
Sitwell family was born behind the scenes at a performance of
Mozart's *Figaro*. Sacheverell's *Italian Air* is a lyric based wholly
upon this favorite opera. Figaro steps forth again in the last lines
of the second song in his masterpiece, *Hortus Conclusus*:

Till those plumes come,
He will pace his Kingdom by loud starlight
On tiptoe past the windows
Listening to the harp's loud beat,
In case a sash should open while music masks the noise,
And Cherubino, in a flash of stars, be gone again.

Sacheverell sighs for "this virtuoso music, heartless and brilliant." Handel he remembers in his *New Water Music*, although the poem leans also upon the imagery of Shakespeare's
Antony and Cleopatra, whose barge, Sacheverell reminds us,
"burned on the waters."

His songs, certainly among his finest compositions, imitate the
seventeenth-century lyric more closely and successfully than do
those of any living poet. His delicate collection entitled *Sere-*
nades, for example, stands remarkably close to the music of the
Stuart masques. The imitation is highly intelligent and never
servile. The first line, "Sigh soft, sigh softly," was presumably
suggested by a song in Ben Jonson's masquelike drama, *Cyn-*
thia's Revels. These lyrics, like their predecessors, are each of a
mood, with auditory images, calculated echoes, repetitions and
variations of phrase, a pastoral language throughout, and a care-

fully designed harmonious conclusion. Several of his songs follow their originals in depicting the graceful movement of fountains. They prove how thoroughly their author is in tune with the notable revival of English music from Byrd to Purcell. Sacheverell's *Village Bard* is written in direct imitation of the innumerable odes for Saint Cecilia's Day composed in the seventeenth and eighteenth centuries.

The architecture, painting, statuary, and gardening derived from the neoclassical age prove among the most common subjects in his verse. One series of lyrics, *Exalt the Eglantine*, is suggested by "lines inlaid in marquetry upon a table at Hardwick Hall." A majority of his poems suggest the favorite neoclassical maxim: *ut pictura, poesis*. Indeed, he even surpasses his models since he describes not only nature but pictures, assuming the role of a more poetic Ruskin or Pater. *Bolsover Castle*, one of his best and most typical works, is descriptive poetry of the school of Jonson's *Penshurst*, Marvell's *Appleton House*, Thomson's *Seasons*, and Pope's *Windsor Forest*. George Crabbe describes the same scene in one of his best poems, *The Patron*. *Bolsover Castle* summarizes many aspects of its author's neoclassicism. He reminds us, for example, in a foreword, that "William Cavendish, first Duke of Newcastle, entertained Charles I at Bolsover Castle in 1634 with a performance of Ben Jonson's masque of *Love's Welcome*, for which Inigo Jones designed an elaborate stage setting." The piece describes the castle and especially the ruined Caroline banqueting hall. It depicts also a statue of Venus placed by a fountain in the court and recounts a typical day of the idle dwellers in this latter-day Eden. Such a poetical review of a day's leisure at a country house Swift gallantly presented to one of his Irish hosts two centuries before.

Description plays an uncommonly important part in Sacheverell's work. Following the tradition established by Virgil's *Georgics* (and one might add by Hesiod and Homer), Sachev-

erell delights in describing a harvest, a scene naturally attractive to a garden poet. Thus he has pictures of harvests of grape,
apple, and cherry. His *Comendador Turns Burlador*, painting a
grape harvest in a Spanish cloister, is as typical as it is brilliant.
Largely based on what appears to have been the poet's own
observations, the piece describes the ancient architecture as
well as the traditional activities of the monks and like *Bolsover
Castle* comes to its focus in an animated description of a statue.
Like Keats, Sacheverell describes a Greek vase, but his account
is more in the manner of eighteenth-century verse essayists than
in that of the romantic poet. His *Eckington Woods* ("for my
brother who walks there every day") falls halfway between the
subjective sketching of Henry Vaughan's *Priory Walk* and the
objective painting of Pope's *Windsor Forest*. Repeatedly parts
of poems suggest eighteenth-century painting. The swing, for
example, mentioned in *Thoughts in a High Wind Sailing a
Boat* (the wind seems not to have been *too* high) suggests
well-known scenes by Fragonard, Boucher, and other French
painters. His occasional African sketches, as *Three Nights in
Fez*, remind one in their vivid and exotic imagery of the descriptive elements in William Collins's *Persian Eclogues*. The
poet is fond of describing dances, as in his verses on the festivals
of the god Krishna. Sometimes description for Sacheverell embraces several arts including music, as when in one poem he
writes:

> . . . to soft music planned
> We had Italian pantomine by torchlight on the water.

His passion for description certainly leads him at times, as it
led his Augustan forerunners, to superficiality and even to
absurdity. Thus his *Studies in the Black Keys*, nominally dealing with the Negroes of Tennessee, betrays as dark an ignorance
of his literal subject as any poet has ever exhibited.

Since his own verse is modeled upon the Augustans more in

spirit than in technique, it is unprofitable to remark at length specific parallels between phrases in the new verse and in the old. It must be obvious, nevertheless, that he stands in debt not only to the great masters of architecture, painting, and music, to Inigo Jones, to Claude, and to Mozart, but to the English poets. He freely acknowledges his neoclassical favorites, especially Peele, Greene, Marlowe, Lyly, Herrick, Browne, and the Milton of *Comus* and *Il Penseroso*. Although he says little of Fletcher, Dryden, and Marvell, he has profited from knowing them, especially Marvell, with whom he has a closer affinity than with any other poet. Nor has he forgotten "the sweet nightingale of Twickenham." The most modernistic and least typical of his works is the psychopathic study, *Actor Rehearsing*. Yet this in itself suggests the old stage of masque and tragi-comedy and is virtually a meditation upon the closing lines of Pope's *Dunciad*. These not only give the poem its motto, but actually make up the last four lines. Sacheverell works them brilliantly into the pattern of his own verse. In his charming mythological tales in *Canons of Giant Art*, such as *Cephalus and Procris*, *Landscape with the Giant Orion*, and *Battles of the Centaurs*, he closely approximates Renaissance adaptations of Ovid from Golding to Dryden. His songs, often Jonsonian, come closer, perhaps, to the work of such a minor but still memorable poet as that favorite of Charles I, William Cartwright. Cartwright, also, cultivated a cool, aristocratic, and imaginative art. His baroque and sentimental verses on Theseus and Ariadne, for example, well exhibit the affinity between the Augustan and the modern spirit. They might with equal ease have been used as a libretto for Richard Strauss's beautiful Mozartian opera, *Ariadne on Naxos*, or as model for lyrical or narrative verse by Sacheverell Sitwell.

The disillusionment which Sacheverell finds pleasant and sweet to caress inspires in his still more brilliant sister a crackling flame of hard wit. Pope, Prior, Gay, and Swift supply not a little inspiration. The disillusionment which remains everywhere her theme is about equally indebted to exigencies of the life which she leads in the present and to romantic and neoclassical traditions. But the romantic poets seldom lose sight of a faith which Edith has wholly discarded. It is therefore from the neoclassicists that she learns most of the thought and expression that all is vanity and that the wise course is to live, as it were, outside life. Repeatedly she expresses her position, as when she writes of a cold air lost and wandering, of a remote and legendary spirit, of lotus-eaters on whose cold lips the past lingers like a perfume. She envisages a life aimless as wisteria blossoms falling in the rain. The writers of the age of Queen Anne, as Edith observes, said something like this superlatively well. With a happy simplicity unknown to Edith, Gay had written:

> Life is a jest; and all things show it;
> I thought so once; but now I know it.

Moreover Edith herself concedes all too eagerly the superior charms of Queen Anne, whose life she symbolizes by perfumed breezes wafted by eighteenth-century fans. Well, whether or not life was just this to the unfortunate lady, undoubtedly the important thing is that Edith says so and that she has throughout her life meditated upon the Queen's portrait. Her poems are baroque monuments to a romantic longing for the older world. As she herself well observes, the English country houses are inhabited less by the living than by the dead. Nursing her poetic dreams, she hears the garments of ghosts sweeping their deserted floors. Paradoxically, she loves the eighteenth-century life best because from that century she best learns not to love life at all.

Much more frank, nervous, and compressed in her expression than Sacheverell, she comes far closer than he to the stinging pointedness of the Queen Anne wits: only her romantic lack of restraint keeps her from nearing it still more. Unlike the work of Sacheverell and Osbert, her poetry bristles with Augustan allusions. Her first love is also Mozart. Palestrina, Handel, and Scarlatti she also celebrates in rhyme. She recalls the old musical instruments, such as the lute, the dulcimer, the virginals, the spinet, and the *chapeau chinois*. Her poems have the air of a concert on old strings. They resemble sad, cold madrigals. They contain fewer allusions than Sacheverell's to the fine arts of architecture, painting, and sculpture as practiced by the Augustans, but vastly more references to the more decorative and socialized arts and crafts. While he, it seems, admired the Louvre, she explored the Musée des Arts Decoratif. Of her delight in eighteenth-century costume there is no end. Her life itself seems an elegy on dead fashions. Not only her longest poem, the fairy tale *The Sleeping Beauty*, but the majority of her verses concern ladies of the court. She depicts perfumed silks, dresses of sarcenet, Cupid in Oriental trousers, angels clad in mohair, trees like periwigs, buttercups like glazed chintz, silk pavilions of the waves, waterfalls of sprigged muslin, forests of green baize, sheep periwigged like William and Mary, leaves resembling the petticoats of Alsatians, and the sun as a gold and peruked conqueror. Bushes seem to her like gauze parasols, winding roads have dust like gilded bindings made for *Paul et Virginie*. The perfumed dressing table of the Dowager Queen in *The Sleeping Beauty* strongly suggests Belinda's toilet in *The Rape of the Lock*. The scene breathes odors of pomander. Beneath the dressing table plays the Dowager's beloved griffin, Dido, Queen of Carthage. In this society, as in the pictures of the times, appear numerous Negro servants and even dwarfs, kept more for curiosity than for use. The Dowager is commonly seen with her missal and her parrot, although the parrot is stuffed and only thought by the old woman to be alive. (The poetry, all suggestions to the contrary, remains alive and not stuffed.) Pompously dressed monkeys from time to time appear. The poet lingers affectionately over old dances, as the minuet, pavane, saraband, polka, mazurka, and hornpipe. She refers to many old games like ombre and quadrille. Even for things still in use the old name is often preferred, as when, apparently with a memory of Pope, she depicts the Queen's dwarfs drinking bohea.

Edith's elegies on the Bourbon age abound, as does the polite literature of that period itself, with scornful or amused pictures of the servant and middle classes. They contain many a bucolic clown. Jane, the kitchenmaid, is on different occasions the object of ridicule and condescension. Aubade depicts Jane's awkwardness, while lines to Jane in The Sleeping Beauty are softened by a perceptible tenderness. Popular superstitions, and particularly those current in the seventeenth and eighteenth centuries, give life to a considerable number of her bizarre productions, as, for example, to her "bucolic comedy," Three Poor Witches.

The furniture of her mind is old, her most natural mode of conveyance the sedan chair. But her spirit is hardly less Augustan. Her disillusionment places in her hand not the sledge hammer of the typical pessimist but a jeweled knife, for her mind has been sharpened by close contact with the Queen Anne wits. From Swift, Gay, and their associates she learns the habit of seeing life through a diminishing glass. She symbolizes the world as a toy ball of gold, hard, dry, and barren of love. People are half-human puppets. Life is a hurdy-gurdy waltz. The sun is a bucolic mime; the moon, a bucolic clown. She declares that hell has no vastness. We are merely weeping marionettes. In Clown Argheb's Song she views poetry and philosophy as mere greenhouse growths. Philosophy she depicts elsewhere as a mountebank and a blind bat. Serious human words are vain, a mere tinsel and meaningless jargon. A man is a mere Jumping Jack. The Doll is a profoundly disillusioned poem viewing faith as a child's folly, in Pope's stinging words, "all that the nurse has taught." In scores of images the vastness of nature is belittled by imagery drawn from the arts, as when she writes of gilded and rococo waves. The philosophy of life, in short, remains identical with that of *The Rape of the Lock*. That Pope is also the author of idealistic verse, Edith seems not to recall. Even the funeral elegy suffers a sad diminution at her hands. One of her wittiest poems (and there can hardly be any wittier) is a burlesque elegy of a dead hen.

Edith is much less pedantic in her literary allusions than Sacheverell. One poem she properly describes as an imitation of Skelton. Like her younger brother, she praises the French Pléiade. She adds the name of Margaret of Navarre. Dryden she quotes at least once. But this gives no conception of the value which the Augustan poets possess for her. Her prose, especially her critical volume on Pope, as well as her anthologies, proves this. It would be unthinkable for so skillful a poet to enjoy, as she clearly does, all the manners and fine arts of the times and to escape the influence of her predecessors in her own art. And she has neglected neither the intervening age of the romantics nor her own times. The fox trot is as familiar to her as the minuet. She writes as an Augustan poet might be imagined to write had he drunk an elixir of immortality and remained the being that he was in the times of Queen Anne, but youthfully sensitive to the present century.

Although Osbert is neither so historically minded nor so poetically gifted as his brother and sister, he plays a consistent role in their neo-Augustan trinity. His appreciation of the fine arts has not chilled his verses as it chills his brother's. His masculine mind rejects his sister's enthusiasm for the effeminate eighteenth-century bric-a-brac. Yet he has written some garden and fountain poetry almost as abstract and brilliant as Sacheverell's poems modeled on the school of Marvell; and with the manlier aspects of eighteenth-century thought he has more in common than Edith. His satires maintain a ferocity which Edith attains only once, namely, in her *Gold Coast Customs*. And his political satire comes remarkably close to lampooning by Swift. His *England Reclaimed*, generally regarded as his best work, is a series of character sketches of the servants surrounding the English country-house aristocracy. A gardener, a carpenter, a servant girl, and a score of others pass before a gaze as cool and keen as that of Cowper and Crabbe, as witty and genial as that of Addison and Steele. Although the meters are modern, the metaphors are conceits of which Fuller, Walton, and other men of the seventeenth century might have been proud. Osbert states his purpose to be a literary record of rapidly vanishing representative types. But his people are no more obsolete than those similarly described in Chaucer's *Prologue*. Fundamentally this series of eclogues expresses the genial side of its author and of the human spirit tried by such natural ills as flesh is heir to. Secondarily it is neither personal nor universal, but Augustan. Its colloquial style comes closest to the easy, fluent vein of such wits as Gay or Prior. Any one of Osbert's eclogues may be compared with Prior's affectionate lines to his lifelong mistress, Jinny. The book belongs to a type of writing—the verse character—never so widely or successfully cultivated either in verse or prose as in the Augustan period. It preserves the image of a culture belonging not to the age of Wells and Galsworthy but to that of Henry Fielding and Doctor Johnson. Two or three times, it may be noted, Edith also cultivates this vein. Thus her portrait of the tragically trivial governess, Mademoiselle Richarde, in *Troy Park*, is one of her most human poems; while *Colonel Fantock*, in the same collection, being at the same time autobiographical and biographical, unites the happiest graces of Wordsworth's introspections with Prior's incomparable poetry of manners. These two pieces, obviously exceptional in Edith's repertoire, conform to a venerable genre cultivated much more widely, if no more successfully, by Osbert.

Although the rare conjunction of family tradition and genius present in the Sitwells has produced results almost impossible to duplicate, a fastidious poetry infused with the Augustan spirit is still occasionally written by others, and by none more successfully than the American poet Wallace Stevens, one of the wittiest and most exacting of modern craftsmen. Stevens is author of three volumes, *Harmonium*, *Ideas of Order*, and *The Man with the Blue Guitar*. The first and longest of these is both the most attractive and the most clearly under the Augustan spell. His later verse greatly enlarges a theme only occasionally present in his first book—the analysis of the aesthetic attitude. His poems on this subject, whatever may be their style or merit, have a subjective vision and a philosophical method closer to Wordsworth and Coleridge than to Pope and Dryden or, in other words, closer to *The Prelude* than to *The Essay on Criticism*.

Stevens shows an interest in the French language and the French spirit that makes him especially accessible to Augustan influences, since the French spirit dominated European culture throughout the eighteenth century. *Harmonium* contains striking evidence of his Gallic predilections. He alludes to travels in France. Four of the poems bear titles in French. Several contain phrases or even lines in that language. The number of French words boldly introduced proves quite extraordinary; and he shows a fondness for other words unusual in English and common in French. One poem is prefaced by a quotation from the *Revue des Deux Mondes*. The French classics are obviously in his thought, as evidenced when the resounding surf on the Californian shore reminds him of the eloquence of Racine or Bossuet. English custom, on such occasions, is to evoke the memory of Milton.

Stevens is a better exponent of the Augustan spirit than the leading Sitwells, as witty as Edith, as detached as Sacheverell, and a more impeccable artist than either. To be sure, he rarely alludes to the *ancien régime*. His title *Gallant Chateau* is one of his closest approximations. He seldom paraphrases or refers to the older writers. It is typical of his school of thought, however, that he cannot resist specific allusion to Bach and Mozart. One is not surprised to find him referring to "the mountainous coiffures of Bath." His *Peter Quince at the Clavier*, one of his best-known lyrics, although without definite allusions was certainly suggested by works of Augustan musicians and by old paintings of Susanna and the Elders. Without imitating the actual technique and without specifically acknowledging his debt to the thought and spirit of the Augustan age, he follows paths which he knows to have been laid out by a European culture at its height two centuries ago. To examine this condition more fully it is necessary to consider the spirit rather than the body of his work, to view his end rather then his means, to remember his distinctly traditional view of art and life, and to forget his emphatically modern technique.

The theory of Augustan poetry observed by its typical leaders, Pope, Prior, and Gay, dictated a neatness of expression, an agile wit, a cool heart, a critical spirit, a deal of the salt of satire, an aristocratic temper, and a meticulous avoidance of vulgarity. It preferred a strictly humanistic outlook, an urban and a cosmopolitan spirit, an adaptability to town and country life, and a disillusionment that abhorred uncontrolled enthusiasms. These are not vague generalities, but definite standards. And in his own peculiar idiom Stevens satisfies them as fully as any poet of the eighteenth century. While he also achieves certain romantic and distinctly modernistic attitudes, the best part of his art remains a splendid vindication of the Augustan tradition as perfected in France and more or less successfully imported into England. Stevens is not only an aesthete seeking for a perfection of style and taste in life and art; he values a particular kind of style and taste. Expression must be clean, economical, cheerful—in a word, neat. In significant collaboration with Stevens his publisher has produced his poetry in volumes almost as exquisite in taste as the work itself.

In *The Comedian as the Letter C*, one of his longer pieces devoted to a discussion of his own artistic principles, Stevens makes a number of helpful observations. He seeks, he tells us, a style "desperately clear." These may seem strange words from a writer generally regarded as singularly precious and difficult to understand. But Stevens does not aspire to the dramatic clarity of Molière. He refers to a lucidity perceived only by the specially qualified reader to whom his works are addressed. For while Stevens prefers a social aristocracy, he emphatically demands an intellectual one. He even hopes to carry his neatness to new heights of perfection, striving for "beautiful barenesses as yet unseen." Stevens means that each word must be fastidiously chiseled and in its exact place. Hence his shorter poems resemble the epigrams or inscriptions so popular on monuments throughout the neoclassical period. Not only tombs and statues, but every manner of object from garden seats to books suffered this rage for inscription. Over a score of pieces by Pope fall into the category. A considerable reputation in this coveted art was achieved by that cool and competent poet, Mark Akenside. Although our social customs deprive Stevens of the opportunity to write formal inscriptions as these were freely used in the Augustan age, several of his poems achieve the ideal of such a style. Such are *The Snow Man, From the Misery of Don Joost, The Worms at Heaven's Gate, Nomad Exquisite,* and *The Death of a Soldier.* It is noteworthy in this connection that *Harmonium* includes a series of sixteen epigrams, or witty couplets, headed *New England Verses.*

Stevens's poetry resembles that of Prior and Gay not only in the prevalence but in the quality of its wit—a tone smooth and polite, a temper sharp, disillusioned, and ironical. Speaking of the ideal poet, Stevens remarks, "Nota: his soil is man's intelligence." Even his tender elegy, *Two at Norfolk,* shows a keen mind. Where he depicts a meeting between two lovers, as in *Two Figures in Dense Violet Light,* we recognize his characters as equally humorous and intelligent. Here one lover pleads with the other to speak, even if the words are utterly trivial. The same thought, more wittily expressed, appears in *The Plot against the Giant*. Even the titles of the poems in *Harmonium* are among the most delightfully witty and imaginative that any poet has devised. His amused irony appears to advantage in that distinctly cosmopolitan little poem in which a young German girl explains that her plan during her courtship to decorate a black dress with bright trimmings is no romantic folly. In *The Weeping Burgher* the poet, apparently speaking in his own person, acknowledges the strange malice that leads him to distort the world. Such a mock-heroic poem as *Cortège for Rosenbloom*, with its sharp irony and fantastic imagery from animals and flowers, is identical in spirit with Gay's *Fables*. When describing starlight, Stevens consciously describes his own verse:

> A sheaf of brilliant arrows flying straight
> Flying and falling straightway for their pleasure,
> Their pleasure that is all bright-edged and cold . . .

With the temper of the true wit and aristocrat, he hates above all else banality. Shun banality as you would shun the plague, is the meaning of any number of his most imaginative pieces, such as *Banal Sojourn* and *In the Clear Season of Grapes*. He mocks the prosaic rationalists who envisage all things in cubes and squares. This doctrine, as well as the obscurity of much of his verse, may at first seem to clash with the Augustan love for common sense. But we should recall that the best of the eighteenth-century poets, as Pope, Gay, and Prior, never allow clarity to stand in the way of wit. The bourgeois rather than the aristocratic faction in the Augustan age emphasized common sense. Prior, the least contaminated of the poets with middle-class ideas, is the least touched by the heavy hand of reason and is at the same time the most lambent and playful in his wit.

Although Stevens does not actually imitate the style of the Augustans he is certainly indebted to their ideals.

His poetry adheres to the humanistic tradition in demonstrating that the proper study of mankind is man, and man as a social animal. Indeed, a good deal of Stevens's poetry is *vers de société*. A fair specimen would be *Tea:*

> *When the elephant's-ear in the park*
> *Shrivelled in frost,*
> *And the leaves on the paths*
> *Ran like rats,*
> *Your lamp-light fell*
> *On shining pillows,*
> *Of sea-shades and sky-shades,*
> *Like umbrellas in Java.*

It was, of course, Pope writing from Hampton Court who first sang the delights of "taking tea." It was Pope, too, who popularized the word taste as well as the idea, a conception which becomes the guiding theme of so great a part of Stevens's verse. This appears best in one of his most original and striking poems, *Floral Decorations for Bananas*. Here the poet violently objects to his "nuncle's" error in placing bananas as a centerpiece on a dining-room table. His uncle's fundamental error lay in introducing a symbol of a tropical hurricane into a delicately toned and feminine room.

> *You should have had plums tonight,*
> *In an eighteenth-century dish,*
> *And pettifogging buds,*
> *For the women of primrose and purl,*
> *Each one in her decent curl.*
> *Good God! What a precious light!*

It is hard to praise this poem enough or to regret too much

that so few works of the sort are written. Many other of Stevens's lyrics depict the social world, both in its outer and inner reality. Thus we read of fabrics, fans, and coiffures and enjoy specimens of polite irony and condescension. His splendid *Domination of Black* shows a fine sense for the color and gloss of cloth. Such lines as the following are typical of his social verse:

> How explicit the coiffures became,
> The diamond point, the sapphire point,
> The sequins
> Of the civil fans!

His subtler verses of the sort are very polite, very ironical, and very French. So in his imagined address entitled *A High-toned Old Christian Woman* he casts a philosophical and supercilious smile upon religion, speaking with a cool courtesy entirely in the manner of the old deistical aristocrat. His little lyric *Gubbinal* affords a similar instance of his worldly-wise condescension.

This distinguished citizen of Connecticut is the better Augustan for being more cosmopolitan than provincial in his tastes and more orthodox than heterodox in such religion as he countenances. It seems natural for him to weigh, as in *The Surprises of the Superhuman*, the "palais de justice" with the "Übermenschlichkeit." Nor are we in the least surprised to find him on shipboard in the Caribbean sipping "Chinese chocolate." While he is hardly a religious poet, such lines as *Lunar Paraphrase*, with their tender allusions to the Holy Family, assume the presence of a Catholic society. Whatever may be the philosophical implications of his exquisite and highly formal hymn, *To the One of Fictive Music*, its imagery is inspired by hymns to the Virgin, and as such an address the first stanza might assuredly be read:

> Sister and mother and diviner love,
> And of the sisterhood of the living dead

Most near, most clear, and of the clearest bloom,
And of the fragrant mothers the most dear
And queen, and of diviner love the day
And flame and summer and sweet fire, no thread
Of cloudy silver sprinkles in your gown
Its venom of renown, and on your head
No crown is simpler than the simple hair.

Stevens writes with the humanist's fondness for seeing nature
with the aid of the accumulative interpretations of the fine arts.
Such a poem as *The Public Square* with its emphasis upon hard
surfaces is nicely attuned to the vision of modern painting. In
the eighteenth century, as previously noted, painting and poetry
held to a firm alliance—*ut pictura, poesis*. The imagery of
Thomson's *Seasons* is itself largely based on painting of the
Dutch school and was itself repeatedly used by such leading
painters of the French school as Boucher. Sacheverell Sitwell
paints nature as though his eyes had been closed to it since 1700,
when Claude Lorrain died. But, after all, Stevens actually remains closer to the vital Augustan temper by following in the
steps of Braque or Matisse than in those of Claude or Boucher.
And everywhere he sees man as the measure of all things and
art as the measure of nature. This is the meaning of *Anecdote
of the Jar*:

> I placed a jar in Tennessee,
> And round it was, upon a hill.
> It made the slovenly wilderness
> Surround that hill.
>
> The wilderness rose up to it,
> And sprawled around, no longer wild.
> The jar was round upon the ground
> And tall and of a port in air.

> It took dominion everywhere.
> The jar was gray and bare.
> It did not give of bird or bush,
> Like nothing else in Tennessee.

His beautiful and subtle description in *Idea of Order at Key West* also declares that form is subjective (or within man), not objective (or within nature).

No poem by Stevens has been more generally admired than his panorama of the tropical ocean, *Sea Surface Full of Clouds*. It shows not only his art at its best, but his grasp of one of the ultimate ideals of the Augustan humanist, a harmony between man the dweller in houses and man the inhabitant of the enveloping outdoor world which we call nature. The school of poetry which produced *Cooper's Hill, Windsor Forest, The Seasons,* and *The Task* (and, one may add, *Paradise Lost*) certainly did not neglect nature. Its object so far as the external world is concerned was to harmonize nature and man. Only the lesser Augustan poets confined themselves to *vers de société*, just as lesser romantic poets confined themselves to a wholly barbarous exploitation of a vast and uninhabitable wilderness. One mark of the equilibrium achieved by the Augustans is their fondness for periwigged trees—for metaphors that express nature in terms of artificial productions or artificial productions in terms of nature. Such images we have seen in large number in the verse of Edith Sitwell, imitating not only the spirit but the letter of the Augustans. *Harmonium* is one of the few books of verse since the eighteenth century which gives the reader an impression of its author as equally at home indoors and out of doors. In this respect Stevens is the more complete man. His achievement is particularly evinced in this wisest and most beautiful of his poems. One of its refrains, echoed with subtle variations, deals with chocolate and umbrellas. How Stevens harmonizes chocolate and umbrellas with a sea surface full of clouds is equally a secret of his art and doctrine. It is clearly a learning transmitted from one mind and generation to another by the humanism which came to full ripeness in the Augustan spirit.

FROM THE ROMANTICS

Loud protests of the oncoming age against the departing one conceal a regard which the present always owes to the immediate past. Misled by the seductions of novelty and mistaken as to the pace at which evolution actually occurs, a superficial judgment overlooks the continuity of thought. Today it is fashionable rather than wise to decry the romantics from Wordsworth and Shelley to Tennyson and Swinburne and to deny the value of the more reflective of the Victorian poets, such as Arnold, Meredith, and Browning. Yet recent verse has been no more able to break completely with the nineteenth century than Renaissance poetry was able wholly to dismiss medieval tradition. Although the unprecedented rapidity of change in the industrial state has made the repudiation of the immediate past more marked today than ever before, the human spirit, which is also the soul of poetry, changes less rapidly than the lines of physical communication. And the more progressive of the Victorians actually stand closer to ourselves than we are generally willing to admit. The dilemmas regretted by Arnold, the problems broached by Carlyle, and the attitudes developed by Browning obviously retain a vital meaning. E. A. Robinson at times followed Wordsworth, Elinor Wylie preferred Shelley, Wilfred Owen emulated Keats, and recently W. H. Auden has imitated Byron. Virtually all the leading American poets today have derived a considerable part of their craft and vision from Poe, Whitman, and Emily Dickinson. Browning and Arnold of the older school, Meredith and Francis Thompson of the younger, have been especially strong influences. Severe attacks by critical factions against the romantic philosophy have proved unable to blind our poets to the splendor of Keats and Shelley or to undo the profound achievements of Wordsworth and Coleridge. Even when we regret our intellectual heritage, we are powerless to disown it. Just as the ardent atheist grows to resemble the believer whom he opposes, those who revolt against the romanticists become themselves unmistakably romantic. Several writers peculiarly sensitive to modern social and intellectual developments have followed with unusual fidelity on paths cut out by the romanticists whom they have studied and admired. While the leading poets have invariably discarded certain features, both strong and weak, of the romantic poets, they have also discriminated between what among their immediate predecessors is of temporary value and what is of lasting value. On the whole the nineteenth century left a richer legacy of the spirit than of poetic technique. Thus contemporary writers often express a romantic point of view in an idiom reminiscent of medieval, Elizabethan, or Cavalier verse.

Before examining a few poets typical of the marriage of the distinctively modern with the undisputably romantic, it is helpful to consider some outstanding qualities which make the romantic writers attractive to their successors. Although the outlines are too well known to bear emphasis, it may be of use to sketch them briefly. Two major waves of poetical activity, alike in their fundamental aims, passed over England during the course of the century. The first, more properly called romantic, led by the Lake School and Byron, Keats, and Shelley, enjoyed the youthful qualities of emotionalism, high hopes, zeal for radical reform in art and society, marked introspection, and an unbounded faith in the development of the individual. To these qualities were added somewhat paradoxical addictions to nature worship and to the fantastic. The second, or Victorian group, felt the growing pressure of disturbing circumstances and ideas, in many cases yielding to confirmed despair or seeking release in aestheticism or in transcendental or Catholic mysticism. In

the second half of the century also the intellectual climate produced in braver men a poetry more realistic and more intellectual than the hyperemotional verse favored by the early
romantics. Thus as Browning's art developed he became increasingly sensitive to this new and vigorous appetite among
his more intelligent readers. Meanwhile American poetry produced at least three highly original masters of poetic technique
whose stature has grown continually since their death. All now
seem manifestly in advance of their times and accordingly to
belong with movements most vigorous towards the close of the
century. Poe was destined to inspire writers of the ultra-aesthetic
school both in America and Europe, while Whitman and Emily
Dickinson contributed importantly to the realism and the
mysticism increasingly powerful during the later decades.

As an instance of a poet who fuses modern psychology with
the romantic pessimism expressed by such a poet as the later
James Thomson, we may consider Conrad Aiken. As an example
of a writer who combines far different aspects of modern
democracy with the optimistic hopes and aspirations of the
early romantics, we may examine Vachel Lindsay. Finally, as
a variant upon the phase of rationalism and realism explored by
Browning, we may glance at E. A. Robinson. All these men
have written original and modernistic verse which still has strong
roots in nineteenth-century traditions. All have specific debts
to poets of that strenuous age.

Aiken himself acknowledges his sympathetic interest in the
thought and poetry of the last century. He has never joined in
the raucous protest and loud-mouthed cry of American critics
against the romantic quest. In *Scepticisms*, his collection of early
criticisms and reviews, he rarely speaks of a modern poet without some censure or of an older one without some praise. In one
of his *Preludes for Memnon* he singles out Shelley for special
commendation as a man who frankly expressed his own heart.
In the same volume he several times refers to Blake, of whose

writings he has obviously been a sympathetic student. Aiken has edited a comprehensive anthology of American poetry chiefly devoted to the nineteenth century. He is a reader of Verlaine, Rimbaud, Baudelaire, Mallarmé, Vildrac, and Laforgue.

It is true that Aiken remains in a sense one of the most modernistic of poets, since it is doubtful if any literary figure has studied certain fields of modern thought more closely than he. Like Eugene O'Neill, he is devoted to psychology. Much of his poetry, such as *Changing Mind*, for example, is merely a poetizing of one or another scientific theory. He is one of the few men who have actually pronounced the name of Freud in rhyme. *The Melody of Chaos*, by Houston Peterson, affords an exhaustive study of Aiken's intellectual background, considering in particular his "mania psychologica." The work of this scholar makes exceptionally clear the genesis of modern psychology in the introspections of the early romantic period dominated in England by Wordsworth and Coleridge, as well as the subsequent allegiance between poets and philosophers who consider the individual as such and are therefore students of the soul. Aiken's extensive reading in nineteenth-century philosophical prose gives a harmonious background for his study of romantic verse. In short, his modernity itself has firm roots in nineteenth-century schools of thought.

Romanticism is a product of modern individualism. In their mood of extroversion the romantics champion the political liberty of the individual; in their mood of introversion they dwell upon the infinite potentialities and sufferings of the private soul. Aiken emphatically belongs to the school of the introverted romantics. No other group of poets is so consistently addicted to this attitude—not even the so-called metaphysical poets of the seventeenth century. For Donne, we sometimes forget, is author of trenchant social satires paraphrased by Pope as well as of lyrics, secular and divine, imitated by Carew and Herbert. Aiken's mood of intense and merciless introspection, his complete absorption in the plight of the soul, would alone be sufficient to establish him as a direct heir of the romantic movement.

Along with relentless introspection in Aiken goes a profound melancholy, defeatism, and despair, such as only the romantic school has fostered. It is true that the wits of the times of Rochester and Swift held mankind in sufficiently low regard; but the Augustans enjoyed either a savage and manly wit or a gay and urbane humor to refresh their scorching hearts. Though Hamlet discovered the gorgeous o'erhanging firmament to be a foul congregation of vapors, he was himself a noble prince, a glass of fashion, and a mold of form. Although the Middle Ages preached de contemptu mundi, they also believed in the glory of heaven and in the praise of God and his hallows. No previous age, in short, knew the utter abandonment to despair typical of Thomson, author of *The City of Dreadful Night*, and of not a few writers from the romantic period to our own. Romantic poets, careless of the mean, are now uplifted by a boundless optimism, now depressed in fathomless despair. Lindsay belongs to the school of hope and day, Aiken to that of misery and night. The latter is a romanticist not only because of his introspection, but because of his unbridled pessimism.

Although romantic influences are still strong upon us, romantic ideas and idioms themselves are steadily being either discarded or transformed into material more adapted to the present age. In keeping with the current of the times, therefore, Aiken's latest work is less markedly romantic than his earlier. This is not so much because his essential views have changed but because his reading has enlarged and his temperament hardened. His first book, *Earth Triumphant*, with echoes of Keats and Masefield, is exclusively romantic and sentimental, while his two volumes of "preludes" more recently published are eclectic and chiefly stoical. Especially since his residence in rural England he has acquired a taste for earlier English literature—not for the Augustans or the Cavaliers but for the Chaucerians and the Elizabethans. His *Preludes for Memnon* proves a series of poems as severely intellectual as they are deeply felt; and these are based largely on the form of the Elizabethan blank-verse dramatic soliloquy. The sententious thirty-first Prelude, for example, beginning, "Where is that noble mind that knows no evil," may easily be imagined as spoken on the Elizabethan stage. Shakespeare is mentioned and sometimes considered at length over a score of times in *Preludes for Memnon*. Among Aiken's most mature poetry is a series of distinctly Shakespearean sonnets. A number of pieces in *Time in the Rock* are echoes of "to be or not to be." His *John Deth*, suggested to him by names in a medieval parish register, shows a fondness for a grotesque medieval imagery not found in his earlier poems. *John Deth* retells the fine old medieval story of Horn Child and Rimenhild. In qualification, then, it must be conceded that Aiken today is less exclusively romantic than twenty years ago; but it must also be insisted that he remains at heart romantic still. His two fundamental attitudes of pessimism and introspection are unchanged. He has merely added a touch of Elizabethan romanticism to his more native attitude, an infusion of Renaissance stoicism as a partial restraint to his emotions, and an occasional coloring from the Elizabethan and medieval imagery now thoroughly familiar to him at first hand.

While his powerful imagination sufficiently transforms what he borrows, his indebtedness to the major romantic poets remains unmistakable. His earliest loves are in some respects the most fruitful. At thirteen this young Southerner began carrying about in his pocket an edition of Poe's poems. Repeatedly his own works reflect this unceasing devotion. We trace it in a fondness for phrases repeated with slight variations in a dreamy and trancelike tone, as in his early poem *Evensong*:

> She looked into the west with a young and infinite pity,
> With a young and wistful pity, as if to say . . .

Similarly in his brilliant *Senlin:*

> *Quietly watching the burial of its dead?*
> *Dumbly observing the cortège of its dead?*

And in the same poem:

> *Phrases again his unremembering mirth,*
> *His lazily beautiful, foolish, mechanical mirth.*

Poe's famous line, so rich in preciosity, "The viol, the violet and the vine," is echoed in Aiken's line, "Viol and flute and violin." And Poe's morbid eroticism seems reproduced in such a passage as the following:

> *This night I dreamed that you shone before me*
> *Colder and paler than rose-flushed marble,*
> *With dark hair fallen across your shoulders*
> *And face half hidden.*

The fifteenth lyric in *Priapus and the Pool* beginning, "There was an island in the sea," is throughout an unblushing imitation of Poe's dreamy verses, *The City in the Sea.* The latter poem has undoubtedly been one of Aiken's favorites.

He is chiefly indebted to Coleridge among the earlier romantic poets. The kinship between the two men, almost equally lyrical, morbid, melancholy, and mystical, can hardly escape notice. Once Aiken quite outdoes Coleridge. The latter, we are told, because of an unhappy interruption left us only some fifty lines of his dream-poem, *Kubla Khan;* but Aiken's *Cliff Meeting,* similarly transcribed, if we may trust his biographer, from a dream, is a considerably longer piece of eeriness. Many images in the episode of the vampire in *The Jig of Forslin* show parallels to the magical scenes in *Christabel* and *The Ancient Mariner.* These are typical:

> *. . . whereat her eyes*
> *Peered, and darkened, and opened wide,*
> *Her white brow flushed, and by my side*
> *Laughing, with little ecstatic cries,*

> She kissed my mouth, she stroked my hair,
> And fed upon my fevered stare. . . .
> I heard my heart hiss loud and slow;
> A gust of wind through the curtains came;
> It flapped the upright candle-flame.
> Her famishing eyes began to glow,
> She bared my arm; with a golden pin,
> Leaned, and tenderly pricked the skin.
> And as the small red bubble rose,
> Her eyes grew bright with an evil light,
> She fawned upon me; and my heart froze . . .

Similarly one may well detect Coleridgean echoes in such a couplet as the following from *John Deth:*

> And Deth, and the Demons, turning slowly,
> Tongueless went from the wood unholy . . .

Several times one is reminded of Coleridge's magnificent ode on dejection—for instance, when Aiken repeats the earlier poet's phrase "luminous cloud" or writes thus:

> If you could solve this darkness you would have me.
> This causeless melancholy that comes with rain . . .

With Shelley and the more rhetorical of the romantic poets Aiken has much in common. His verse occasionally has Shelley's vagueness:

> Secretly in your depths of sleep
> Among the unresting rocks and roots
> A dream, a gleam, a warmth will start,
> A whorl of winds and lutes . . .

The *Ode to the West Wind* may well have suggested the romantic couplet:

> Dead leaves stream through the hurrying air
> And the maenads dance with flying hair.

When the introverted egoist fancies his hero, Festus, "alone, immense and dark on a pinnacle of the world," his mind travels back to Shelley's "Pinnacled dim in the intense inane." The lyric dialogue between Festus and the Old Man at the end of *The Pilgrimage of Festus* has many reminiscences of the last pages of *Prometheus Unbound*. One sees the relationship, for example, in a couplet spoken by the Old Man:

> *We are the earth: this music is our tree . . .*
> *And yet what misery it wakes in me!*

What the Shelleyan tradition became in the hands of Swinburne and his followers may be seen in Aiken's anapaestic lines:

> *Beauty the dream will die with the dreamer,*
> *None shall have mercy, but all shall have death.*

Aiken's relations with Whitman prove at once more elusive and more important. His entire *House of Dust* is a morbid inversion of the optimistic poetry of *Song of Myself*, especially Whitman's passages descriptive of Brooklyn, Manhattan, and their adjoining waters. Whitman found imaginative excitement and mystic unity in a great city. Aiken discovered an equal excitement in the same scene, but also evidence of the total discontinuity and frustration of modern urban life. He is wholly Whitmanic when he describes the excitement of a city fire. One recalls also those splendid romantic prints by Currier and Ives, *The Life of a Fireman*. It is the soul of Whitman speaking when Aiken writes, "My veins are streets. Millions of men rush through them." But it is Aiken's peculiarly romantic and introspective anguish that adds: "Which, in this terrible multitude, is I?" The romantic, Whitmanic manner appears in these sentimental lines on death:

> *Death is never an ending, death is a change;*
> *Death is beautiful, for death is strange;*
> *Death is one dream out of another flowing;*

> Death is a chorded music, softly going
> By sweet transition from key to richer key.
> Death is a meeting place of sea and sea.

In the casual manner of *Song of Myself* and *Crossing Brooklyn Ferry*, we read:

> Two lovers move in the crowd like a link of music,
> We press upon them, we hold them, and let them pass.

The opening of Part Three of *The House of Dust*, too long to quote, echoes Whitman's passion for cataloguing individuals as typical specimens of the city's throng. Wholly in Whitman's familiar, democratic vein are Aiken's words, "What do you whisper, brother? What do you tell me?" Again in the cosmic vein of the earlier poet Aiken writes:

> How many aeons returning have whispered and thrilled me!
> Rocks, how many, have crashed into dust beneath me!
> Lovers, how many, have loved me and blown on the wind!

With the author of *Leaves of Grass* Aiken depreciates deity and deifies grass:

> Yet god, though no smaller he be than the shell of the world
> No greater is, truly, than the green blade of grass.

The exquisite metaphysical ending of *Song of Myself* is duplicated in the last page of *Senlin*:

> Will I not answer you as clearly as now?
> Listen to rain, and you will hear me speaking.
> Look for my heart in the breaking of a bough.

Many of Aiken's poems, such as *Forslin* and *The House of Dust*, deal extensively with the dreams of men and women in the day and night. They are utterly introverted, amoral, fantastic, and spiritual. And such is one of the most modernistic of Whitman's own poems, *The Sleepers*. A great part of Aiken's work is an expansion of this poem in terms of modern idiom and modern psychology. Finally, the first lines of *The House of Dust* reproduce much of the spirit of such a transcendental piece as Whitman's *Answerer*. As a disciple of Whitman, Aiken writes:

> And the wandering one, the inquisitive dreamer of dreams,
> The eternal asker of answers, stands in the street . . .

Although definite echoes are heard of other romantic poets besides the four considered so far—for example, of Arnold's rich sonorities in *Tristram* and other of his poems—Aiken's indebtedness is best seen by considering his major poems in turn. These may be viewed from first to last as successive revelations of his literary character. His considerable writing as a young man resembles the work of other gifted and uncritically prolific romanticists. *Earth Triumphant*, for instance, begins as a romantic elegy and ends in romantic praise of the healing powers of nature. One early poem expresses the ethics of Nietzsche with settings in a New York barroom and a cabin in the Wild West. Aiken's own preface to his *Charnel Rose* describes this work concisely: "This theme might be called nympholepsy—nympholepsy in a broad sense as that impulse which leads us from one dream, or ideal, to another, always disillusioned, always creating for adoration some new and subtler fiction. . . . Thus, beginning with the lowest order of love, the merely carnal, the theme leads irregularly, with returns and anticipations, as in music, through various phases of romantic or idealistic love, to several variants of sexual mysticism; finally ending, as I have said, in a mysticism apparently pure. It scarcely needs to be said that the protagonist of the poem is not a specific man, but men in general. Man is seen seeking in many ways to satisfy his instinct to love, worshipping one idol after another, disenchanted with each in turn; and at last taking pleasure not so much in anticipation as in memory." A program for a more purely romantic poem could hardly be found. During his earliest years of authorship Aiken wrote also a number of minor poems, vague, melancholy, and sentimental, in the approved romantic manner. He turns naturally to nocturnal sins and to dreamy vicarious experience. Few of the poems thus far mentioned, however, were thought by their author worthy of inclusion in his generous volume of selected poems published in 1929. They serve chiefly in reminding us of his thorough training in romantic schools of thought and expression, from which as yet he has not seriously digressed.

His chief ties with the romantic poets are to be found in a brilliant series of eight fairly long poems published in the *Selected Poems* and in *John Deth and Other Poems*. The first of these, *The Jig of Forslin*, depicts the vicarious dreams and excitements of a man significant only in typifying the miserable failure of modern life. Romantic not only in its dreamlike form and luxurious despair, this work is based on the vulgar murder stories in fiction and in the daily press that form so large a part in the perverted mental diet of the modern man. If it should be urged that no poem presents a more unfavorable or more scornful view of degenerate romance, it may at least be added that none is more exclusively concerned with this phenomenon.

In numerous details *The Jig of Forslin* exhibits its literary inspiration. These, for example, are eminently romantic thoughts:

> Let us succumb to a soft blue wave of music. . . .
> But yield our depths to the silent flow of change. . . .
> Here is no striving, no choosing. We do not know
> Whither we drift, but shut our eyes and go.

Fancies and realities tumble illogically together. The poet expresses his aim as "seeking the strange cool secret of ourselves." In a thoroughly romantic mood he writes of how "the tired heart forgets." The beautiful lyric on twilight beginning Part Four has a peculiar sensitivity scarcely to be found in English verse before the rise of the romantic spirit. Aiken entertains the most extreme views of the vicissitudes of the ego. In his own words, "ever like smoke I am blown and spread and die." In this poem, too, is much of the paraphernalia of Georgian romance, shown in scenes of mad terror, mermaids, witches, lamias, elfin horns, and passionate mouths withdrawn into a mystery of mist.

The Jig of Forslin depicted the individual lost in the pitiable confusion of self-deception. The Whitmanic House of Dust shows him lost equally in himself and in his community. To the chaos of the ego is added the chaos of the city. One futility echoes another. Although the conclusion is the same, and no really objective writing occurs, the imagery is at least enlarged. Man's dreams are shown to be vain not only because of the nature of self, but because of his so-called community. The poem is a wedding of two typical nineteenth-century works, Whitman's Song of Myself and Thomson's City of Dreadful Night; it possesses the amplitude of the former, the darkness of the latter.

Like The Jig of Forslin, The House of Dust is romantic not only in theory but in execution of detail. As Aiken himself observes, "You have been always, let me say, romantic." Carrying on his theme of the nullity of the will, he pictures the individual as a musical instrument breathed upon by nature or as seaweed tossed helplessly by the waves. Nevertheless man experiences a violent desire to express his own nature. There are passages of extreme tenderness or idealism, as well as passages of violent antirationalism, with magic, crystal gazing, witches, maenads, a red bat, dead leaves in a whirl, and green light from a moon in partial eclipse.

Senlin: a Biography, is a subtler indictment of the individual in terms of romantic despair. Senlin himself, for all we can see, is an exceptionally fortunate and happy man, as far as man can be fortunate and happy. He certainly is not a mote off the metropolitan scum, like poor Forslin; nor do we find him lamenting a life tossed away in a chaotic modern city. But an examination of the mind and fate of any man, his dark origins, his futile preoccupations, and his cloudy destiny convinces the poet of the human tragedy. Caught between the vanity of an unknown God and the triviality of a necktie, poor Senlin proves as unhappy as any of Aiken's rain-besotted heroes. This is the most lyrical and ingratiating of its author's philosophical poems. It flows from the pen of a new Shelley as thoroughly disillusioned as he is inspired. Adolescent doubts are sublimated into the commonplaces of metaphysical poetry.

In this "poetical symphony," too, are many minor echoes of romantic writing. Thus we read of "the star flesh longed to be but could not be," an image and a thought much in the manner of Shelley. More such vague imagery appears in quatrains such as the following:

> It takes my hand and whispers to me
> The melodious mystery of flesh,
> It draws the web of the moonlight down
> And spins for my heart a mesh.

We encounter, also, some fine lines in the best romantic manner, as, "A helpless gesture of mist above the grasses." We note tender childhood reminiscences, the passionate crying of a violin, some lines that read very much like lovely nonsense, and one passage on pale unicorns by the sea suggested by a mystical and symbolic painting by the American artist, Arthur Davies. Incidentally, Aiken more than once shows his imagination touched by a memory of one of the most romantic of all nineteenth-century works of art, Boecklin's *Island of the Dead*.

Similar to *Senlin* in general purpose and effect is *The Pilgrimage of Festus*. This, too, deals, in Aiken's words, with the "soft ascension of despair," teaching the nihilistic view that "only in nothingness we have our being." It deals with a ro-

mantic hero who walks "in a moonlight wind of dream," and
with

> . . . the myriad eyes that in his veins went to and fro
> Seeking a dream forever and finding no ease.

One passage seems to have been suggested by the misery of
Arnold's Empedocles momentarily assuaged by the innocent
music of a flute. Another long passage describing an autopsy on
the body of a beautiful woman outdoes Poe and has been well
described as "a masterpiece of decadent horror." "Thus," says
Peterson, "would Festus epitomize in a single act that incor-
rigible sadism which colors almost half the acts of human beings." Mysticism, in certain forms always agreeable to romanticism, reigns in the section entitled He Enters the Forest of
Departed Gods. The section ends with a vision of unmitigated
evil, where Mephistopheles transforms himself into a whore.
There follows a keen account of the spiritual strife of the man
who shudders at the thought of renouncing a God objectively
perceived for a God wholly within his own breast but who finds
himself fatefully drawn to the latter creed. The passage epitomizes one of the sharpest spiritual struggles of the last century.
This poem ends with a dialogue between Festus and an Old
Man, an allegorical emanation of his own spirit. Their talk is
wholly disillusioning. Festus, ever guilty of nympholepsy, fancies
that he has found truth in beauty, when he is merely driven
back on the coarseness of his own bestial origins. The orchestra
which has ravished his senses appears as a band of butchers
with white aprons spotted and green in the moonlight. In
thought and tone Festus differs in no way from The Charnel
Rose and the other "symphonies" of this series except that it
is one of the more mature in poetic texture.

Aiken's Priapus and the Pool is a lyrical account of a romantic
and unsatisfied passion, with a point of view going back at least
to Petrarch but an art learned by Aiken primarily from nine-

teenth-century romantics. The series which begins with a hymn to Priapus ends with a chant to the eternal Virgin. On its course it passes through such galling extremes as the yearning of a lonely heart and the sadism of the soul enflamed by a love that in reality is hate. This lyric chaplet is as romantic as it is artful.

One interesting poem of moderate length, *Medusa*, well exhibits Aiken's romantic individualism. It is divided into twelve sections, each representing the thoughts of one of the twelve jurors in a trial of a woman who has been abused by a worthless, lying man and led by blind love and hate to kill her rival. Not the action as a whole or its social significance, but the twelve portraits of the hopelessly self-centered and egotistical jurors draw Aiken's attention. This is obviously the work of a man more concerned with the soul than with society, although for once he consents to consider twelve egoists instead of the more usual one.

Two of Aiken's longer poems stand somewhat apart because of their brilliant use of a grotesque and macabre imagery especially beloved by many romantic authors. *Punch, the Immortal Liar*, his most popular and imaginative poem, supplies the flesh and blood which the shadowy Forslins, Senlins, and Festuses so signally lack. Punch, too, is the human soul, but the soul revealed in a remarkable allegory. Like the poor puppet, the soul is forever romantically deluding itself as to its grandeur and forever receiving the hard blows of fate and the conclusive evidence of its tragic insignificance. Man, like Punch, is a dreamer, a ribald, sensitive, paradoxical clown. Punch's troubles over Judy and Polly merely indicate the eternal trouble in which man finds himself. He fancies himself Solomon and his doxy the Queen of Sheba, only to discover that he is a fool and she a trull. In the opinion of an indulgent Old Man, Punch is somehow lovable despite all his lying, brutality, and sensuality. In the eyes of a respectable Elder he appears the devil incarnate.

The doctrine of the poem is itself romantic, but the execution far more so. It ranks as the ablest macabre extravaganza written in recent years. Edith Sitwell's frequent use of the image of Punch and the old puppets, considered in the preceding section, is in a totally different spirit. Concerned only with fatalistic and materialistic implications of her mechanistic symbols, she keeps the witty spirit of the cool Augustans. Aiken's poem, to be sure, concludes with the same mechanistic pessimism, but it includes romantic notions and spiritual depths of which the wittier and less profound author is incapable. For Edith Sitwell's puppets are made only of wood and wire, while Aiken's Punch is tremblingly alive with flesh and blood and the most human weaknesses. She makes men resemble puppets, he makes puppets resemble men. He envisages that contradictory creation, a biological machine, while to her man becomes wholly mechanical. Aiken, in short, successfully romanticizes the Punch legend.

His almost equally fascinating *John Deth* is even richer in macabre imagery, being a new poetic version of the dance of death and certain episodes in the medieval Passion play. Mythology, mysticism, and orientalism join to produce an extremely bizarre effect, with an eclecticism not uncommon in the romantic period and virtually impossible at an earlier date. The most immediate tie with romantic poetry proves a curious one. Attar, the Sufi mystic of the twelfth century, wrote *The Parliament of Birds*, a poem as profound in mystic doctrine as it is brilliant and realistic in its imagery. In it a host of birds about to go on pilgrimage debate the pros and cons of various types of mysticism. Edward Fitzgerald, translator of Omar's *Rubaiyat*, paraphrased Attar's work in a condensed version almost as admirably poetical as his work on Omar. The third canto of *John Deth*, in which a parliament of birds gives to Deth their views on beauty, closely approximates Fitzgerald's art, dazzling as the finest painting in Persian miniature. Indeed much of Aiken's poem is a romanticized orientalism. It concludes, for example, with an image of Buddhistic impassiveness. His sadistic romanticism, equally familiar to the Oriental and the Christian world, is conspicuous in the gruesome crucifixion of Venus Anadyomene. Whether the romanticism of the earlier cantos describing the wineshop and Deth between his lovers, Millicent Piggistaile and Juliana Goatibed, proves specifically romantic in the Elizabethan or medieval rather than in the strict Victorian sense, a romantic fantasy this dance of death always remains. The poem has well been likened to *Death's Jest Book*, a volume by the excellent Georgian poet, Beddoes.

Only the briefest mention need be made of Aiken's minor poems as instances of his untiring romanticism. *Sound of Breaking*, for example, is an idealization of grief; *Poverty Grass* is unrivaled in its Timonian misanthropy, *Samadhi* in its nostalgic mysticism. In *Seven Twilights* Aiken prefers decay to growth, laments the vanity of all intellectual effort, declares that the gross always defeats the fine, and offers a dark stoicism as the one human hope. His two volumes of *Preludes* show a more austere technique but no change in spirit. The language and symbolism of all these exquisite poems are the natural development of the art and philosophy of the romantic school from Coleridge and Poe to James Thomson and Thomas Hardy.

Vachel Lindsay represents romanticism in its converse form, as optimistic and rude as Aiken's is dejected and refined. Nevertheless it is a pity that in his volume of criticism Aiken should have written so unfavorable a review of a poet with whom in some respects, at least, he has much in common. For each has roots going deep into the romantic earth, though one is as overcultivated, sensitive, and decadent as the other is undercultivated, spontaneous, and crude. One is the romantic seed as sown in a metropolitan window box, the other as sown on the Western plains. In short, the two poets differ more in circumstance than in substance.

So truly romantic is Lindsay that clarity demands some state-

ment of the elements in his work that make him at once
individual and modern and not merely a conventional follower
of the nineteenth-century poets. No tradition, of course, actually
tyrannizes over a true artist. It assists him; it does not repress
him. And the romantic movement in particular left the individual free to speak as his impulse required. Lindsay was one of
the first true poets to express American life of the Midwest and
of the lower classes. The school of Longfellow primarily addressed the middle and upper classes of the long-settled Atlantic
seaboard. Whitman was too much an egotist to give expression
to any intimate thoughts not his own. Consequently when a
poet arose to express in sound art the raucous urge of the auto-
mobile along the Sante Fe Trail, the rhythms and longings of
the Negroes, the fervor of the Salvation Army, the vigor of
Nebraska from the reign of the buffalo to that of Bryan, the
rudeness of primitive California and Tennessee, and the vulgar
vitality of American popular music and the early motion pictures, critics were quickly aware of a new voice in literature.
Whatever Lindsay had learned from literary and nonliterary
sources—from Poe, Kipling, and Swinburne on the one hand
and from popular hymns, lyrics, and ballads on the other—he
undeniably had a fresh and invigorating sense of rhythm. His
idea of poetry as a chant, and even as a choral chant, his strong
sense for the affinity of verse with music and with the dance,
marked his originality among poets of the second decade of the
present century. Even if his successful poems were less numerous or fully accomplished than might be wished, he immediately
inspired some of the most progressive minds in literature and in
the arts. His verse mannerisms were in some respects not easily
imitated; Lindsay's identification of himself with the under-
privileged classes meant more to the development of American
prose, from Lewis and Dreiser to Faulkner and Steinbeck, than
to the progress of American verse. He made a deep impression,
however, upon all his poetical fellow Westerners, and specially

on Sandburg and Masters, as the latter observes in his biography. Such romantic radicals from the Middle West as Paul Engle are today his heirs. But perhaps the most interesting clues to Lindsay's modernity lie in his influence upon musicians and painters. Percy Grainger, one of the most popular of contemporary composers, became a close friend in Lindsay's later years; and there are numerous musical settings for his poems. The Middle West has witnessed advances in painting even more notable than those in poetry and music. One easily sees an affinity between the lyrical poet and the satirical and democratically inspired paintings of Thomas Benton and Grant Wood which deal with the Middle Western scene. Benton, an acquaintance and admirer of Lindsay, has literally followed in his footsteps, taking walking trips in the South and West as Lindsay did, recording his adventures with the brush as the poet had always vainly wished to do. Benton has painted pictures of Fords clattering through the dust and sunset glow of the Western plains which are perfect illustrations to Lindsay's *Sante Fé Trail*. And his Negroes are the same beings so vigorously sung by Lindsay in *The Congo* and *The Booker Washington Trilogy*. Lindsay, then, still holds a forward-looking position in American literature, art, and culture. Whatever may be his stature as a poet, he is certainly original and modernistic. Indeed there are few more original or historically significant figures in American letters. Even his drawings prove his independence. Practically everyone who has thought them worthy of comment agrees that they are negligible artistically. But they reveal a unique personality. No one else has been romantic in precisely the same way.

Although extraordinary as a writer and unusual as a man, Lindsay is thoroughly representative in his education and ideas. His romantic poetry is as barren in thought as it is rich in feeling. Although the work of a wide reader, its basic ideas are scarcely more developed than the thinking of any average citizen of the Middle West fifty years ago. Lindsay was the more truly romantic in that he never grew up. He remained slightly mad, both as a boy and as a man. The average Middle Westerner may not have, as astringent critics have declared, a sixteen-year-old's mentality. But Lindsay himself confessed that he never passed adolescence. He is the more characteristically romantic because of this arrested mental and spiritual development. Certainly one of his finest poems is that memorable picture of political excitement in a Middle Western town, *Bryan, Bryan, Bryan, Bryan*. In this piece Lindsay, then thirty-nine years old, recalled his feelings at the age of sixteen. He hardly need have done so, however. Even by his fiftieth year, when he was apparently exhausted, so far as he was alive he remained youthful. On the night of his death his mind wandered in delirium to his days in Hiram College. Lindsay remained the incurable undergraduate, chanting to the end of his life the "Kallyope" yell. Wholly in the spirit of praise, not in the least of censure, Masters observes that he voiced the youthful spirits of a youthful nation. His originality lay primarily where a poet's genius may be expected to lie, namely, in his power of expression.

His native emotionalism and lack of the critical faculty associate him with much romantic practice. In place of rational thinking he commonly shows a religious zeal. His first successful poem depicts the spiritual life of the Salvation Army. His second success portrays the religious fanaticism of the American Negro. He was forever in quest of some mystic grail, whose colors glowed for him in some prairie sunset or from some snowy peak in Colorado. Sometimes, as in *The Congo*, the mystical spirit is obvious, sometimes, as in the symbol of the prairie bird in *The Sante Fé Trail*, it lies half-hidden in the background. Democracy for him becomes virtually a religion. Lincoln, Boone, St. Francis, and Bob Taylor, Governor of Tennessee, are alike to him not real men or historical figures but deities in a mystic heaven. Lindsay is a perfect example of a Protestant fashioning his own God and his own saints. Historically considered, no element is more important in English romanticism than nonconformist "enthusiasm." And Lindsay becomes the ideal instance of religious enthusiasm run wild as a prairie fire. Nominally of the Campbellite sect, he was in fact a worshipper in no sect, but a Protestant saint, chaste, ascetic, visionary, pressing his revelations of God out of the joys and agonies of sore feet and sunstruck brow. His entire world became the winepress for his "poetical" madness. Lindsay would have experienced even keener suffering than he did, had there been a wider gap between his verse and his religion. In fact they were continually united. Sometimes poor verse and conventional piety were the result, as when he wrote poems in praise of the Campbellites. More often the stream of his religious enthusiasm poured into less conventional and more imaginative channels—such as Salvation Army devotions, Negro revivals, or sublimations of sexual passion—yielding a richer crop of poetry. His symbolical method and boundless zeal are marks of his romantic background.

Lindsay's romanticism was literary, but it was even more a consequence of his general social heritage. There was romantic feeling aplenty in American youth of nineteen-hundred, as well as in the elders of these youngsters. Here lay the soil from which Lindsay's verse was to spring. Mark Twain had painted a slightly more sober picture, but the grounds of romantic feeling are evident also in the work of the great storyteller. Popular preachers, political orators, propagandists, and social leaders of all sorts exploited the public emotions of the times. Lindsay's mother was forever doing the most extraordinary things, quite as rash and preposterous as the conduct of her son. And the community accepted her eccentricities. The eccentrics are the romantics; and life in the Middle West in 1896 had as yet found no center. Here a romantic poetry of some consequence was bound to arise, if only the essential conditions of poetic genius blessed and blighted some individual mind.

It is the vital paradox of Lindsay's mind that at the same time he represented this romantic culture and fanatically and illogically clashed with it. He detested jazz, yet certainly imitated its violent, syncopated rhythms; he despised vaudeville, yet produced what he himself termed "the higher vaudeville." He passionately loved and hated his native town, Springfield: hated it for what it was, admired it for what he believed it to have been and hoped it might become. The dim horizon always held a fascination for him. He compared himself with Dante, exiled from Florence. His own beloved people had turned against him. But he altogether lacked the classical and scholastic discipline, the philosophical and theological systems, the support of Aristotle and Aquinas, to give his character or art Dante's stability. Lindsay's art is necessarily dreamy, vague, lyrical, abrupt, and romantic. Thus to sum the matter up, he became an American Shelley, without the blessings of Oxford and a British gentleman's education. Instead of meditating stanzas among the ruins of Rome, he listened to his own shouts returned to him in the echoing canyons of Colorado. The two poets thoroughly agreed on such cardinal issues as the present depravity of mankind, the religion of beauty, and a living hope for social salvation. Lindsay revolted against America not only because it failed to give him the appreciation which as a poet, artist, and prophet he believed that he deserved, but because from early childhood he found himself a rebel against its ways. Manhood merely confirmed him as the radical which he had been fated to be from his birth.

Although the romantic Lindsay was incapable of imagining another culture or even another character than his own, he read widely, never in the classics or the Romance languages, but in many other fields. He knew, for example, Matthew Arnold's definitions of Hellenism and Hebraism and accepted his own place among the Hebraic minds. He knew well that he was a prophet, a dreamer, an enthusiast, and an eternal child. We in turn see him as a perfect example of romantic wanderlust. He possessed the romantic's boundless appetite for experience without rational plan or organization. Hence came his feeling that his best education as a poet consisted in living the life of a tramp and a beggar, walking prodigious distances across the country, avoiding the larger towns, getting a ride when he could, and securing food and lodging in three ways: by selling his poems for a few cents, by working for a few hours, or by downright begging. Such a life seemed to him as honorable as it might have appeared to a saint. His romanticism was never the sentimental brand of the middle classes but the Bohemian brand of the vagrant artist.

Art and life were made up for him from these passionate and idealistic devotions. He was continually swinging censers over some new man or building, generally in adoration, sometimes, as Masters points out, with the opposite motive of fumigation. The censers seen in his drawings resemble about equally Christmas-tree ornaments and the tinsel decorations of merry-go-rounds. Life he declared to be a merry circus, though he often found it to be a tragic one. He worshipped his mother, his sweethearts, the Socialist martyr Eugene Debs, the Springfield High School, his English teacher Susan E. Wilcox, Hiram College, his friend Sara Teasdale, Buddha, Confucius, the United States, and each state contained within it. He was a partisan of Swedenborgianism, prohibition, the single tax, and any number of schemes which he believed to hold some hope for human betterment. Swinburne himself might have learned a lesson from him in spontaneous and unreflecting ardors. His optimism is as typically a romantic mood as Aiken's pessimism.

He followed another well-beaten track of romantic theory and practice in relying heavily upon folk art. Folk dances and folk music interested him greatly. He tried to cultivate poetry-games, applying in a novel form current theories on the popular origin of the ballads. By far his chief technical discovery came to him on an eventful walking trip in Colorado. There he conceived the notion of writing poems in the rhythms of Negro spirituals and of popular American music generally. The refrain of *General William Booth Enters into Heaven* is taken from a revivalist hymn. He was really putting new words to old tunes, from *Casey Jones* and *The Old Time Religion Is Good Enough for Me* to the football cheer of the University of Kansas. Lindsay is full of romantic precepts of a democratic nature, as when he writes: "Let us seek rather to live the fullest, most self-expressive life possible, to unravel the secret of the imagination, or the hand that still dwells hidden, to bring these before my average fellow man on the road, and to trust him." He might have added, "and to hear America singing."

What verse Lindsay read and what verse influenced his poetry are two distinct questions, and while it is only with the latter that we are directly concerned, the former is useful as a preliminary inquiry. Once he observed: "Angels and ministers of grace defend us from current literature. By all means let us read the dead masters." And he read avidly. He was passionately devoted to Shakespeare and to Milton, understanding both from a romantic point of view. Shakespeare he loved on the stage no less than in print; and two of his better poems deal with performances of *Hamlet*. Milton he admired both as poet of love and of religion. "It was Milton," he said, "made me a poet and blessed and cursed me at nine years of age." Masters remarks that Lindsay read *Paradise Lost* "at eight years of age, and fell in love with Eve, dreaming about her day and night." Again, one of his more readable poems deals with Eve, romantically representing Milton's epic as written in her honor. He spoke disparagingly of Herrick and of Pope. Believing, as he said, that "the moods of poetry are for the most part the moods of solitude," he could hardly have relished Augustan verse. Nine tenths of his poetical reading was accordingly in the leading English and American writers of the last century. Only his love for his

native locality and his native land kept him from complete sub-
mersion in this romantic ocean. "My mother," he wrote, "took
an especial pleasure in those poets who dealt also in art, and
filled me full of the Brownings and the Pre-Raphaelites." Moreover, he never wearied of this diet or escaped beyond the literary
influence of his parent. As a lecturer in various settlement houses
and clubs for men and boys, he spoke on Tennyson, Henley,
Kipling, Poe, and other of his favorite authors. The cynical
Byron he disliked early in life, although he came to admire him
later. Shelley and Keats he esteemed highly, knowing them best
in the latter part of his career. In his own chanteys and lilting,
balladlike poems Lindsay owed something to Kipling. The British poet had written songs dealing with the laboring classes and
composed in radically new and brilliant meters; Lindsay used
at times a similar subject matter with still newer and subtler
rhythms. From the first he was devoted to Poe. In one of Lindsay's infinite proposals for literary work he looked forward to
showing, in the case of Poe, "how real his touch in influence is
when it can be seen at all; how he calls forth all the originality
to be possessed by the disciples affected, even when they swallow
but a morsel of him." There can be no question that Poe's
mastery of lyric rhythm inspired Lindsay, even if in the obscure
manner which he himself describes. His fondness for repetitions
suggests the eloquence of Poe's *Bells*. As Masters remarks, Poe's
poems "enthralled the imagination of the sensitive boy from
the first." One might add, to the last.

As a romantic spokesman for American democracy, Lindsay
was in a sense the continuator of Whitman, serious tempera-
mental differences notwithstanding. It is obvious that the
breadth and maturity of Whitman's mind, his grave, resigned,
and almost Oriental calm, his evenhanded treatment of good
and evil and impartial view of the American scene, lay wholly
beyond Lindsay's understanding. Yet Lindsay studied Whitman carefully as early as 1902 and never lost touch with his

great predecessor. He rejoiced in Whitman's religious view of life and art, in his intense patriotism, in his picture of the submerged classes, in his exuberant love of life and fresh and unconventional expression. Lindsay nevertheless drew more from the ideas in *Democratic Vistas* than from the art of *Leaves of Grass*. The former he quotes, the latter he seldom if ever imitates.

Among the great romanticists deeply affecting Lindsay were Blake and, in prose, Ruskin, Thoreau, and Tolstoy. As he strove to illustrate his own mystical poems and to develop his romantic theories of the saving power of imagination, he naturally turned to Blake, reading with special enthusiasm the *Songs of Innocence* and the tender biography by Gilchrist. His artistic interests led him first to Ruskin; socialism, another of his mental brides, later confirmed this affection. Ruskin's books proved sweet poison for the tooth of a young man addicted in a thousand ways to a romantic view of life. He composed poems on Egyptian hieroglyphics with as blithesome superficiality as Ruskin wrote prose on Amiens cathedral. Lindsay esteemed Thoreau for insight into both nature and society. The Tolstoy whom he knew best was the reformer of Yasnaya Polyana, the man who had, Lindsay thought, accomplished in a Russian village what he dreamed of achieving in Springfield, Illinois.

One of Lindsay's most fantastic and charming poems, *The Chinese Nightingale*, the dream of a Chinese laundryman, ultimately derived, the poet held, from Andersen's fairy tales. Andersen in turn drew his legend of the speaking bird from Grimm; and thus Lindsay's poem may be regarded as one of the more recent of the countless fantasies to spring directly or indirectly from this celebrated romantic source. It is of interest to note the chief magician of the Western plains, a region generously settled by German immigrants, showing his indebtedness to the wellspring of so much romantic poetry. By virtue of his exceptional environment Lindsay became in American poetry the most recent of the notable romantics, as he also is one of the pioneers among the moderns.

Aiken, Lindsay, John Gould Fletcher, and many other moderns are alike in feeling most strongly the influence of the ultra-romantic poetry of the last century. But the leading authors of Georgian and Victorian verse produced poems which cannot easily be called romantic. Browning's *Parleyings* is such poetry. And it is chiefly from the nonromantic and rationalistic type of verse that the greater part of the work of one of the chief American poets, E. A. Robinson, lineally descends. Robinson achieved originality without romantic eccentricity and genuine modernity without a harsh break with Victorian verse. Quietly, industriously, and with the modesty of a sound New England craftsman, he built his own house on foundations of the recent past.

Elsewhere in this book have been noted various aspects of Robinson's indebtedness to the past, almost always to verse of the nineteenth century. The cool, rationalistic quality of his style—a leading feature of his language—has been examined. He has been shown at work on the dramatic monologue, the short story, and the romantic novel, all forms much cultivated by Victorian poets. His frequent borrowings from the verse forms of both Wordsworth and the Pre-Raphaelites have been observed. It remains only to glance a little more deeply at the spiritual ties between Robinson and his immediate forerunners.

With the cool deliberation and high purpose of one who believes equally in reason and inspiration, Robinson winnows chaff from grain, preserving the emotional and intellectual richness of nineteenth-century verse with the poise of spirit representative of humanity at its best or, to be specific, of the classical world. He steers shrewdly between the Scylla and Charybdis of romantic exultation and despair. Thus he acquires a richer tragic sense than Aiken because he avoids the sentimental morbidity to which Aiken is heir; and he has a richer affirmative nature than Lindsay because he shuns the latter's uncritical and mawkish optimism. In Robinson we find the strength and delicacy of the romantic tradition without its weakness and effeminacy. He uses an exquisite nature imagery which romantic poetry has made possible for him without falling into the error of bowing his knee to nature. Above all he shows an interest in psychological and occasionally in sociological problems already faced, though as a rule less successfully, by poets before him. Romanticism has two aspects: a fulfillment of a promise of emotional and intellectual subtlety seldom achieved in earlier verse and a foppish indulgence in affectations together with an uncommon indulgence in personal weaknesses. The sentimentality nursed in the eighteenth century reached its most abundant flowering in the nineteenth. Robinson possessed the strength of mind to embrace the first aspect and to repudiate the second. He recognized the peculiar virtues and universal aims of romantic poets while shunning their moral delinquencies and affected posturings.

This mature attitude led Robinson to look with favor upon poets of other periods than the romantic, although pasturing his mind chiefly upon nineteenth-century literature. Perhaps because he was not a particularly wide reader of verse or a lover of the specious glitter and polish of Augustan style, he read superficially in the eighteenth century. The contemporary vogue of the metaphysical poets barely touched him. But he showed a fondness for Chaucer, whom in broad sanity he often resembles; and the author of *Ben Jonson Entertains a Man from Stratford* had certainly studied both Jonson and Shakespeare.

It is more significant still that throughout his life he was devoted to the classics. Classical professors in two of the New England colleges remained among his closest friends. Cestre, a French scholar, observes that Robinson is "a modern classic," meaning that he is a modern example of the classical ideal. That Robinson wrote several minor poems on Greek themes and translated felicitously from the Greek Anthology is of secondary importance here. More truly classical are his scrupulous workmanship, his unwavering intelligence, his unfaltering poise. His instinctive classicism harmonized as naturally with his inherited romanticism as the classical colonnades in his native Gardiner with their overhanging elms. Cestre errs in describing Robinson as wholly classical, for he achieved a harmony between the definitely classical and the definitely romantic.

In examining this unpedantic and spiritual classicism one may turn again to Robinson's mean between the opposite horns of romantic hope and despair. He is not without hope. He can view with equanimity the fall of things which he prizes, such as liberty and democracy, envisaging for truth neither an ultimate victory nor defeat. He believes in truth, honors science, hopes for democracy, but wisely expects all these causes to suffer frequent reversals. In more personal fields he shows the same restraint. On the whole his mind is tragic; whether or not his own physical and mental sufferings are a contributing factor is irrelevant here. His finest work is in his long poems—there are thirteen of them—the great majority of which end sadly. But crude violence or unrelieved despair are equally distasteful to him. He is no sentimental pessimist. *The Glory of the Nightingales*, for example, ends with a death that is equally merciful and heroic and with the spiritual redemption of the second character. The subject of *The Man Who Died Twice* at least glimpsed his ideal in his death. The soul of man, or Zoe, survives the quiet demise of the aged King Jasper. *Amaranth* concludes with its central figure a happier and a wiser man than at the beginning of the story. *Cavender's House* threatens to end violently but does end quietly. The leading characters in *Matthias at the Door* and *Roman Bartholow* undergo a spiritual purification. A violent conclusion is averted. We have a tragic atmosphere without a tragic ending. Yet how much more profound Robinson's mood is than that of Jacobean tragicomedy, a comparison with John Fletcher's plays might immediately show. An idealistic philosophy and an innate nobility preserve Robinson's Arthurian romances from the tragic darkness with which their stories threaten us. Finally, *Captain Craig* depicts the life and death of a man whose philosophy is equally humorous and tender. A classical restraint is of the essence of Robinson's spirit. He ponders this ideal so deeply that in the end he gives it a mark of genuine originality.

His treatment of romantic themes is similarly broad and vital. Beginning with aims as old as civilized literature itself, with the aid of the nineteenth century he realizes certain of these aims more fully than it has been possible to realize them hitherto. Romanticism is a phase of individualism. The Renaissance had stressed the differences of men. Shakespeare's plays are largely based on the delineation of contrasting characters. The nineteenth century, however, acquired new tools and achieved new subtleties for analysis of the individual. Varieties of personality become increasingly the study of nineteenth-century thinkers, in poetry and the novel as well as in laboratories of biologist and psychologist. Robinson's poems avail themselves of these advantages. He writes, therefore, along lines which we might imagine Shakespeare or Chaucer following had they lived in our own period.

Robinson is a difficult poet. His *Tristram*, least representative of his work, was forced by its critics and its publishers into a fame surely not greater than it deserved but out of all proportion to the reception of his other works. All his long poems are admirable, and all are based on his catholic understanding of life and letters which led him to value the poetic legacy of many periods but chiefly that nearest his own. It is evident from his freedom from all doctrinaire views that he realized his own position correctly. He knew the continuity of art, from the ages of Sophocles and Virgil to those of Malory, Shakespeare, Wordsworth, and Browning. His critics commonly found his work perplexing and presumably modernistic. They commonly missed its classical foundation, by which is meant not only its kinship with Sophocles but with Chaucer, Malory, Shakespeare, Wordsworth, and Browning as well. The same misunderstanding arises in all the arts. A true artist, possessing an idiom of his own, almost invariably has strong ties with the more progressive movements of his age. The public, uninitiated in the nuances of art, sees the originality and the modernity. But the artist knows also his allegiance to all sound art and the extent of his indebtedness to the past. Modernistic nonsense, exclaims the Philistine at the music of Stravinsky, who replies that so far as he can see he is giving to his own age the equivalent of what Bach and Handel contributed to theirs. Modernistic nonsense, also exclaims the Philistine at the paintings of Picasso, who calmly replies that he conceives himself in communion with Giotto and El Greco. Robinson left others to discourse on the modernity of his art, knowing well that it was both sincerely modern and sincerely personal. He also said little of his reading and of what he learned from it. But as a poet he must certainly have learned much, not only from the prose of Meredith and Henry James but from the verse of Wordsworth and Browning. His strength is owing to the naturalness with which his art evolved from the great Victorians. In his sagacious silence as to its literary origins we find the best conclusion to our present study. The public at large may assume an artist to be without precedent, but the artist knows in his own heart how deep are his roots in the art and social structure of the past.

V: THE RIGHT USE OF THE PAST

ALTHOUGH NO SYSTEMATIC ATTEMPT HAS BEEN MADE in the foregoing chapters to repress every trace of my personal dislikes or enthusiasms, it is hoped that these pages have given a representative, an impartial, and a substantially objective picture of the relation of the old poetry to the new. Any value which they may possess rests on the degree to which they offer a fair and comprehensive presentation of the subject. From the somewhat forbidding mass of evidence now completed certain conclusions have been steadily emerging. These views have been kept in the background during the presentation of the evidence and have been indicated only lightly in the opening chapter. The facts having been reviewed, it is now possible to state the case with a new emphasis.

Just as ample evidence exists that poetry from all the major periods of our literary history is now read, we have proof that this poetry is also being used. Modern poets find suggestion and inspiration from writers in all these ages of our literary history from *Beowulf* to George Meredith. Evidence has been given of ample and brilliant use by the moderns of the technique of poetry from Anglo-Saxon and Middle English, from the Elizabethan, the Augustan, and the romantic ages. Not merely one but all these periods contribute to the rich variety of modern verse.

This proves how doctrinaire are the merely personal views of critics who speak of modern poetry as wholly divorced from literary tradition. Far from being utterly new, it is widely eclectic; and genuinely fresh as many of its innovations are, its roots lie deep in the past. That a knowledge of the older verse affords little or no aid for an understanding of contemporary verse is sometimes assumed. But in view of the degree to which the moderns have been shown to lean upon their predecessors, this seems an unwarranted counsel of despair. It is, as we have recently seen in examining the verse of E. A. Robinson, the superficial critic and not the poet himself who feels this alleged detachment from his antecedents. Not only is the poetic art today basically what it was a thousand years ago—English and American poetry has, in fact, the priceless heritage of at least a thousand years of literary tradition. On the whole modern verse is presumably not radical enough, or at least not directed as successfully as might be hoped along new courses. On many scores it has failed to express the modern spirit as fully as might be expected. But the overwhelming probability is that were it vastly more modern and radical than it actually is, it would still have roots firmly in the past. For the English language has accumulated a vast poetic capital too valuable not to be used in serving the unprecedented needs of today.

Partisans of one or another literary movement at times assert the past, present, and future of English poetry to rest with them. A generation or two ago the Romantic Revival undoubtedly loomed out of all proportion to its abiding significance. Thus it is an error to suppose that the age of Wordsworth and Shelley was either the most or the least brilliant in the history of English verse. Soberly considered it is merely one more glory in the crown of English poetry. The most violent current of partisanship in recent years has been that in favor of the so-called metaphysical verse as written by Donne. This view naturally arose after Donne's true poetic stature was rediscovered by critics about twenty years ago. The view has lent its aid to the partisans of wit and obscurity in modern verse and to poets who might well be termed the twentieth-century transcendentalists. This school has unquestionably produced rich and valuable fruits; but in view of the evidence gathered in this book, it may not be untimely to emphasize the limitation of its critical perspective. Poets had been witty, subtle, and inspiring before Donne and were destined to comparable achievements after him.

All periods, then, have not only contributed verse delightful to read today but verse profitable for the modern poet to study. And each has of course its special contribution. In each period rhythms and genres have arisen which flourish lustily today. We not only write as our predecessors, but our poets, at least, know that they are doing so. All periods contribute something to our style. The Anglo-Saxon rhetoric and alliteration have surprisingly reëmerged in recent years. Medieval colloquialism has assisted a number of our younger poets in vivifying their style and freeing it from gilded chains of Victorian eloquence. An intellectualized style has been learned not only from Donne but from Meredith, Browning, and a large number of poets flourishing in the latter part of the nineteenth century. More often than generally supposed, modern verse is obliged to the splendor and especially to the wit of the age of Pope. Finally, a truly metaphysical and mystical symbolism is inherited rather from Dante, Langland, and Blake than from Donne's profound but somewhat narrow school.

The past enhances not only our technical mastery but our spiritual strength. The apocalyptic splendor of Cynewulf inspired Hopkins, the epic strength of *Beowulf* inspired MacLeish. Because the great Elizabethans have written, our verse possesses much of its profound grasp of tragedy, of its refined sense for purity of lyric tone. Our most fastidious poets are also heirs of the ripest of European culture from Monteverde to Mozart, and consequently the admirers and followers of Dryden, Pope, Prior, and Gay. And although they may philosophize and ridicule to the height of their bent, the antiromantics cannot prevent imaginative and inward-looking poets from discovering that Blake and Coleridge, Keats and Shelley, Whitman and Emily Dickinson, have opened springs of poetry still sparkling and refreshing. While it may be questioned in what sense the remote and mysterious medieval spirit still survives in literature, the medieval art of poetry emphatically does survive. And in addition to their technical accomplishments Elizabethan, Augustan, and romantic poets have bequeathed us much of their spirit as well. The evidence of this book is thus for a distinctly catholic view of the living heritage of English poetry. We have noted that major poets, such as Yeats, have drawn inspiration from every century.

Since no one moderately well read in modern poetry finds it difficult to recall some writers, usually of modest reputation, who have leaned unimaginatively and academically on predecessors, the invidious and tedious task of quoting such versifiers may here be omitted. It is more useful to recall the skill with which not only poets discussed in detail in this book but still others of note have in various ways successfully assimilated the literary past. Some, resembling Yeats, borrow from a wide range of sources, others principally from only a single fountain of inspiration. Mark Van Doren, editor of an anthology of poetry translated from many languages and an able critic of Elizabethan, Cavalier, Augustan, and romantic poetry, illustrates the most catholic attitude. His sonnet sequence owes much to Shakespeare, his short, witty poems to the metaphysical school, his *Winter Diary* to Augustan verse essayists, and his delicate lyrics to romantic poetry from Wordsworth to Hardy. Carl Sandburg, on the contrary, who is less affected by a wide reading of verse and probably less widely read in the field, stands in a singularly happy relation to Whitman. While far too original and truly modernistic a poet to follow any master servilely, he has most legitimately and profitably studied Whitman's technique in metrics and design and his moods, feelings, and ideas. Although not wholly free from Whitman's vulgarity, he keeps his democratic sympathy and imaginative fecundity. No more vital relationship can be imagined between two poets: the younger thoroughly true to himself and his times and yet deeply inspired by his compatriot of three generations earlier.

It is eloquent of the power which the old poetry still exercises over the new that even writers justly reputed for their bold, fresh, and imaginative style reconcile some notable traditionalism with their modernity. No poet is more widely recognized for his modernity than William Carlos Williams. Yet the last, the longest, and by no means the least interesting piece in his *Collected Poems* he himself describes as in the rococo style. Its central image of a man baptized in the waters of a stream by a symbolical figure is reminiscent of allegories from Dante to Spenser. Generally devoted to a sparse impressionism, Williams employs in this, possibly his strongest and most serious poem, an almost baroque eloquence. And he seems rightly to discover no hostility between the two extremes. The same mind creates the two types of work; the same volume harmoniously contains them. This affords good evidence that no part of our poetical tradition is actually alien to the modern spirit.

With their extraordinary rhythms and abrupt references, few leading poets are at once more original and more closely in key with the modern spirit than Marianne Moore; yet in his introduction to her *Selected Poems* T. S. Eliot discerningly observes that despite her experimentalism her descriptive style suggests the Augustans. One might go further, using a profusion of detail to show beyond the least doubt that Miss Moore often—although, of course, not always—is a direct follower of the Augustan element in the Renaissance spirit. As a singularly civilized and well-educated person, she has made this phase of our tradition in art, literature, and sensitivity a part of herself. The first word in her volume, significantly enough, is "Dürer." Her masterpiece, *The Jerboa*, celebrates the formal perfection of little things according to the finest and most fastidious Augustan taste. Her feeling for disciplined form is itself fundamentally classical. The moral satire of eighteenth-century poetry is brought up to date by such phrases as "presidents who have repaid sin-driven senators by not thinking about them." Her poems on cats at the same time surpass the similar verses by T. S. Eliot, her most generous admirer, and remind one of the many lightfooted, feline verses by Cowper. One notes typical references to Scaramouche, Molière, Handel, Rasselas, Will Honeycomb, Poor Richard, Chippendale furniture, ornamented toilet boxes, goldfish, French wines, and "the dead fountains of Versailles." A poetic love of understatement and conversational bagatelle proves her familiarity not only with the spirit but with the letter of neoclassical verse. Nor is she by any means forgetful of Shakespeare's richness or of Victorian fancy. Here again we recognize how subtly a leader in new fields relies upon the old for at least a part of her sustenance.

The example of Merrill Moore is in a different way equally instructive. His work has already been mentioned in this book as, of all recent poetry of high merit, the least indebted to the verse of the past and the most refreshingly modern. In a volume discussing the aesthetic merits of contemporary verse I should deal with no writer at greater length; in one on its poetic heritage I am constrained to mention no distinguished poet so seldom. None is less obliged to specific predecessors, none more successful in the use of a modern idiom or in the expression of the modern spirit. Yet it also remains true that, while Moore avoids all such literary borrowings as may be found not only in Chaucer, Shakespeare, and Milton but in Hopkins, Wylie, and Crane, consciously or unconsciously he follows much of the poetical tradition even though he neglects to pursue the letter. Not only does Moore like his predecessors write admirable verse; his lyrics in his principal volume, *M*, as arranged chiefly by the skillful hand of Louis Untermeyer, clearly fall into long traditional categories. Thus his contemplations upon time and love are in harmony with Shakespeare, his meditations on death with Donne, his satirical character sketches with Chaucer, while his verses under the heading *Dreams and Symbols* parallel visionary flights of romantic fancy. In his vitality, fluency, and intellectual courage he suggests Byron. One of his own sonnets reminds us of the old truism that there is nothing wholly new under the sun. Like the lion in Milton's account of the creation, his poetry is born half in a maternal earth, half pawing the ground to be free.

We have seen a number of sidelights on the road by which the old poets reach the new. There is a tendency for our poets, or at least for our poems, to divide themselves into two groups. Works inspired by an objective outlook upon life, a strongly marked social or satirical sense, owe most to the periods of the *Canterbury Tales* and *The Essay on Man*. Works inspired by a subjective vision, an outlook upon the infinity of the soul, are more often inspired by the poetry of the periods of Shakespeare and Donne, Wordsworth and Coleridge. There is, in short, a marked tendency for one group of poets to borrow from medieval and Augustan sources, another group from Elizabethan and romantic. These groups are respectively the realists and the idealists. If it is true, as appears to be the case, that the pendulum of history swings alternately between these two extremes, it would seem that the age on whose threshold we now stand is destined to incline toward realism. But the two tendencies clearly represent two undying attributes of human nature, one at any single time usually in ascendancy over the other. The actual death of one or the other would presumably mean the death of both.

Modern poetry is not only literary in the sense that it is partially derivative, but often positively learned. Since modern life has created a new intellectual class frequently with a selfish indulgence of its intellectual pleasures wholly foreign to the great majority of the people, schools of esoteric poetry have arisen. As the nineteenth century wore on, the Muse of English poetry tended to become a prisoner of the British Museum. Terrified by the alien appearance of the London streets, she retired among the Elgin Marbles. W. H. Auden and others give some evidence that she at last wearies of her retirement. To maintain, as Archibald MacLeish has asserted, that the modern poet should utter a genuinely "public speech" and at the same time to write in a style which must appear cryptic to all but a small group of initiates is a contradiction not only in terms but in deeds. As T. S. Eliot has reminded us, theoretically a true poem may have meaning merely for two persons, its author and one other. But there is nothing, at least in theology, leading one to suppose that grace may not descend upon a gathering of two or three thousand, or even two or three million as well.

The happiest poet is generally one who profits by a wide reading of verse without showing too clearly that he has done so. Such was the manner of Chaucer, Spenser, Shakespeare, Milton, Pope, and Shelley. And such today is the manner of MacLeish, Jeffers, Frost, Auden, Lewis, and MacNeice. To the old maxim that true art conceals art may be added a corollary that the poet's learning should also tend to conceal itself. The proposition might seem too obvious to be restated, were it not that Eliot, Pound, and other gifted poets so frequently violate its precept. Among the humanists of the Renaissance it is nowhere recorded that art should conceal meaning. Finally, poets like De la Mare, who are overliterary and imitative while at the same time renouncing the vanity of literary allusions, merely exchange pedantry for insipidity.

This book is in no sense intended as a review of modern poetry. Because of its avowed purpose, it has focused attention upon those poets who have used, and especially who have used legitimately, a wide literary heritage. It has accordingly given scant attention to many highly talented men and women who have succeeded in writing admirable verse with only slight or indirect aid from their predecessors. A few such sturdily self-sufficient writers were mentioned in the introductory chapter, such as Merrill Moore, Stephen Spender, and James Stephens. The list might easily be much enlarged by other names, such as Gogarty, Masters, Rukeyser, Gregory, and Louise Bogan. Obviously the mean between the extremes is best, for complete innocence of poetic tradition is undesirable and virtually impossible, exactly as servile imitation in any art is incompatible with sincerity. When a writer subjugates the expression of his own personality and of the spirit of his times to an attempted reproduction of the expression of another age, he forfeits his claim to be held a creative artist, becoming at best a historian, at worst a pedant. In any true poem the present is always more conspicuous than the past, the near than the far. Such a poem may exist without any tangible relations to the past whatsoever, other than the most elementary aspects of language and form. But the work cannot exist without such relations to the man who writes it and to the public for which it is written. Although modern poetry, even in its least pedantic practitioners, is certainly more traditional than is usually supposed, there is still no sounder admonition than the famous line written over three and a half centuries ago by Sir Philip Sidney:

Fool, said my Muse to me, look in thy heart, and write.

A SELECTED BOOK LIST

Abercrombie, Lascelles, The Poems of Lascelles Abercrombie, 1930.

Aiken, Conrad, Selected Poems, 1929.

—— John Deth and Other Poems, 1930.

—— Preludes for Memnon, 1931.

—— Time in the Rock, 1936.

Auden, W. H., Poems, 1934.

—— The Dog beneath the Skin (with Christopher Isherwood), 1935.

—— The Ascent of F 6 (with Christopher Isherwood), 1937.

—— Letters from Iceland (with Louis MacNeice), 1937.

—— On This Island, 1937.

—— Journey to a War (with Christopher Isherwood), 1939.

—— Another Time, 1940.

Belloc, Hilaire, The Bad Child's Book of Beasts, 1936.

—— Sonnets and Verse, 1938.

Benét, Stephen Vincent, John Brown's Body, 1928.

—— Burning City, 1936.

Bridges, Robert, Poetical Works of Robert Bridges, 1913.

Campbell, Roy, The Flaming Terrapin, 1924.

—— Adamastor, 1930.

—— The Georgiad, 1931.

—— Mithraic Emblems, 1936.

Crane, Hart, The Collected Poems of Hart Crane, 1933.

Cummings, E. E., Collected Poems, 1938.

Davies, W. H., The Poems of W. H. Davies, 1935.

De la Mare, Walter, Collected Poems 1901–1918, 1920.

—— Poems for Children, 1930.

Eliot, T. S., Collected Poems 1909–1935, 1936.

Engle, Paul, Break the Heart's Anger, 1936.
——— Corn, 1939.
Frost, Robert, Collected Poems, 1939.
Gogarty, Oliver St. J., Selected Poems, 1933.
Hardy, Thomas, The Dynasts, 1904–8.
——— Collected Poems, 1930.
Henderson, W. B. D., The New Argonautica, 1928.
Hillyer, Robert, Collected Verse, 1933.
Hopkins, G. M., Poems of Gerard Manley Hopkins, 1930.
Jeffers, Robinson, The Women at Point Sur, 1927.
——— Cawdor and Other Poems, 1928.
——— Dear Judas and Other Poems, 1929.
——— Solstice and Other Poems, 1935.
——— Such Counsels You Gave to Me, 1937.
——— The Selected Poetry of Robinson Jeffers, 1938.
Lawrence, D. H., Collected Poems, 1928.
——— Last Poems by D. H. Lawrence, 1933.
Lewis, C. Day, Collected Poems 1929–1933, 1935.
Lewis, Clive Staples, The Pilgrim's Regress, 1933.
Lindsay, Vachel, Collected Poems, 1925.
MacLeish, Archibald, Poems 1924–1933, 1933.
——— Public Speech, 1936.
——— The Fall of the City, 1937.
MacNeice, Louis, Poems, 1935.
Moore, Marianne, Selected Poems, 1935.
Moore, Merrill, The Noise That Time Makes, 1929.
——— Six Sides to a Man, 1935.
——— M, One Thousand Autobiographical Sonnets, 1938.
Moore, T. Sturge, The Poems of T. Sturge Moore (4 vols.),
   1931–33.
Owen, Wilfred, The Poems of Wilfred Owen, 1931.
Pound, Ezra, Selected Poems, 1928.
——— A Draft of XXX Cantos, 1933.
——— Eleven New Cantos, XXXI–XLI, 1934.

—— The Fifth Decad of Cantos, 1937.

Ransom, John Crowe, Chills and Fever, 1924.

—— Two Gentlemen in Bonds, 1927.

Robinson, Edwin Arlington, Collected Poems of Edwin Arlington Robinson, 1937.

Sackville-West, Victoria, Collected Poems, 1933.

Sandburg, Carl, Chicago Poems, 1916.

—— Cornhuskers, 1918

—— Smoke and Steel, 1920.

—— Slabs of the Sunburnt West, 1922.

—— Selected Poems of Carl Sandburg, 1926.

—— Good Morning America, 1928.

—— The People, Yes, 1936.

Schwartz, Delmore, In Dreams Begin Responsibilities, 1938.

Sitwell, Edith, The Collected Poems of Edith Sitwell, 1930.

Sitwell, Osbert, The Collected Satires and Poems of Osbert Sitwell, 1931.

Sitwell, Sacheverell, Collected Poems, 1936.

Spender, Stephen, Poems, 1934.

Stephens, James, Collected Poems, 1926.

Stevens, Wallace, Harmonium, 1931.

—— Ideas of Order, 1936.

—— The Man with the Blue Guitar and Other Poems, 1937.

Taggard, Genevieve, Collected Poems 1918–1938, 1938.

Tate, Allen, Selected Poems, 1937.

Todrin, Boris, 5 Days, 1936.

—— 7 Men, 1938.

Van Doren, Mark, Collected Poems 1922–1938, 1939.

Warren, Robert Penn, Thirty-six Poems, 1935.

Weismiller, Edward, The Deer Come Down, 1936.

Wylie, Elinor, Collected Poems of Elinor Wylie, 1932.

Yeats, William Butler, The Collected Poems of William Butler Yeats, 1933.

—— Last Poems and Plays, 1940.

INDEX